SKILLS FOR LIFE

A TEEN'S GUIDE TO HEALTH, MONEY, AND SUCCESS

Kyan Montague

DEDICATION

For my 19-year-old daughter, stepping into adulthood with courage, talent, and determination, carrying a touch of anxiety but endless excitement for the journey ahead.

And for my 12-year-old son, filled with curiosity, wonder, limitless potential, and an undeniable passion for gaming.

TABLE OF CONTENTS

INTRODUCTION

Congratulations! You're either a teenager, on the verge of becoming one, or perhaps stepping into adulthood. Kudos to you for picking up this book instead of getting lost in a flood of memes and dance videos on your favorite app. It shows you care about your future—and that's a fantastic first step, my friend.

This book dives into the topics school often skips over but that are more relevant and useful in today's world. Ever wondered why school teaches you to solve for X in algebra but doesn't teach you how to find yourself? Or why you can name every planet but struggle to identify your own strengths? You might know all the major events of World War II, but understanding the battles inside your own mind remains a mystery.

Think of this book as your personal guide to life—the kind that covers what school doesn't, but what you genuinely need to know. We'll explore the life skills that build a solid foundation, shape your future, boost your confidence, and help you tackle real-world challenges. From staying physically healthy in a world of screens and sugar to embracing mental and emotional wellness, this book is all about the skills you need to thrive—whatever "success" means to you. Together, we'll delve into self-acceptance, resilience, and the power of grit. We'll look at how mindfulness and meditation can transform your mindset, cover the basics of finance, and discuss how Artificial Intelligence is changing the job landscape.

And that's not all—we'll get into skills like communication, collaboration, creativity, confidence, critical thinking, continuous learning, time management, and leadership, which are more important than ever. You'll also find practical advice on career planning, building a standout résumé, and nailing interviews.

Above all, my main goal with this book is to help you feel happy and comfortable with who you are. I've packed this book with scientific insights to give you a deeper understanding—and a few silly pictures to keep you entertained (or maybe make you cringe just a little).

Your future is bright, and I hope this book helps you start thinking more about who you are and gives you the tools and knowledge to make better choices along the way. Just a heads-up: this book is meant for educational and informational purposes only. While I've researched these topics thoroughly, I'm not a licensed medical or mental health professional. For any specific medical advice, diagnosis, or treatment, please consult a qualified healthcare provider.

And don't worry—I've kept things bite-sized so you won't be yawning through endless pages of text. Ready to get started? Let's go!

CHAPTER 1:

Nothing Is More Important Than Health

Let's start with something simple: breathing. Yes, just breathe. In a world buzzing with screens and noise, we often forget that breathing is more than just taking in air; it's a chance to clear your head and reset. So, close your eyes, relax your forehead, release the tension in your shoulders, and take a deep breath. Notice how the air feels entering through your nose and filling your lungs.

"You don't get what you want in life. You get who you are!" - Les Brown.

I'm beginning this book with health because, without it, getting what you want out of life becomes so much harder. Good health fuels the energy and confidence you need to excel in anything you pursue. Reaching your best health is the first step in reaching your potential in other areas. And reaching that peak requires discipline and knowing both what to do—and what to avoid. We have all been gifted this amazing complex machine to experience this beautiful world, and we

HEALTHY + HEALTHY = HAPPY
BODY   MIND   LIFE

must take care of it to have a quality life. Sure, your brain is like the command center, but your body is the real star of the show. Without it, your brain wouldn't get very far. Imagine trying to ace a test when you're exhausted, hungry, and can't sit up straight. Yeah, not gonna happen.

Our bodies are like the most complicated machines ever built—way more intricate than your phone, laptop, or even a spaceship. But here's the kicker: unlike machines, our bodies can heal themselves, grow stronger, and adapt to almost anything life throws at them.

Imagine having a car that not only fixes itself when it breaks down but also gets faster and more efficient the more you drive it. That's your body in a nutshell! It's like the ultimate superhero with superpowers we don't always appreciate. But to keep this superhero in peak condition, you need to understand how it works, what it needs, and how to treat it right.

When your body is run-down, tired, or neglected, your mental clarity suffers, your social relationships weaken, and it becomes nearly impossible to focus on higher-level goals like finding meaning or purpose in life. Health isn't just one part of the equation; it's the base that supports everything else. If you're not taking care of your body, the rest of the pyramid—your psychological, social, and spiritual well-being—will struggle to stay balanced.

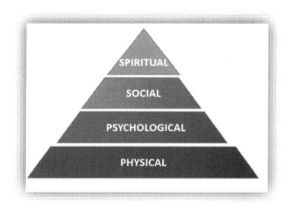

Here are five random mind-blowing facts about the human body, but there are so many more:

1. **Your bones are stronger than steel**: Pound for pound, human bones are stronger than steel. While they may not seem like it, the femur (thigh bone) can support up to 30 times the weight of a person. The structure of bone, made up of mineral crystals and collagen fibers, gives it both strength and flexibility.

4

2. **You're more bacteria than human**: The human body contains trillions of microorganisms, including bacteria, which outnumber human cells by about 10 to 1. Most of these bacteria are harmless or even beneficial, living in your gut and on your skin, helping with digestion, and protecting against harmful microbes.

3. **Your brain can generate enough electricity to power a light bulb**: The brain is an energy powerhouse, using around 20% of your body's total energy. Neurons, or brain cells, communicate through electrical impulses, and when all neurons fire together, the brain produces enough electrical energy to light up a 25-watt bulb.

4. **You shed about 40 pounds of skin in your lifetime**: Your skin constantly regenerates, shedding old skin cells to make way for new ones. In fact, your entire outer layer of skin replaces itself about every 2-4 weeks. Over a lifetime, you shed about 40 pounds (18 kilograms) of skin cells!

5. **Your stomach lining regenerates every few days**: The acids in your stomach are so strong they could dissolve metals, but your stomach is protected by a lining that regenerates quickly. Every 3-4 days, your stomach lining completely renews itself to prevent the acids from eating away at it.

Your body is like the magic wand in a wizard's hand—it's the source of all your power, creativity, and energy. Imagine trying to cast spells or create something amazing, but your wand is cracked and weak. No matter how much magic you have inside, it won't come out right. That's what happens when you don't take care of your body. Without a strong body, even the most brilliant ideas and exciting plans can fall apart like a sandcastle at high tide. Keep it strong and vibrant, and there's no limit to the magic you can create. Now that you know how amazing your body is, it's time to talk about how to keep it in top shape. We will talk about some key areas in the coming chapters.

From Cavemen To Couch Potatoes

Imagine waking up in the morning, and the first thing you do is check your phone. You scroll through memes, reply to messages, and maybe even watch a video or two before you get out of bed. This routine is so normal today that we don't even think twice about it. But what if I told you that, not too long ago, our ancestors' idea of "getting up" was rolling out of a cave, grabbing a spear, and chasing down breakfast? There is no Wi-Fi, no Netflix, and definitely no couches: just survival, all day, every day.

The journey from chasing mammoths to chasing high scores in video games is a wild one. It's the story of how humans went from being one of the most active species on the planet to becoming, well, a bit lazy.

The Caveman's Daily Workout

Back in the day, our ancestors, often referred to as "cavemen" (though they didn't always live in caves), had a very different lifestyle. Imagine a world where you have no grocery stores, no Uber Eats, and no fridges stocked with snacks. If you wanted to eat, you had to go out and get it. This meant running, climbing, hunting, and gathering—activities that required serious physical effort. They didn't have gyms, but they didn't need them. Their daily survival was a full-body workout.

The Slow Shift: Agriculture and Settling Down

Around 10,000 years ago, something huge happened. Humans discovered farming. Instead of constantly moving to follow the herds of animals, people started to settle down and grow their food. This was a game-changer. For the first time, humans could stay in one place, build communities, and focus on things other than survival.

But with farming came a new lifestyle. People didn't need to move around as much. They started to stay in one place, working the land, raising animals, and eventually building towns and cities. While this meant more reliable food sources, it also meant less daily exercise. The need to hunt and gather slowly faded, and with it, our ancestors' highly active lifestyle.

Industrial Revolution: The Birth of Convenience

Fast forward a few thousand years to the Industrial Revolution in the 18th century. This is when things really started to change. Machines were invented to do work that people used to do by hand. Factories popped up, and people moved to cities to work in them. This was the beginning of modern society, but it also marked the decline of physical activity for many people.

Instead of working on farms or in fields, people started working in factories, offices, and, later, in front of computers. Jobs became less about physical labor and more about sitting and managing machines—even the simple act of getting around changed. Instead of walking, people could now ride on trains, buses, and eventually cars. Life was getting easier, but it was also getting more sedentary.

The Rise of Technology: The Couch Potato Era

Enter the late 20th and early 21st centuries. Technology exploded, and with it came the rise of the Internet, video games, smartphones, and streaming services. Suddenly, entertainment was at our fingertips, and social

interaction didn't require leaving the house. You could chat with friends, watch movies, play games, and even work—all from the comfort of your couch.

This convenience led to a new phenomenon: the couch potato—a term used to describe someone who spends a lot of time sitting and not much time moving. Instead of chasing down our food, we now chase after the latest episodes of our favorite shows. The human body, once built for endurance and activity, now faces a new challenge: staying healthy in a world where it's easy to be lazy.

The Science of Laziness

Our bodies are designed to move. Our muscles, bones, and even our brains work best when we're active. Physical activity helps regulate our metabolism, keep our hearts healthy, and even improve our mood.

But when we sit too much, things start to go downhill. Extended periods of inactivity can lead to a host of problems like obesity, heart disease, diabetes, and even mental health issues like depression and anxiety. Our bodies just aren't built to sit still for long periods. It's like using a Ferrari ⯑ to drive around a parking lot—completely underusing its potential.

There's a reason why we feel better after a workout or a good walk. Exercise releases endorphins, the "feel-good" chemicals in our brains, which is something our caveman ancestors experienced daily just by surviving. Today, we have to make a conscious effort to move, something that used to be as natural as breathing.

Evolution vs. Modern Life: The Big Disconnect

The problem is that evolution hasn't caught up with modern life. Our bodies are still wired for the caveman or cavewoman lifestyle. We're built to move, hunt, gather, and stay active. But our environment has changed drastically. We've created a world where we don't need to move to survive. Food is abundant (sometimes too abundant), and entertainment is instant. This creates a disconnect between what our bodies need and what our environment offers.

This is why it's so easy to fall into the couch potato trap. Our brains are also wired to conserve energy. Back in the caveman days, conserving energy was crucial because food was scarce. But now, with food readily available and movement optional, this energy-saving mode can backfire, leading to laziness. Don't conserve energy! Spend it!

How to Avoid Becoming a Couch Potato

So, what can we do to avoid becoming couch potatoes in a world that's designed to make us lazy? Get uncomfortable!

1. **Move More, Sit Less**: Find ways to add movement to your day. Take the stairs instead of the elevator, walk or bike instead of driving, and try to stand or stretch every hour if you're sitting for a long time.

2. **Exercise, Play, Dance, or whatever**: This doesn't mean you have to start running marathons (unless you want to). Find an activity you enjoy, whether it's dancing, swimming, hiking, or playing a sport. The more fun it is, the more likely you are to stick with it.

3. **Get off that Screen**: It's easy to get sucked into the endless scroll of social media or binge-watching shows. Set limits for yourself, and try to balance screen time with active time.

4. **Eat Like Our Ancestors**: Focus on whole, natural foods—fruits, vegetables, nuts, and lean meats—just like our ancestors ate. Avoid too much-processed food, which is often packed with sugar and unhealthy fats.

5. **Stay Social 'physically'**: Connect with friends and family in person when possible. Social interaction is important for mental health, and it often involves more movement than chatting online.

Go back to your roots and think about your body as a Ferrari or Lamborghini (or whichever brand you like), and don't let it rot in the parking lot of our couch. Move it, use it, enjoy it. You will be amazed by how much better you will feel. And if you have done it already, you know what I am talking about! Write down what one new change you will do starting today to respect your wonderful machine more:

2. Junk Food: Why do we love them so much when we shouldn't

Our ancestors lived in a world where food wasn't something you picked up at the store in a trolley —it was something you hunted or gathered. Back then, finding food wasn't easy. So, **our bodies evolved to love high-calorie foods.** It was a survival mechanism. If you came across something sweet like fruit or honey, you'd eat as much as you could because you didn't know when you'd find it again. Fatty foods were the same—if you found something rich in fats, like meat, you ate as much as possible to store that energy.

Fast forward to today. We no longer have to chase after our food, but our bodies still crave those same high-calorie foods. The problem is, our bodies haven't caught up to our modern world, where food is everywhere and mostly junk, processed, and loaded with sugar and chemicals!

The Trickery of Processed Foods

Processed foods are the ultimate tricksters. They're designed to hit all the right spots in your brain, making you want more and more. They're not just about feeding you—they're about keeping you coming back. That's why you can't eat just one chip or why fast food tastes so good even when you know it's bad for you.

Let's break it down. Processed foods are loaded with sugar, salt, and fat. These ingredients don't just make food taste good; they also make your brain happy. When you eat something sugary, your brain releases dopamine, a chemical that makes you feel pleasure. The more dopamine your brain releases, the more you want that food. It's like your brain is giving you a high-five every time you eat a cookie.

But there's a catch. The more junk food you eat, the less sensitive your brain becomes to dopamine. That means you need to eat more and more to get the same happy feeling. It's a vicious cycle that food companies know all too well. They create foods that are "hyper-palatable," meaning they're so tasty that you keep eating them, even when you're full. Think about that for a second. They're literally engineering food to make you overeat.

The Impact on Your Body

So, what happens when you eat all this junk? At first, it might seem harmless. However, over time, the effects can be significant. Eating a diet high in processed foods can lead to weight gain, heart disease, diabetes, and

other serious health problems. Your body doesn't get the nutrients it needs to function properly, and over time, this can lead to feeling sluggish, getting sick more often, and even affecting your mental health. Well, none of this will happen at your age, but if you get addicted to eating junk, you will continue in your adult life and then find it very hard to get off the junk treadmill.

But it's not just about physical health. Junk food can mess with your brain, too. Studies have shown that a diet high in processed foods can affect your mood, leading to issues like depression and anxiety. It's like a double whammy: you eat junk food because it makes you feel good in the moment, but in the long run, it can actually make you feel worse.

Breaking the Cycle

So, how do you break the cycle? It's not easy, but it's possible. The first step is awareness. Understand what's in your food and how it affects your body. Start reading labels and making informed choices. It's not about never eating junk food again—it's about finding a balance.

Try to replace some of the processed foods in your diet with whole foods.

Instead of reaching for a bag of chips, try snacking on fruits, nuts, or yogurt. These foods give your body the nutrients it needs without all the added junk. And when you do indulge in junk food, enjoy it—just do it in moderation.

What is processed food?

Go to a supermarket and observe 2 types of foods:

(1) With no label of Ingredients - Well, like an Apple or Banana or Egg or Chicken or Carrot

(2) With a label of ingredients - usually a long list of chemicals something like this:

INGREDIENTS: WHOLE CORN, VEGETABLE OIL (CONTAINS ONE OR MORE OF THE FOLLOWING: CORN, SOYBEAN, AND/OR SUNFLOWER OIL), SALT, CHEDDAR CHEESE (MILK, CHEESE CULTURES, SALT, ENZYMES), MALTODEXTRIN, WHEAT FLOUR, WHEY, MONOSODIUM GLUTAMATE, BUTTERMILK SOLIDS, ROMANO CHEESE FROM COW'S MILK (PART-SKIM COW'S MILK, CHEESE CULTURES, SALT, ENZYMES), WHEY PROTEIN CONCENTRATE, ONION POWDER, PARTIALLY HYDROGENATED SOYBEAN AND COTTONSEED OIL, CORN FLOUR, DISODIUM PHOSPHATE, LACTOSE, NATURAL AND ARTIFICIAL FLAVOR, DEXTROSE, TOMATO POWDER, SPICES, LACTIC ACID, ARTIFICIAL COLOR (INCLUDING YELLOW 6, YELLOW 5, RED 40), CITRIC ACID, SUGAR, GARLIC POWDER, RED AND GREEN BELL PEPPER POWDER, SODIUM CASEINATE, DISODIUM INOSINATE, DISODIUM GUANYLATE, NONFAT MILK SOLIDS, WHEY PROTEIN ISOLATE, AND CORN SYRUP SOLIDS.

There are no prizes for guessing which one is Processed food!

Can you even pronounce those chemicals? Forget about knowing what those are. Go and search on the web and see what those chemicals mean. Are we not all supposed to know what we are putting inside our bodies?

Corporations producing those foods only care about 2 things:

1. Foods should look colorful, appealing, and appetizing. (i.e., more sales)

2. Foods should not rot soon (i.e., stay on supermarket shelves longer)

Our minds, bodies, and the microorganisms in the gut are all getting trained to like junk food, and as soon as we see them, our bodies release the feel-good Dopamine - even if those foods are not healthy for our bodies. We are being tricked into eating more Sugar and Chemicals, and we crave it more and more.

In the last 100 years, humans have invented thousands of processed foods to suit our taste buds and support our fast-paced lives where there is no time to cook. Go to any supermarket, and it is filled with colorful and attractive food items, which the companies have spent millions on marketing to convince you that consuming these will make you happy.

Fake Alert: There are also a lot of misleading products that claim that they are natural and are loaded with Vitamins and natural stuff. In reality, more than 90% of the stuff is junk, and less than 10% is natural.

Identifying junk food is simple. Just read the ingredients. Unless you are a Chemistry expert, you won't even understand what those things are; if you don't understand what you are eating, it's better to stay away from it.

Don't fall into the trap that there has been research and these things are safe. Humans have made a lot of progress, but we still don't understand how our bodies and brains work. There are so many things unexplained. We don't know how all these factory-made chemicals work in our bodies.

The combination of junk food and a sedentary lifestyle is a recipe for disaster.

The Bubble Invasion

Did you know something as ubiquitous as soda wasn't even around a hundred years ago? How did we go from sipping on water, tea, or milk to guzzling gallons of sugary, carbonated beverages and start acting as if it is normal to have it with every meal?

The history of soda started in the 18th century when scientists began experimenting with carbonating water. Joseph Priestley, an English clergyman, was the first to infuse water with carbon dioxide, creating soda water in 1767. It wasn't until the 19th century that flavored sodas began to emerge, initially marketed as medicinal drinks. The first soda fountain was installed in a pharmacy, and pharmacists would mix the syrup with carbonated water. Coca-Cola, one of the

most famous sodas today, was created by Dr. John Stith Pemberton in 1886, originally intended as a patent medicine.

By the early 20th century, soda had transformed from a health tonic to a popular beverage—the introduction of bottling technology allowed for mass production and distribution. With aggressive marketing and the rise of fast food culture post-World War II, soda consumption skyrocketed. It became a symbol of American consumerism and spread globally, making its way into homes, schools, and workplaces.

3. The Chemistry of Soda: What's Really in Your Can?

Sugar: The Sweet Culprit

A standard can of soda contains about 39 grams of sugar, roughly equivalent to 10 teaspoons. Just one can alone is far above the recommended daily intake.

High Fructose Corn Syrup (HFCS)

HFCS is a sweetener made from cornstarch. It is cheaper than cane sugar and is commonly used in sodas. HFCS has been implicated in the obesity epidemic and is associated with an increased risk of metabolic diseases.

Phosphoric Acid

This ingredient gives soda its tangy flavor and extends its shelf life. However, phosphoric acid can interfere with the body's ability to absorb calcium, leading to bone density loss and increased risk of osteoporosis.

Caffeine

Caffeine is a natural stimulant found in many sodas. While it can increase alertness, excessive consumption can lead to restlessness, insomnia, and increased heart rate. Dependence on caffeine can also lead to withdrawal symptoms.

Artificial Flavors and Colors

Many sodas contain artificial flavors and colors to enhance their taste and appearance. For example, caramel color (E150d) is used to give cola its distinctive brown hue. Some artificial colors have been linked to hyperactivity in children and other health concerns.

Aspartame

Diet sodas often come with the promise of zero sugar and zero calories, making them seem like a healthier alternative to regular soft drinks. However, when you dig deeper into what's inside these fizzy drinks, you'll find that they might not be as harmless as they seem. Diet sodas are loaded with artificial ingredients that have raised concerns about potential health risks. Let's break down what's really inside and why you might want to reconsider your next can. Aspartame is an
artificial sweetener found in many diet sodas and sugar-free products. It is about 200 times sweeter than sugar. There has been controversy over its safety, with studies suggesting potential links to cancer, neurological issues, and other health problems. However, regulatory agencies maintain that aspartame is safe for consumption within established limits. Can we trust a new chemical that humans have never consumed in millions of years? Some

studies suggest that our bodies get confused when the taste buds signal that sweet sugar is coming, but the stomach never has any sugar!

Other Additives and Harmful Chemicals in Modern Foods

Monosodium Glutamate (MSG)

MSG is a flavor enhancer commonly found in processed foods. While generally recognized as safe, some people experience an "MSG symptom complex," which includes headaches, sweating, and chest pain after consumption.

Sodium Nitrite

Sodium nitrite is used to preserve and color-cured meats like bacon and hot dogs. It can form nitrosamines and carcinogenic compounds, particularly when exposed to high heat during cooking.

Trans Fats

Trans fats are artificially created by hydrogenating vegetable oil, making it solid at room temperature. They are used to improve texture and shelf life in processed foods. Trans fats are strongly linked to heart disease, inflammation, and an increased risk of type 2 diabetes.

BHA and BHT

Butylated hydroxyanisole (BHA) and butylated hydroxytoluene (BHT) are preservatives that prevent oils in foods from oxidizing and becoming rancid. There are concerns about their potential as carcinogens and their effects on the liver and kidneys.

The Rise of Artificial Colors

Before artificial colors, people used natural sources to color their food. Ancient civilizations used spices, fruits, and vegetables to enhance the appearance of their meals. For example, saffron was used for a rich yellow, while beet juice provided a deep red. These natural dyes were safe and often added nutritional value.

In the mid-19th century, the Industrial Revolution brought synthetic dyes into the food industry. The first artificial color, Mauveine, was discovered by accident in 1856. By the early 20th century, a rainbow of synthetic dyes was available, promising consistent and vivid colors. The convenience and low cost of these dyes made them popular with manufacturers.

Common Artificial Colors

1. Red 40 (Allura Red AC)

    o Source: Derived from petroleum.

    o Uses: Found in candies, drinks, baked goods, and more.

    o Health Concerns: Linked to hyperactivity in children and potential carcinogenic effects.

2. Yellow 5 (Tartrazine)

    o Source: Also derived from petroleum.

    o Uses: Common in cereals, snacks, and desserts.

    o Health Concerns: Associated with allergic reactions, especially in people with asthma or aspirin sensitivity.

3. Yellow 6 (Sunset Yellow FCF)

    o Source: Petroleum-based.

    o Uses: Used in beverages, candies, and baked goods.

    o Health Concerns: May cause adrenal gland and kidney tumors, as well as hyperactivity in children.

4. Blue 1 (Brilliant Blue FCF)

    o Source: Synthetic dye from petroleum.

    o Uses: Seen in beverages, candies, and ice cream.

o   Health Concerns: Can cause allergic reactions and has been linked to cancer in animal studies.

5. Blue 2 (Indigo Carmine)

   o   Source: Another petroleum-based dye.

   o   Uses: Used in candies, cereals, and pet foods.

   o   Health Concerns: Associated with brain tumors in animal studies.

6. Green 3 (Fast Green FCF)

   o   Source: Derived from petroleum.

   o   Uses: Found in drinks, desserts, and candies.

   o   Health Concerns: Linked to bladder and testes tumors in animal studies.

How These Dyes Affect Our Bodies

Artificial colors are made from synthetic chemicals, primarily derived from petroleum. When ingested, these dyes are metabolized by the liver and can have various effects on the body. Some are excreted unchanged, while others may be broken down into potentially harmful compounds.

Regulatory Actions and Public Awareness

The U.S. Food and Drug Administration (FDA) regulates artificial colors, setting limits on their use in foods. However, despite evidence from animal studies, many of these dyes are still approved for use in the U.S. The FDA maintains that they are safe when used within established limits.

The European Union has stricter regulations regarding artificial colors. Some dyes are banned, while others require warning labels indicating that they may have adverse effects on activity and attention in children.

Color Psychology: The color of food can influence our perception of its taste. For example, a strawberry-flavored drink may taste sweeter if it's bright red.

Marketing Magic: Brightly colored foods are often marketed to children, who are more attracted to vibrant hues. After all, it is all about how companies can make more MONEY. Natural colors are costlier!

Remember, it's all about balance. You don't have to give up your favorite treats completely. Enjoy them in moderation, and focus on making healthier choices most of the time. Your body will thank you.

Now, an assignment for you. Read the label of your favorite food or drink and Google the ingredients. Write if you found something that didn't look very healthy to you:

4. Food: More Than Just Fuel

As we talked about in the last chapter, your body is a powerful machine—like a Formula 1 race car. You wouldn't fill up that car with adulterated cheap gasoline and expect it to win races. You'd choose the highest quality fuel to ensure it performs at its best.

Food is a complex combination of nutrients that interact with your body in fascinating ways. It doesn't just keep you alive—it can boost your mood, sharpen your focus, enhance your energy levels, and fortify your immune system. But the reverse is also true: the wrong foods can drag you down, making you feel sluggish, unfocused, and even unhappy.

How Food Impacts Your Mood

Your brain is like a command center, directing everything your body does. But it's not just the boss; it's also very needy. Your brain demands a constant supply of energy and nutrients to function properly. What you eat directly affects how your brain works and, consequently, how you

feel.

Carbohydrates, for instance, are your brain's main source of energy. But not all carbs are the same. **Simple carbohydrates**, like those in sugary snacks and drinks, are quickly absorbed into the bloodstream, leading to a rapid spike in blood sugar. This can make you feel a sudden burst of energy, followed by a crash that leaves you feeling tired and irritable. Imagine a rocket shooting up quickly only to fall back to Earth just as fast.

Complex carbohydrates, on the other hand, found in foods like whole grains, fruits, and vegetables, are digested more slowly. They provide a steady release of glucose, keeping your blood sugar levels stable and your brain happy. This is more like a steady, controlled flight that keeps you cruising smoothly.

Proteins also play a crucial role in your mood. They are broken down into amino acids, which are used to produce neurotransmitters—chemicals that transmit signals in the brain. One important neurotransmitter is serotonin, often called the "feel-good" chemical. Foods rich in tryptophan, an amino acid found in turkey, eggs, and dairy products, help your body produce more serotonin. This can lead to feelings of well-being and happiness.

Different cultures have long recognized the connection between food and mood. For example, in India, the concept of "sattvic" food refers to pure, natural foods that promote calmness and clarity of mind. These include fruits, vegetables, whole grains, and dairy. In contrast, "tamasic" foods, which are overly processed, fried, or stale, are believed to lead to sluggishness and negative emotions.

In the Mediterranean, the diet is rich in fruits, vegetables, nuts, and olive oil. People who follow this diet tend to have lower rates of depression and anxiety. This isn't just a coincidence—foods high in omega-3 fatty acids, like fish, nuts, and seeds, are known to reduce inflammation and improve brain health, which can directly impact your mood. See the tables below:

Food Category	Scientific Explanation
Fruits & Vegetables	High in vitamins, minerals, and antioxidants that protect brain cells and promote neurotransmitter production (e.g., serotonin).
Whole Grains	Provide a steady release of glucose, which is essential for brain function and mood stabilization.
Nuts & Seeds	Rich in healthy fats, magnesium, and tryptophan, which are precursors to mood-boosting neurotransmitters like serotonin.
Lean Proteins (e.g., fish, turkey, chicken)	High in amino acids like tryptophan and tyrosine, which are converted into serotonin and dopamine.
Fermented Foods e.g., yogurt, kefir, auerkraut)	It contains probiotics that support gut health, which is closely linked to mood regulation through the gut-brain axis.
Legumes (e.g., beans, lentils)	High in fiber, protein, and B vitamins, supporting steady energy levels and serotonin production.
Dark Chocolate	It contains phenylethylamine and serotonin precursors that have mood-enhancing effects.

Processed/Junk Foods	Scientific Explanation
Sugary Snacks & Beverages	This leads to rapid spikes and crashes in blood sugar levels, causing energy fluctuations and irritability.
Refined Carbohydrates (e.g., white bread, pastries)	Rapidly digested, causing blood sugar spikes and crashes, leading to mood instability and fatigue.

Trans Fats (e.g., fried foods, margarine)	Disrupt cell membranes and inflammation in the brain, negatively affecting mood and cognitive function.
Processed Meats (e.g., sausages, hot dogs)	High in preservatives and low in essential nutrients, leading to poor brain function and increased inflammation.
Artificial Sweeteners (e.g., aspartame, saccharin)	Disrupt neurotransmitter production and can alter gut bacteria, negatively affecting mood.
High-sodium foods (e.g., chips, canned soups)	Excessive sodium can disrupt fluid balance and increase blood pressure, leading to physical stress and mood disturbances.

How Your Body Uses Food for Energy

Your body converts the food you eat into energy through a process called **metabolism**. Carbohydrates are broken down into glucose, which is used by your cells for energy. Proteins and fats can also be used for energy, but they're primarily used for building and repairing tissues and supporting cell functions.

Simple sugars, like those found in candy, soft drinks, and pastries, provide a quick but short-lived burst of energy. This is because they are rapidly absorbed into the bloodstream, causing a spike in blood sugar. However, this quick energy doesn't last, and soon, your blood sugar levels drop, leaving you feeling tired and hungry again. This is often referred to as the "**sugar crash**."

Complex carbohydrates, such as those in whole grains, legumes, and starchy vegetables, are digested more slowly. They provide a steady source of energy that lasts longer, helping you avoid the rollercoaster of energy highs and lows.

Fats, particularly healthy fats like those found in avocados, nuts, and fish, are a more concentrated source of energy. While they take longer to break down, they provide sustained energy and are essential for absorbing certain vitamins.

Real-World Examples

Athletes are particularly aware of how food affects their energy levels. Take Kenyan marathon runners, who are known for their endurance and speed. Their diet is rich in complex carbohydrates, primarily from staple foods like ugali (a type of maize porridge), sweet potatoes, and beans. These foods provide the slow-burning energy needed for long-distance running.

In Japan, sumo wrestlers consume a high-calorie diet to maintain their large size, but they also include a variety of nutrients to ensure they have the energy and strength needed for their sport. Their meals often include fish, rice, vegetables, and a hotpot dish called chanko-nabe, which is rich in protein and healthy fats.

Brain Foods That Boost Focus

Your brain is constantly working, even when you're sleeping. It requires a steady supply of nutrients to maintain cognitive functions like memory, focus, and decision-making. Certain foods have been shown to boost brain power, making them essential for students, professionals, and anyone looking to enhance their mental performance.

Omega-3 fatty acids, found in fatty fish like salmon, walnuts, and flaxseeds, are crucial for brain health. They help build and repair brain cells, improve memory, and support cognitive function. In fact, studies have shown that people who consume high levels of omega-3s have a lower risk of developing neurodegenerative diseases like Alzheimer's.

Antioxidants, found in berries, nuts, and dark chocolate, protect the brain from oxidative stress, which can damage cells and lead to cognitive decline. These foods also enhance communication between brain cells, improving memory and learning.

The Role of Nutrients in Immune Function

Your immune system is your body's defense mechanism against infections and diseases. It relies heavily on the nutrients you consume to function effectively. Vitamins, minerals, and antioxidants play a critical role in supporting your immune system, helping it respond to threats and recover from illnesses.

Vitamin C, found in citrus fruits, bell peppers, and strawberries, is one of the most well-known immune boosters. It helps stimulate the production of white blood cells, which are essential for fighting infections.

Vitamin D deficiency is becoming a big problem worldwide, affecting people of all ages, including kids and teens. Vitamin D is important because it helps keep our bones strong, supports our immune system, and keeps us healthy overall. But many people aren't getting enough of it, mostly because they spend a lot of time indoors and don't get enough sunlight, which is the best source of Vitamin D. This can happen more in places with long winters or where the air is really polluted. Plus, not everyone eats enough foods that have Vitamin D, like fish, eggs, and fortified milk. When our bodies don't get enough Vitamin D, it can lead to problems like weak bones, a higher risk of getting sick, and other health issues. To fix this, we need to encourage safe time outside, eating foods rich in Vitamin D, and sometimes taking supplements to stay healthy.

Here's a table that includes some essential vitamins, minerals, and other nutrients, along with their benefits, food sources, and some interesting or fun facts.

Vitamin/Mineral/ Nutrient	Benefit	Food Sources	Interesting Fact
Vitamin A	It keeps your eyes sharp and your skin healthy.	Liver, carrots, sweet potatoes, fish oils, spinach	Carrots really can help you see in the dark!
Vitamin B1 (Thiamine)	It helps your body turn food into energy.	Pork, whole grains, beef, beans, nuts, seeds	Called the "anti-stress" vitamin!
Vitamin B2 (Riboflavin)	Supports energy production and healthy skin.	Eggs, almonds, milk, mushrooms, spinach	It's responsible for your pee turning bright yellow!

Vitamin B3 (Niacin)	It boosts energy and helps digestion.	Chicken, peanuts, avocados, turkey, whole wheat bread	High doses can cause a "niacin flush"!
Vitamin B5 (Pantothenic Acid)	It helps your body produce hormones and energy.	Avocados, broccoli, chicken, beef liver, whole grains	It is found in almost every food, hence the name "pantothenic"!
Vitamin B6	Supports brain health and mood regulation.	Bananas, fish, potatoes, chickpeas, chicken	It helps with making serotonin, the "feel-good" hormone!
Vitamin B7 (Biotin)	Strengthens hair, skin, and nails.	Eggs, almonds, sweet potatoes, liver, spinach	Often called the "beauty vitamin"!
Vitamin B9 (Folate/Folic Acid)	It helps make new cells, which is crucial for growth.	Lentils, liver, asparagus, oranges	Pregnant women must prevent congenital disabilities!
Vitamin B12	It is important for brain health and energy levels.	Beef, fortified plant milk, fish, eggs, nutritional yeast	Vegans often need to supplement this!
Vitamin C	It boosts your immune system and helps heal cuts.	Oranges, strawberries, bell peppers, liver, broccoli	Sailors used to carry lemons to prevent scurvy!
Vitamin D	It builds strong bones and teeth and improves mood.	Salmon, fortified plant milk, egg yolks, mushrooms	You can make it from sunlight!
Vitamin E	It protects your cells and keeps your skin glowing.	Almonds, shrimp, sunflower seeds, fish, spinach	Great for skin, often in lotions and creams!
Vitamin K	It helps your blood clot and keeps bones strong.	Kale, liver, spinach, eggs, broccoli	It got its name from the German word "koagulation"!
Calcium	Essential for strong bones and teeth.	Dairy products, tofu, fortified plant milk, almonds, cheese	The most abundant mineral in the body!
Iron	It powers up your blood to carry oxygen and keeps you energized.	Red meat, lentils, spinach, quinoa, poultry	Iron deficiency is the most common worldwide!
Magnesium	It helps muscles relax and supports a steady heartbeat.	Spinach, chicken, fish, almonds, black beans, whole grains	Involved in over 300 biochemical reactions in your body!
Potassium	It keeps muscles and nerves working well and balances fluids.	Bananas, beef, potatoes, chicken, spinach	Bananas are radioactive (but don't worry, it's safe)!
Zinc	It boosts your immune system and helps you grow.	Beef, chickpeas, pork, pumpkin seeds, lentils	It helps you taste and smell!
Selenium	It protects cells from damage and supports immune function.	Tuna, Brazil nuts, beef, sunflower seeds, mushrooms	Just one Brazil nut can give you your daily dose!

Copper	It helps make red blood cells and keeps nerves healthy.	Nuts, liver, seeds, shellfish, whole grains, mushrooms	Copper deficiency can turn your hair gray!
Iodine	Supports thyroid function, which controls growth.	Iodized salt, fish, dairy, seaweed, cranberries	Iodine deficiency can cause goiter!
Phosphorus	Strengthens bones and teeth and helps produce energy.	Chicken, beans, turkey, lentils, fish, nuts, whole grains	It is the second most abundant mineral in the body!
Chromium	It helps regulate blood sugar levels.	Beef, broccoli, poultry, potatoes, whole grains	It helps insulin do its job better!
Fluoride	It keeps teeth strong and prevents cavities.	Fish, tea, fluoridated water	Too much can cause fluorosis and white spots on teeth!
Sodium	It helps control blood pressure and supports nerve function.	Table salt, processed meats, cheese, soy sauce	Too much can raise blood pressure!
Chloride	Works with sodium to balance fluids and support digestion.	Table salt, seaweed, processed meats	It is also found in the stomach as hydrochloric acid!
Sulfur	It helps make proteins and supports joint health.	Meat, garlic, fish, eggs, onions, cruciferous vegetables	Found in every cell of the body!
Omega-3 Fatty Acids	Supports heart health and brain function.	Salmon, flaxseeds, walnuts, chia seeds, sardines	Important for brain development in babies!
Omega-6 Fatty Acids	Supports brain function and normal growth.	Vegetable oils, nuts, seeds, poultry	Often over-consumed in Western diets!
Pantothenic Acid (Vitamin B5)	Helps with energy production and hormone synthesis.	Avocados, chicken, whole grains, mushrooms	Its name comes from the Greek word "pantothen," meaning "from everywhere"!
Vitamin B12 (Cobalamin)	Essential for red blood cell formation and brain function.	Eggs, fortified cereals, fish, nutritional yeast	It is only found naturally in animal products!
Vitamin D3	It helps absorb calcium and promotes bone health.	Cod liver oil, salmon, fortified foods, sunlight exposure	Your body makes it when your skin is exposed to sunlight!
Vitamin K2	It works with calcium to build strong bones and teeth.	Natto, cheese, egg yolks, butter	Often overlooked but crucial for heart health!
Beta-Carotene	A precursor to Vitamin A, it supports vision and immune function.	Carrots, sweet potatoes, kale, spinach	It can give your skin a yellow-orange tint if you eat too much!
Lutein	It supports eye health and may reduce the risk of cataracts.	Kale, spinach, eggs, corn	Known as the "eye vitamin" – important for vision!

Lycopene	It protects cells from damage and supports heart health.	Tomatoes, watermelon, pink grapefruit, red peppers	Cooking tomatoes increases lycopene availability!
Silicon	Supports bone health and collagen synthesis.	Whole grains, oats, bananas, beer	Silicon is in your hair, nails, and skin!
Boron	It supports bone health and improves wound healing.	Apples, nuts, raisins, avocados	Boron helps the body use other minerals!
Carnitine	It helps convert fat into energy.	Red meat, fish, poultry, dairy, avocado	Popular in sports supplements!
Taurine	Supports cardiovascular function and bile salt formation.	Meat, fish, dairy products, seaweed	Often added to energy drinks!
Cobalt	A component of Vitamin B12, essential for red blood cells.	Liver, dairy products, fish, green leafy vegetables	Cobalt is also used in batteries!
Nickel	Supports iron absorption and enzyme function.	Nuts, legumes, grains, chocolate	Nickel is essential in small amounts!
Vanadium	It may help with blood sugar control.	Shellfish, mushrooms, black pepper, parsley	Vanadium is found in the Earth's crust!
Tryptophan	An amino acid that helps with serotonin production.	Turkey, eggs, cheese, nuts, seeds	Known for causing post-Thanksgiving drowsiness!
Glutamine	Supports gut health and immune function.	Meat, eggs, dairy, beans, cabbage	Most abundant amino acid in the body!
Valine	Helps with muscle growth and energy production.	Meat, fish, eggs, dairy, beans	Third, BCAA is essential for muscle recovery!
Serine	Helps with brain function and metabolism.	Soy products, meat, eggs, dairy, legumes	Important for the production of cell membranes!
Glycine	Supports collagen production and muscle repair.	Meat, fish, dairy, gelatin, soy products	Found in collagen, the most abundant protein in the body!
Proline	Supports joint and skin health through collagen synthesis.	Meat, fish, dairy, egg whites, gelatin	Critical for maintaining skin elasticity!
Threonine	Supports immune function and collagen production.	Meat, fish, dairy, eggs, lentils	Essential for healthy skin and connective tissues!
Aspartic Acid	Helps with hormone production and nervous system health.	Meat, fish, eggs, soy products, legumes	A building block for other amino acids!
Pyrroloquinoline Quinone (PQQ)	Supports mitochondrial health and energy production.	Fermented soybeans, spinach, kiwi, green tea	Known as a "longevity" nutrient!
Lipoic Acid	It acts as a powerful antioxidant and supports energy production.	Spinach, broccoli, organ meats, potatoes	It helps regenerate other antioxidants like Vitamin C and E!

27

Polyphenols	It protects cells from damage and supports heart health.	Berries, tea, coffee, red wine	Known for their antioxidant properties!
Resveratrol	Supports heart health and longevity.	Grapes, red wine, peanuts, dark chocolate	Found in the skin of red grapes!
Flavonoids	It supports heart health and reduces inflammation.	Citrus fruits, berries, onions, tea	Over 6,000 types of flavonoids exist!
Curcumin	Supports anti-inflammatory and antioxidant activity.	Turmeric root, turmeric powder	It gives turmeric its bright yellow color!
Anthocyanins	It supports heart health and reduces inflammation.	Berries, red cabbage, purple potatoes	Give berries and red cabbage their rich color!

Phew! Pretty sure you haven't heard most of these names, and this is not even a complete list. But this gives an idea of the complexity of who we are and what our bodies need.

Now, digesting food is as important as eating. Here are the top 10 tips:

1. Chew Slowly and Completely

Thoroughly chewing your food until it becomes a paste-like consistency aids digestion by breaking down food mechanically. Mixing it with saliva helps pre-digest carbohydrates through enzymes like amylase. This process reduces the burden on your stomach and intestines, allowing for smoother and faster digestion. Slowly sipping drinks allows digestive enzymes to stay at optimal levels, preventing bloating and aiding nutrient absorption.

2. Avoid Mixing Fast and Slow-Digesting Foods

Some food combinations can hinder digestion. For example, mixing fast-digesting fruits with slow-digesting proteins like meat can cause fermentation in the gut, leading to bloating and gas. Fruits digest quickly, while proteins require more time and effort, causing a mismatch. However, pairing proteins with vegetables improves digestion, as fiber helps move proteins more effectively through the intestines.

3. Incorporate Fermented Foods

Fermented foods like yogurt, kefir, sauerkraut, and kimchi are rich in probiotics, which are beneficial bacteria that aid in digestion. These bacteria help break down complex carbohydrates, lactose, and fibers that can otherwise cause bloating or discomfort. They also enhance gut flora balance, promoting efficient digestion and reducing inflammation in the gut lining.

4. Eat Enzyme-Rich Foods

Certain raw foods contain natural digestive enzymes that can boost your body's enzyme production. For example, pineapple contains bromelain, which aids in the digestion of proteins, and papaya contains papain, another protein-digesting enzyme. Including these foods in your meals can help break down tougher components of food and ease digestion.

5. Time Your Fiber Intake

While fiber is crucial for good digestion, consuming too much insoluble fiber at once can cause bloating and gas. Insoluble fiber, found in foods like whole grains and leafy greens, adds bulk to stool but isn't digested by the body. Soluble fiber, found in oats, legumes, and some fruits, forms a gel-like substance in the intestines, aiding in smooth transit. Balancing both types of fiber and introducing them slowly is key to avoiding digestive discomfort.

6. Use Bitter Foods as Digestive Stimulators

Bitter foods like arugula, dandelion greens, and endives can stimulate the production of digestive juices such as bile and stomach acid. Bile helps emulsify fats, making them easier to digest, while stomach acid is essential for breaking down proteins. A small serving of bitter greens before a meal can prime your digestive system, improving nutrient breakdown and absorption.

7. Eat Smaller, Frequent Meals

Instead of eating large meals that overwhelm your digestive system, smaller, frequent meals can promote smoother digestion. Overloading your stomach with too much food at once can delay gastric emptying, leading to discomfort and bloating. By eating smaller portions more frequently, you allow your digestive system to handle the workload more efficiently, promoting faster digestion and reducing gas.

8. Avoid Cold Drinks with Meals

Drinking cold beverages during meals can slow digestion by solidifying fats in the food and reducing stomach acid's efficiency. Digestive enzymes also work best at body temperature, so that cold drinks can hinder their activity. Opt for room temperature or warm beverages to maintain optimal enzyme function and improve digestion.

9. Include Prebiotic Foods

Prebiotics, such as inulin and fructooligosaccharides (found in foods like garlic, onions, and bananas), feed the beneficial bacteria in your gut. These bacteria play a crucial role in digesting certain fibers and producing short-chain fatty acids, which support the health of the gut lining. A healthy balance of gut bacteria can improve digestion, reduce inflammation, and enhance nutrient absorption.

10. Eat Fat in Moderation, but Don't Eliminate It

While fat slows down digestion, moderate amounts of healthy fats can actually aid in nutrient absorption, particularly fat-soluble vitamins (A, D, E, and K). Eating too much fat at once, however, can delay gastric emptying and cause bloating. Pairing healthy fats, like olive oil or avocado, with fiber-rich foods helps optimize digestion and prevents the digestive process from becoming sluggish.

Consider a time when you were feeling down or anxious. What did you eat that day? Could your diet have played a role in your mood?

5. Get Moving or Get Rusty

From the moment we take our first breath, we're set on a course of constant motion. Think about it. As babies, we're wiggling, squirming, and doing everything we can to explore the world. Crawling becomes rolling, which turns into stumbling attempts at walking. We're like little scientists, testing the limits of our new abilities. We reach for anything we can get our tiny hands on, and we're not satisfied until we've knocked it over, tasted it, or tried to shove it into our mouths.

As kids, movement is second nature. Playgrounds become our battlegrounds. We run, jump, climb, and tumble, burning off energy as if our lives depend on it—because, in many ways, they do. We're not thinking about exercise; we're just playing. Whether we're playing tag, riding bikes, or simply running around like wild animals, we're in our element. **We're doing what humans have always done: moving.**

But then something changes. As we get older, our world becomes smaller. School means sitting still for hours at a time, focused on books, screens, and assignments. After school, we might head home to relax, which often means more sitting—scrolling through social media, watching videos, or gaming. Before we know it, we've gone from being in constant motion to spending most of our time on our butts. It's like someone hit the pause button on our natural urge to move.

The Sedentary Trap: What Happens When We Stop Moving

Picture this: You're at your desk, hunched over your homework or scrolling through your phone. Hours pass, and you barely move. Maybe you're comfortable, but deep down, your body's not happy.

When we don't move enough, our bodies pay the price. Our muscles weaken, our joints stiffen, and our energy levels plummet. **It's no wonder**

that sitting for too long has been called "the new smoking." Studies have shown that long periods of sitting can increase the risk of everything from heart disease to diabetes to depression. It's like our bodies are shouting, "Hey! I was made to move! What are you doing to me?"

The irony is we live in a time when technology makes it easier than ever to be sedentary. Need to talk to a friend? Text them. Want to know something? Google it. Need to entertain yourself? Endless streams of videos are just a click away. It's all so convenient, but convenience comes at a cost. We've traded movement for comfort, and our bodies are feeling the effects.

The Science of Movement: Why It Matters

So, why is movement so important? Let's break it down. Your body is like a complex machine, with hundreds of different parts working together to keep you alive and well. And just like any machine, it needs to be used to stay in good condition.

1. **Muscles and Bones:** When you move, you're not just burning calories—you're building strength. Every time you walk, run, lift, or stretch, your muscles are getting stronger. And when your muscles are strong, they support your bones, which reduces the risk of injuries and keeps you agile. It's like a protective armor that you build over time.

2. **Heart and Lungs:** Your heart is a muscle, too. Like all muscles, exercise is needed to stay strong. When you're active, your heart pumps more blood, which delivers oxygen and nutrients to your cells. This keeps your body energized and helps your lungs work more efficiently.

3. **Brain Power:** Movement isn't just good for your body—it's essential for your brain. When you exercise, your brain releases chemicals called endorphins. These are like natural mood boosters that make

you feel happier and more relaxed. Plus, regular physical activity improves memory, concentration, and creativity. It's like giving your brain a turbo boost.

4. **Mental Health:** Ever notice how you feel better after a good run or a long walk? That's not just in your head—well, actually, it is! Physical activity reduces stress, anxiety, and depression. It helps you sleep better, feel more confident, and cope with challenges. It's like having a superpower that makes life a little easier.

Why Do So Many of Us Dread Exercise?

Picture this: It's a beautiful morning, the sun is shining, and birds are chirping. Your alarm goes off, signaling it's time for your daily run. But instead of jumping out of bed with excitement, you groan, hit the snooze button, and roll over. Why does the thought of exercise often fill us with dread? Why do we hate exercise so much, even though we know it's good for us?

1. Our Bodies Are Hardwired for Energy Efficiency

The human body is an incredible machine designed for efficiency. Our ancestors needed to conserve energy for survival, whether it was for hunting, gathering, or escaping predators. This energy conservation instinct means our brains are wired to avoid unnecessary exertion whenever possible.

In the modern world, where food is abundant and physical danger is minimal, this instinct can work against us. Our bodies still prefer to conserve energy, making us more inclined to choose sedentary activities over physical exercise.

2. The Discomfort Factor

Exercise can be uncomfortable, especially when starting a new routine. Muscle soreness, fatigue, and the feeling of being out of breath are all deterrents. These sensations are our body's way of signaling that we are pushing it beyond its usual comfort zone, which can be off-putting for many.

3. The Reward System in Our Brain

Our brains are motivated by rewards. Activities that release dopamine, the feel-good neurotransmitter, are the ones we are likely to repeat. Unfortunately, the immediate rewards from exercise, like the endorphin rush or the sense of accomplishment, often don't come until after the workout. In contrast, activities like watching TV or eating comfort food provide more immediate gratification, making them more appealing.

Our ancestors only engaged in physical activity out of necessity. They didn't run marathons for fun; they ran to catch dinner or avoid becoming dinner.

This evolutionary background makes **modern voluntary exercise a relatively new concept that our brains are still adapting to**. In a way, modern exercise is like trying to speak a new language that our bodies are still learning to understand. The motivation to move, once driven by survival, now needs to be cultivated in a world where physical activity isn't strictly necessary. This is why it's important to find ways to make movement enjoyable or meaningful, whether that's through sports, dance, or simply walking in nature.

The Big Three: Types of Exercise

1. Aerobic (Cardio) Exercise: Get That Heart Pumping

What It Is:

Aerobic exercise, often called cardio, is all about getting your heart rate up. This type of exercise includes activities like running, swimming, biking, and even dancing. The goal is to move your body in a way that makes your heart beat faster, which strengthens your heart and lungs.

Why It's Important:

Cardio is great for your cardiovascular health. Think of your heart as a muscle—it needs regular exercise to stay strong. When you do cardio, you're improving your endurance, which means you can keep going longer without getting tired. Plus, it helps burn calories and improve your overall energy levels. Ever notice how you feel more awake after a run? That's the power of cardio.

Examples:

- **Running or Jogging:** Start small, maybe just a few minutes a day. Gradually increase the time as you get stronger.

- **Swimming:** If you have access to a pool, swimming is a fantastic full-body workout that's easy on your joints.

- **Biking:** Whether it's cycling outdoors or on a stationary bike, it's a great way to get your heart pumping while exploring new places.

- **Dancing:** Put on your favorite music and dance like nobody's watching. It's fun, and you'll break a sweat without even realizing it.

2. Strength Training: Building Muscle and Power

What It Is:

Strength training involves exercises that make your muscles work harder than they're used to. This can include lifting weights, using resistance bands, or doing bodyweight exercises like push-ups, squats, and planks.

Why It's Important:

Building muscle isn't just for bodybuilders. Strength training makes you stronger, improves your posture, and helps prevent injuries. It also boosts your metabolism, which means you'll burn more calories even when you're not exercising. Plus, strong muscles support your bones and joints, making everyday tasks easier. And you don't need to go to the Gym to build muscles;

there is plenty you can do with your body weight.

Examples:

- **Push-ups:** Start with as many as you can, even if it's just one or two. Over time, you'll build up strength.

- **Squats:** These are great for your legs and core. You can do them anywhere—no equipment is needed.

- **Lifting Weights:** If you have access to weights, start with light ones and focus on your form. If not, use household items like water bottles.

- **Resistance Bands:** These are portable and great for adding extra challenge to exercises like bicep curls and leg lifts.

3. Flexibility and Balance: Stay Limber, Stay Balanced

What It Is:

Flexibility and balance exercises are all about keeping your body flexible and stable. This includes activities like yoga, stretching, and Pilates. These exercises help you move more easily and reduce the risk of injuries, especially as you get older.

Why It's Important:

Flexibility keeps your muscles and joints healthy, allowing you to move freely and perform daily activities without pain. Balance exercises improve your coordination and stability, which can prevent falls and improve your performance in other types of physical activity.

Examples:

- **Yoga:** Yoga combines flexibility and balance with strength and mindfulness. It's a great way to relax while still getting a good workout.

- **Stretching:** Simple stretching exercises can be done daily to keep your muscles loose and limber.

- **Pilates:** Pilates focuses on strengthening your core muscles, which improves your balance and stability.

- **Balance Exercises:** Try standing on one foot for as long as you can. It's harder than it sounds, and it's great for your balance.

Find What You Love: Make Exercise Fun

The best exercise is the one you enjoy. If you're not into running, don't force yourself to do it just because it's popular. Maybe you love playing soccer, hiking in nature, or dancing in your room. The key is to find something that gets you moving and makes you happy.

When you enjoy what you're doing, you're more likely to stick with it. Exercise shouldn't feel like a chore—it should be something you look forward to. Plus, when you're having fun, you'll naturally push yourself harder and get better results.

Make It Social: Exercise with Friends

Exercising with others can make the experience more enjoyable and keep you motivated. Whether it's a group fitness class, a sports team, or just a workout buddy, being active with others adds a social element that makes exercise feel less like work and more like fun.

When you exercise with others, you're more likely to stick with it because you have accountability. Plus, it's a great way to bond with friends and make new ones. Socializing while being active can make time fly, and you might even push yourself harder when you're working out with someone else.

Incorporate Movement into Your Day: Stay Active Without a Gym

Not all exercises have to be planned or take place in a gym. You can find ways to stay active throughout your day by making small changes to your routine. These little bursts of activity add up over time and keep your body moving.

Modern life often involves a lot of sitting—at school, in front of the TV, or while scrolling through your phone. But sitting too much isn't good for your health. By finding ways to incorporate more movement into your day, you can stay active even when you're busy.

Final Thoughts: Make Movement a Habit

Remember, exercise doesn't have to be complicated. The most important thing is to find what works for you and make it a regular part of your life. Start small, be consistent, and keep trying new things until you find what you love. Over time, you'll feel stronger, more energized, and ready to take on whatever life throws at you. The best thing is that you don't have to go out or join an expensive gym. You can do push-ups, squats, and 100s of other exercises in your bedroom itself. All we need is discipline. Cannot run outside, no problem - just jump. Cannot go biking - no problem - lie down and move your legs like you are pedaling in the air.

Remember, the main goal of being physically active and looking after your body is not to impress others or look like a model or whatever. The main goal is to feel good, confident, and healthy, which is the foundation for a good life. Without health, there is nothing.

6. Sleep Is Your Superpower

You're lying in bed, eyes closed, drifting off into dreamland. While you're completely zonked out, something amazing is happening. Your body isn't just resting—it's working overtime to make sure you wake up the next day ready to conquer the world. All the good things happen when you sleep. You grow taller, you build muscle, your brain builds long-term memories, and man, those crazy vivid dreams - By the way, did you ever wonder if the dream was the reality and maybe reality is a dream?!

Alas, in today's world, we have managed to screw a simple natural act of sleeping. For millions of years, the brain has associated darkness with sleep, and it starts producing melatonin, which prepares us for sleep. But then we show it a bright light and wake it up! The blue light from our phone and TV fools the brain into thinking it is still day - no need to sleep!

If that was not enough, we overeat and have caffeine-laced drinks with dinner. The quality of sleep suffers if the stomach is busy digesting food at night. The vital blood flow is needed in other parts of the body for repair routines, but it gets directed to our big stomachs to digest that chocolate bar we had after a big dinner.

Sleep isn't just for when you're tired. At night, it goes into the shop for repairs, tune-ups, and a fresh coat of paint. This isn't just rest—it's a full-scale maintenance routine. Without enough sleep, your body and mind suffer, and everything from your mood to your immune system takes a hit.

Why Do We Hate Getting Up in the Morning?

You know the feeling: the alarm blares, your eyes flutter open, and an overwhelming urge to hit snooze takes over. You think to yourself, "Just five more minutes." But why is it so difficult to get up in the morning, even when you've had enough sleep? What's the science behind our morning struggle?

Our Biological Clock and Circadian Rhythm

DID YOU EVER WAKE UP EARLY MORNING AND CHECKED YOUR PHONE TO SEE HOW MUCH MORE YOU CAN SLEEP AND IT WAS JUST 1 MINUTE TO THE ALARM?!

Our bodies operate on an internal clock known

as the circadian rhythm. This roughly 24-hour cycle regulates various physiological processes, including sleep-wake patterns, hormone release, and body temperature. Environmental cues like light and darkness influence the circadian rhythm.

During the night, the pineal gland in the brain produces melatonin, a hormone that promotes sleep. As the sun rises, melatonin levels drop, and our bodies begin to wake up. However, if your circadian rhythm is misaligned due to lifestyle factors (like staying up late or exposure to artificial light), waking up can feel like an uphill battle.

Sleep Inertia: The Groggy Morning Feeling

Sleep inertia refers to the grogginess and disorientation we feel upon waking. It occurs because our brains need time to transition from a sleep state to full wakefulness. This period can last from a few minutes to over an hour, depending on how abruptly we are woken up and the stage of sleep we are in.

Waking up during deep sleep (stages 3 and 4) or REM sleep can intensify sleep inertia, making it harder to shake off that sluggish feeling. Alarm clocks often disrupt sleep cycles, causing us to wake up at less optimal times, further exacerbating this issue.

Hormonal Influences: Cortisol and Melatonin

Cortisol, known as the stress hormone, plays a crucial role in waking us up. Levels of cortisol start to rise in the early morning hours and peak around 8 a.m., helping to kick-start our day. However, if our sleep patterns are irregular, or if we wake up too early or too late, the natural cortisol rise may not align properly, leading to a rough start.

Conversely, melatonin, which helps us sleep, is at its lowest in the morning. Disruption in the balance of these hormones due to factors like poor sleep hygiene or irregular sleep schedules can make waking up challenging.

The Symphony of Sleep Cycles

Your sleep is divided into several phases, each with its purpose. These phases are part of what's called the **sleep cycle**, and each cycle lasts around **90 minutes**. You go through several of these cycles every night—ideally about four to six, depending on how long you sleep. Here's a breakdown of the phases:

1. NREM Stage 1: Light Sleep

Duration: 1-7 minutes

This is the stage where you're just drifting off, somewhere between wakefulness and sleep. Your muscles relax, and your breathing slows down. It's super easy to wake up during this phase, like when you jolt awake thinking you're falling—classic Stage 1 move.

2. NREM Stage 2: Deeper Sleep

Duration: 10-25 minutes (gets longer in later cycles)

Stage 2 is where your body starts to prepare for deep sleep. Your heart rate slows, body temperature drops, and eye movements stop. This is like the pre-game show for real rest. It makes up about **50%** of your total sleep time.

3. NREM Stage 3: Deep Sleep

Duration: 20-40 minutes

This is the most important phase for physical restoration. In deep sleep, your body repairs muscles, tissues, and bones, and it also strengthens your immune system. Waking up during this phase can make you feel dizzy and disoriented. That's why getting enough deep sleep is crucial.

4. REM Sleep: Dreaming Stage

Duration: 10 minutes initially, but up to 60 minutes in later cycles

REM (Rapid Eye Movement) sleep is when your brain goes into overdrive, processing emotions, storing memories, and creating the wild dreams you have. Your body is in a state of paralysis to keep you from acting out those dreams. As the night progresses, REM phases get longer, and they account for about **25%** of your total sleep time.

A typical sleep cycle lasts around **90 minutes**, and you go through all the phases multiple times a night. You'll experience a longer REM phase in the morning, which is why you often wake up from vivid dreams.

Nightly Maintenance Routines

When you sleep, your body goes into repair mode. Picture a night crew bustling through your system, fixing and fine-tuning. Here's a sneak peek at what's happening:

- **Mental tuning and Dreams:** Your brain files away the day's experiences, strengthening memory and learning. REM sleep plays a big part here, consolidating information and skills learned during the day. Sleep is just as important for your brain as it is for your body And don't forget about dreams. Dreams aren't just random scenes that play out in your head—they're part of your brain's process of organizing thoughts, emotions, and memories. It's like your brain's own personal workshop, where it can experiment, problem-solve, and even create.

- **Immune System Boost:** Your immune system produces cytokines during sleep, which help fight infection, inflammation, and stress. Cytokines are small proteins that are vital in regulating immune responses. They act as signaling molecules, enabling communication between immune cells and guiding them to areas of the body that require defense or repair. Specifically, cytokines help the body fight off infections by promoting inflammation and directing immune cells to the site of infection or injury. Chronic inflammation, for instance, has been linked to a range of health issues, including the development and progression of cancer. By reducing inflammation and promoting a balanced immune response, **adequate sleep may contribute to a**

lower risk of cancer. The body's ability to detect and eliminate abnormal cells, such as those that could potentially become cancerous, is enhanced when the immune system is functioning optimally.

- **You Grow Taller** - That's right. Have you ever heard someone say, "Get your beauty sleep"? Well, it's more like, "Get your growing sleep." When you sleep, your body releases a hormone called growth hormone, which does exactly what it sounds like—it helps you grow. This hormone is crucial, especially during your teen years when your body is still growing and developing. But here's the kicker: growth hormone is released in its highest amounts during deep sleep.

- **You Build Muscle** - Whether you're lifting weights, playing sports, or just trying to get stronger, sleep is your secret weapon. During sleep, especially during deep sleep, your body repairs and builds muscle tissue. All that hard work you put in at the gym or on the field pays off while you're sleeping.

Beat the Screen: Sleep Better Without Tech

We live in a digital world. From smartphones and tablets to computers and TVs, screens are everywhere. The blue light emitted by screens can suppress the production of melatonin, a hormone produced in the pineal gland in the brain that regulates sleep.

When you use screens before bed, the blue light tricks your brain into thinking it's still daytime. This delays the release of melatonin, making it harder to fall asleep.

Using screens before bed is like drinking a cup of coffee right before you hit the hay. It's not exactly conducive to a good night's sleep.

The Ideal Sleep Routine

The National Sleep Foundation recommends that teens get 8-10 hours of sleep per night. Adequate sleep is linked to better academic performance, improved mood, and overall health. Here are some tips to help you get the best sleep:

1. **Consistency is Key:** Go to bed and wake up at the same time every day, even on weekends. It is hard, but it is the best for your energy levels. Exceptions are fine, of course - those late-nighters are fun sometimes!

2. **Limit Screen Time:** Avoid screens at least an hour before bed.

3. **Environment Matters:** Keep your bedroom cool, dark, and quiet.

4. **Mind Your Dinner:** Avoid very heavy meals just before bedtime. Eat as much as you want, but a couple of hours before bed. Although at your age, the digestive system is strong, this is more so when you become an adult; it is better to create habits early in life, or else it is difficult to change.

So, what one thing you learned in this chapter that you didn't know before?

7. Stand Tall: The Power of Good Posture

Hey, are you sitting with a straight back while reading this? Hope not sitting like this cat?

How's your posture?

It took millions of years of evolution for our ancestors to stand and walk straight. In fact, bipedalism (the ability to walk on two legs) is considered one of the key contributing factors to why our brains evolved and we became intelligent. It frees up the hands to create tools, communicate, travel long distances, etc.

Welcome to the 21st century, where we are all hunched forward, scrolling

something on a rectangular touch screen with our spine discs under immense tension and neck muscles crying in pain silently. If we continue hunching like this, who knows, we will be back on four limbs in a few hundred years!.... I know, I know, that was a lame joke, but the posture is not a joke at all. It is a modern-day epidemic that nobody is talking about enough. We are living in a world where every other adult has a back or a neck problem, and even young adults are reporting back problems that have been unheard of before we got addicted to or got reliant on screens for our work and education.

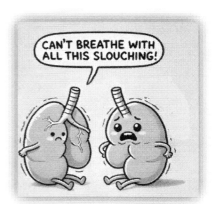

When we slouch, the lungs cannot expand properly, making breathing difficult and shallow. What this means is that you don't get enough oxygen and will feel tired if you continue to sit in bad posture.

Posture is something we don't often think about until we start feeling pain. But the way you sit and stand affects your health in more ways than you might realize. Good posture keeps your bones and joints in alignment, reduces stress on your muscles and ligaments, and allows you to move more efficiently.

Think about how you sit when you're at school or home. Do you slouch in your chair? Hunch over your phone? These habits can cause your muscles to weaken and lead to imbalances that result in pain and discomfort. Good posture helps distribute your weight evenly and reduces the strain on your body.

The Heavy Head: Why It Hurts Our Necks

Our heads weigh around 10-12 pounds, roughly the same as a small bowling ball. When our posture is perfect, our heads are aligned directly above our spines, allowing the weight to be distributed evenly. This alignment minimizes strain on our muscles and bones.

But here's the kicker: most of us don't have perfect posture. Think about how you look at your phone or computer. Your head juts forward, your shoulders hunch, and you may even lean in closer. This is called **"text neck"**. For every inch your head moves forward, the pressure on your neck doubles. So, a 10-pound head leaning forward by 3 inches can feel like 30 pounds. Imagine carrying that around all day!

Where the Weight Should Go

In an ideal world, we would all have perfect posture. Our ears would be aligned with our shoulders, our shoulders with our hips. This way, the weight of our head would be balanced and evenly distributed down our spine, reducing strain on our muscles.

The Role of Core Muscles

Our core muscles, including the muscles in our abdomen, back, and pelvis, play a crucial role in maintaining this alignment. Strong core muscles support our spine and help keep our body in the right position. When our core is weak, other parts of our body, like our neck and lower back, have to work harder, leading to pain and discomfort.

Disc Problems

Poor posture can also lead to disc problems—the discs in our spine act as cushions between our vertebrae. When we have bad posture, these discs can become compressed or herniated, causing significant pain and discomfort.

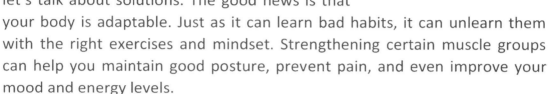

Fixing Our Posture: Tips and Tricks

Now that we've painted a picture of the problem let's talk about solutions. The good news is that your body is adaptable. Just as it can learn bad habits, it can unlearn them with the right exercises and mindset. Strengthening certain muscle groups can help you maintain good posture, prevent pain, and even improve your mood and energy levels.

1. Neck and Upper Back Strengthening

The muscles at the back of your neck and between your shoulder blades are key to holding your head up and keeping your shoulders back. Here's how to give them a workout:

- **Chin Tucks**: Sit or stand tall and tuck your chin towards your chest without moving your shoulders. Hold for a few seconds, then release. This strengthens the muscles at the back of your neck, counteracting forward head posture.
- **Scapular Squeezes**: Sit or stand up straight and squeeze your shoulder blades together as if you're trying to hold a pencil between them. Hold for five seconds, then release. Repeat several times. This helps strengthen the muscles between your shoulder blades.

2. Core Strengthening

Your core isn't just about abs. It includes the muscles around your spine that help you stay upright. Strengthening these muscles can improve your posture and reduce lower back pain:

- **Planks**: Lie face down, then lift your body onto your forearms and toes. Keep your body in a straight line from head to heels, engaging your core. Hold as long as you can without letting your hips sag.

- **Dead Bug**: Lie on your back with your arms extended towards the ceiling and your knees bent at 90 degrees. Slowly lower your right arm and left leg towards the floor while keeping your back flat. Return to the starting position, then switch sides. This exercise targets your deep core muscles.

3. Stretching the Tight Spots

When some muscles are overworked, others get tight. Stretching helps restore balance:

- **Chest Stretch**: Stand in a doorway with your arms out to the side, elbows bent at 90 degrees. Step one foot forward and press your arms against the doorframe, feeling a stretch in your chest.

- **Hip Flexor Stretch**: Kneel on one knee with the other foot in front of you, forming a 90-degree angle. Push your hips forward slightly while keeping your back straight. This stretches the muscles at the front of your hips, which get tight from sitting.

Making it a Habit

The trick is to make them a part of your daily routine. Start small—five to ten minutes a day—and gradually increase the time. Pair them with activities you already do, like brushing your teeth or watching TV. This way, you won't forget, and they'll become as automatic as checking your phone.

Good posture is more than just standing up straight. By making small changes and being mindful of our posture, we can stand tall, reduce pain, and live healthier lives. So, let's get started on the path to better posture.......... Right now!

8. How Living Indoors is Changing Our Vision

Imagine a world where almost everyone wears glasses. This isn't some futuristic science fiction scenario—it's the reality we're heading toward, and in some places, we're already there. Myopia, or nearsightedness, has become a global epidemic, and the numbers are staggering.

Now, there is no problem wearing glasses, and I wear those too, but this is more about caring for your eyes and vision for long-term health.

Myopia, or nearsightedness, is when you can see things up close pretty well, but objects that are far away look blurry. Imagine trying to read a sign that's across the street, but all the letters are fuzzy. It happens because your eyeball is a little longer than it should be, or your cornea (the front part of your eye) is curved too much. Because of this, light focuses in front of your retina (the part of your eye that sends images to your brain) instead of directly on it. This makes distant objects look

blurry. Myopia often starts when you're a kid or a teenager. It's partly due to your genes—if your parents wear glasses for myopia, you might need them too. But it's also about how you use your eyes. Spending a lot of time doing close-up work, like reading, using your phone, or playing video games, and spending less time outdoors can make it more likely or worse.

Let's start with some eye-opening facts. In East Asia, the prevalence of myopia among young people has skyrocketed in just a few decades. In cities like Seoul, Hong Kong, and Taipei, up to 90% of teenagers and young adults are myopic. Compare this with their parents' generation, where only around 20-30% needed glasses. The situation is not limited to Asia. In the United States and Europe, the prevalence of myopia has also risen sharply. In the

U.S., about 42% of people between the ages of 12 and 54 are nearsighted, a significant increase from 25% in the early 1970s. Covid lockdowns had a negative impact on eyesight as we all spent more time on screens and less time outdoors. Research predicts that by 2050, the condition could affect more than half of teens worldwide.

So, what's causing this drastic change? Why are more kids today growing up needing glasses while their grandparents didn't?

A New Way of Seeing the World

To understand this shift, we need to think about how our lives have changed over the past few generations. Our ancestors spent most of their time outdoors, hunting, gathering, farming, and generally living under the sun. Their eyes evolved to handle long distances, scanning the horizon for prey or threats. Today, however, most of us spend the majority of our time indoors, looking at screens, books, or walls that are just a few feet away. This change in lifestyle is having a profound impact on our eyes.

But there's more to the story. It's not just the constant near work that's causing problems; it's also the lack of time spent outdoors. When we spend more time outside, our eyes are exposed to many protective effects that scientists are still trying to understand fully.

Studies have shown that children who spend more time outdoors are less likely to become myopic. For example, a study in Taiwan found that when schools implemented mandatory outdoor time during recess, the onset of myopia slowed down significantly. In Australia, children spend more time outdoors than in many other countries, and the rate of myopia is correspondingly lower—around 30% compared to 80-90% in East Asia.

The Future of Our Vision

So, what can we do to protect our eyes in this screen-dominated world? The answer isn't to throw away your devices but to find a balance between indoor and outdoor activities.

1. Prioritize Outdoor Time

Make it a goal to spend at least two hours outdoors each day. Whether it's playing sports, taking a walk, or just hanging out in the park, time spent outside can help slow the progression of myopia. Encourage outdoor play for children and set limits on screen time.

2. Practice Good Eye Habits

When you're indoors, be mindful of your screen time. Follow the 20-20-20 rule: every 20 minutes, take a 20-second break and look at something 20 feet away. This helps relax the ciliary muscle and reduce eye strain.

3. Create an Eye-Friendly Environment

Ensure that your indoor lighting is bright enough to reduce the strain on your eyes. Position your screens to minimize glare, and keep them at a comfortable distance from your eyes. Adjust the brightness and contrast settings on your devices to match the ambient light in your room.

4. Get Regular Eye Check-ups

Regular eye exams are crucial, especially for children. Myopia often develops during childhood, and early intervention can help manage the condition and prevent it from worsening. An eye doctor can provide advice on lifestyle changes and may prescribe special lenses designed to slow the progression of myopia.

We live in a time where screens are unavoidable, but that doesn't mean we have to sacrifice our vision. By understanding the causes of myopia and taking proactive steps to protect our eyes, we can ensure that we—and future generations—continue to see the world clearly.

So, How much time do you spend outdoors each day? How can you increase your outdoor time?

9. Substance abuse - The Party That's More Dangerous Than It Looks

You're at a party, the kind where the lights are just right, the music makes your bones hum, and everyone's having a blast. Someone nudges you, offering a drink, a puff of smoke, or maybe even a hit from a sleek vape pen. You hesitate because, deep down, you know this isn't just a harmless party favor. You've heard the warnings, the horror stories. But the temptation to fit in, to be part of the moment, is strong. After all, it's just this once, right?

Well, not quite. Here's the thing—they don't tell you what happens after you walk away from the party. The story doesn't end with you just going home and forgetting it all happened. This is where life gets complicated, and the choices you make can affect you for years to come.

Smoking: The Slow Burn That Stunts Your Growth—Literally

Cigarettes have a long history. They've been around since the days when explorers brought tobacco back from the New World. But it wasn't until the 20th century that smoking became a global trend, advertised as the height of sophistication. Back then, nobody knew—or at least, nobody cared—that those "cool" sticks of tobacco were filled with toxic chemicals.

What's Really in a Cigarette?

Let's break it down. A cigarette is basically a delivery system for some of the nastiest chemicals on Earth. We're talking about:

- **Nicotine**: The addictive substance that hooks you faster than you can say, "I'll quit tomorrow."

- **Tar**: The sticky stuff that coats your lungs and turns them black. Lovely.

- **Formaldehyde**: The same chemical used to preserve dead bodies. Now imagine what it does to living tissue.

- **Arsenic**: Rat poison. No, seriously, it's in there.

When you light up, these chemicals get sucked into your lungs, which are designed for one thing: breathing clean air. Your lungs aren't thrilled about this new job description. While you might not feel the effects immediately, the damage happens at a microscopic level every time you inhale.

Now, let's talk about how smoking can mess with your body in ways you might not even notice at first. If you're still growing—like most teens are—smoking can actually stunt your growth. That's right. Smoking can interfere with your body's ability to reach its full potential, whether that's height, muscle development, or brain power. The toxins in cigarettes can restrict the oxygen supply to your bones, organs, and muscles, making it harder for them to grow and develop properly.

And your brain? Well, it's still developing too. Smoking can impair your cognitive functions—things like memory, learning, and even decision-making. So, if you want to do well in school, sports, or just life in general, smoking is a really bad move!

Alcohol: The "Liquid Courage" That's Secretly Sabotaging You

Alcohol has been around forever. Ancient civilizations brewed beer and wine, and it's been a part of social rituals for millennia. But here's the thing: just because it's old doesn't mean it's good for you. Over time, we've learned that alcohol isn't just a drink—it's a drug that can mess with your body and brain in ways you wouldn't believe.

What Alcohol Does to a Growing Brain

Your brain is like a supercomputer, and it's still being programmed. Drinking alcohol is like pouring water on that supercomputer's motherboard. It messes with your ability to think clearly, make good decisions, and remember important things. That's why people do dumb stuff when they're drunk—they're literally not thinking straight.

But here's where it gets really scary. For teens whose brains are still developing, alcohol can cause long-lasting damage. It can impair the growth of certain parts of the brain, particularly the hippocampus, which is crucial for memory and learning. So, if you're hoping to ace that test or remember what you studied last night, alcohol isn't doing you any favors.

Drugs: The "High" That Brings You Low

Drugs come in all shapes and sizes. Some are legal, like prescription meds, while others are illegal, like cocaine or heroin. But whether it's a pill, a powder, or a plant, drugs all do the same thing—they hijack your brain's reward system and make you feel good. But that good feeling is a trick, a chemical illusion that comes with a heavy price.

Drugs can permanently alter brain structure and function, affecting everything from your emotions to your ability to make decisions. For teens, whose brains are still developing, this can mean serious long-term consequences, like decreased intelligence, memory problems, and an increased risk of mental health issues like depression and anxiety.

Drugs don't just mess with your brain; they mess with your entire life. They can wreck your health, destroy relationships, and land you in serious legal trouble. And if you think you're invincible, think again. Overdose deaths are on the rise, and they don't just happen to people who've been using for years. They can happen to anyone, even if it's their first time experimenting.

Vaping: The Sleek, Dangerous New Trend

Vaping is often seen as the "cool" alternative to smoking. After all, it doesn't smell as bad, and the flavors sound harmless—who wouldn't want to puff on something called "Cotton Candy Cloud" or "Bubblegum Bliss"? But here's the dirty secret: vaping isn't harmless. In fact, it might be even worse than smoking in some ways.

Vaping liquids also contain chemicals like formaldehyde (remember that stuff from cigarettes?), acrolein (which can cause irreversible lung damage), and diacetyl (linked to severe respiratory diseases).

So, while vaping might seem like the "healthier" choice, it's still delivering a potent mix of harmful chemicals right into your lungs. And since vaping is relatively new, we don't even know all the long-term effects yet. But what we do know isn't good.

How to Say No Without Feeling Like a Loser

Know Your Reasons

The first step to resisting peer pressure is understanding why you want to say no. Maybe it's because you want to stay healthy perform better in sports, or simply because you've seen what substance abuse can do to people's lives. Whatever your reasons are, keep them at the forefront of your mind.

Find Your Tribe

Having a group of friends who share your values can make a world of difference. When you're surrounded by people who support your decisions, it's easier to stand strong. Plus, it's always more fun to say no when you've got backup.

Be Straightforward

When someone offers you something you don't want, it's okay to be direct. A simple "No thanks, I'm not interested" is often all it takes. If they push, you can always say, "I've got other plans," or "I'm focusing on my health right now." You don't owe anyone an explanation, but having one ready can help you feel more confident.

The choices you make now can shape your future. This chapter isn't about telling you what to do. It's about giving you the tools to make informed choices that set you up for success, not just now but for the rest of your life. Your body and brain are amazing, and they deserve the best care you can give them. Imagine your future self. What kind of person do you want to be, and how does staying substance-free help you get there?

10. Say No to Dieting: Nourish Your Body and Mind

You're scrolling through social media, and every other post is about some new diet, a magic pill, or a quick fix to lose weight. It seems like everyone is obsessed with being skinny. But here's the thing—dieting, especially when you're a teenager, is not just unnecessary. It's harmful.

The Growing Teenager: A Never-Ending Hunger

If you're a teenager, you've probably experienced that intense hunger that seems to come out of nowhere. One minute, you're fine, and the next, you're raiding the fridge like a bear after hibernation. This hunger is no joke, and it's not something to ignore.

When you diet, especially by cutting calories or eliminating key food groups, you deprive your body of the essential nutrients it needs to build and maintain tissues, organs, and systems. For instance, proteins, vitamins, and minerals are crucial for muscle development, bone density, and overall physical strength. Without adequate nutrition, your body may struggle to develop properly, leading to potential issues like stunted growth, weakened bones, and reduced muscle mass. This is particularly concerning during the teen years, as this is when your body lays the foundation for lifelong health.

The Brain Needs Food, Too

We often forget that the brain is part of the body. It's not just sitting up there doing nothing. In fact, your brain is one of the hungriest organs in your body. It consumes about 20% of the calories you eat each day. Now, think about this: If you're not eating enough or if you're depriving your body of essential nutrients, your brain is going to suffer.

The brain, which is still developing rapidly during adolescence, is also highly sensitive to nutritional deficiencies. Essential fatty acids, particularly omega-3s, play a critical role in brain health, influencing everything from cognitive function to mood regulation. A diet low in these nutrients can lead to issues such as impaired memory, concentration difficulties, and even an increased risk of mental health disorders like anxiety and depression. Furthermore, restricting calories can disrupt the production of neurotransmitters, the chemicals responsible for sending signals in the brain. This can lead to problems with learning, emotional regulation, and decision-making.

The Skinny Myth: Why Being Thin Isn't Always Healthy

The world keeps telling us that being thin equals being healthy. But let's bust that myth right now. Health is not just about how you look. It's about how you feel, how your body functions, and how your mind operates.

There are plenty of people who are naturally thin but aren't healthy at all. They might be missing out on essential nutrients, have low energy, or struggle with mental health issues because they're not eating properly. On the flip side, someone with a bit more meat on their bones could be perfectly healthy because they're giving their body what it needs.

Your teenage years are not the time to be obsessed with being thin. They're the time to focus on growing, learning, and enjoying life.

The Science of Starvation: What Happens When You Diet?

Let's get into some science. When you go on a diet and restrict your food intake, your body doesn't just sit there and take it. It fights back. Here's what happens:

1. **Your Metabolism Slows Down:** Your body is smart. It realizes that it's not getting enough food, so it slows down your metabolism to conserve energy. This means you burn fewer calories, which makes it harder to lose weight in the long run.

2. **You Lose Muscle, Not Fat:** When you're not eating enough, your body starts to break down muscle for energy. Muscle is what helps you stay strong and active. Losing muscle can make you feel weak and tired.

3. **You Feel Hungrier:** Your body increases the production of hunger hormones, which makes you feel even more hungry. This can lead to binge eating, which is when you eat a lot of food in a short amount of time.

Social Media: The Skinny Trap

A lot of those "perfect" bodies you see online aren't real. They're filtered, Photoshopped, and posed to look a certain way. Comparing yourself to these unrealistic images is like comparing yourself to a cartoon character. It's not real life. Instead of focusing on what you look like, focus on what your body can do. Can you run, dance, play sports, or just have fun with your friends? That's what really matters.

The Big Picture: It's Not About Dieting; It's About Living

Your teenage years are meant for growing, learning, and having fun—not stressing about diets. Your body and brain need all the help they can get to navigate this crazy time of change. By focusing on nourishing your body rather than depriving it, you're setting yourself up for a lifetime of health and happiness.

So, ignore the noise. Forget the fad diets and quick fixes. Embrace your body, feed it well, and let it do its thing. You'll be amazed at what it can do when you give it the proper fuel.

11. Reducing Chemicals in Everyday Life

We are now surrounded by so many chemicals in our daily lives, and we don't need all of them! From the synthetic fragrances in our soaps and detergents to the plastics we use every day, these substances quietly make their way into our bodies.

In the last century, we've seen a massive shift toward synthetic materials and chemicals in our products. A hundred years ago, most everyday items were made from natural materials—wood, wool, cotton, and glass. But today, our homes are filled with chemicals we can't even pronounce. Here are some of the most common ones, where they're found, and why they matter:

1. Phthalates

Phthalates are chemicals used to make plastics flexible. They're found in products like plastic containers, toys, and even personal care items like shampoos and fragrances. The problem? Phthalates are endocrine disruptors, meaning they interfere with the body's hormones. Studies suggest that long-term exposure to these chemicals can affect reproductive health as well.

Where you find them:

- Perfumes and fragrances (used to make the scent last longer)

- Plastic food containers and wraps
- Vinyl flooring and shower curtains

2. Parabens

Parabens are preservatives used in cosmetics, skincare, and personal hygiene products. While they prevent mold and bacteria, they've been linked to hormone disruption and even breast cancer due to their ability to mimic estrogen.

Where you find them:

- Lotions, shampoos, conditioners
- Makeup and sunscreen
- Shaving creams

3. BPA (Bisphenol A)

BPA is used in plastics and resins and is commonly found in food and drink packaging, especially in cans. BPA is another endocrine disruptor and has been associated with various health issues like fertility problems, obesity, and even heart disease.

Where you find it:

- Plastic bottles and containers
- Canned foods (in the lining)
- Receipts (thermal paper)

4. Synthetic Fragrances

That "fresh laundry" smell or "lavender-scented" dish soap? They might not be as fresh as they seem. Many fragrances are made with synthetic chemicals that can cause allergic reactions, respiratory issues, and skin irritation. Worse, the term "fragrance" can mask hundreds of unlisted chemicals(

Where you find them:

- Perfumes, deodorants, lotions
- Laundry detergents and cleaning products
- Air fresheners

Microplastics: The Unseen Threat in Our Blood and Brain

One of the most alarming developments in recent years is the discovery of microplastics—tiny plastic particles less than 5 millimeters long—that are showing up in our bodies, including our bloodstreams and brains. These microplastics come from the breakdown of larger plastic items, synthetic fabrics, and even the microbeads once found in personal care products.

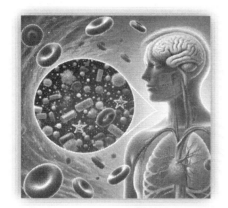

A recent study published in *Environment International* confirmed that microplastics have been detected in human blood, raising concerns about their potential impact on health. Scientists believe that once inside the body, these particles can cause inflammation, interfere with cellular processes, and potentially lead to neurological issues. Another study showed microplastics in brain tissue, sparking research into how they may affect brain function.

Where microplastics come from:

- Breakdown of plastic bags, bottles, and packaging
- Synthetic fabrics like polyester (released during washing)
- Car tires (wear and tear releases microplastics into the air)

Over time, these tiny particles have spread into our food, water, and even the air we breathe. While more research is needed to understand their impact fully, it's clear that

reducing our use of plastics can help limit our exposure.

Life Then and Now: A Century of Change

If we compare life now to 100 years ago, the difference is staggering. A century ago, most people lived surrounded by natural materials—wooden toys, cotton clothing, glass milk bottles. There was no such thing as a plastic bottle or a synthetic fragrance that lingered for hours. Household cleaners were made from simple ingredients like vinegar, baking soda, and soap.

But fast forward to today, and our homes are filled with synthetic chemicals, from the plastic containers in our kitchens to the processed air fresheners in every room. And while these innovations have brought convenience, they've also introduced health risks we're only beginning to understand.

In the past, products were often more labor-intensive, but they didn't carry the same hidden costs—chemicals that seep into our skin, lungs, and bloodstream. By returning to some of these simpler practices, we can reduce the number of chemicals we're exposed to on a daily basis.

Practical Ways to Reduce Chemical Exposure

You don't need to throw away everything you own or live in fear of every product. The key is balance—making small changes that add up over time. Here are some simple ways to reduce your chemical exposure without turning your life upside down:

1. Choose Natural or Fragrance-Free Products

Many companies now offer natural, non-toxic alternatives for cleaning and personal care products. Look for labels that say "fragrance-free" or "phthalate-free."

2. Swap Plastics for Glass or Metal

Use glass or stainless steel containers and water bottles for food storage. Avoid heating food in plastic, as this can cause chemicals to leach into your meals.

3. Air Out New Items

When buying new furniture, mattresses, or rugs, air them out for several days. Many of these products are treated with chemicals that can off-gas (release into the air).

4. Filter Your Water

A good water filter can remove many chemicals, including traces of microplastics. Check to see if your local water supply is tested for contaminants.

5. Wear Natural Fabrics

Clothing made from cotton, wool, or linen releases fewer microplastics than synthetic fibers like polyester or nylon. If you do wear synthetics, consider using a microfiber-catching laundry bag to reduce the amount of plastic entering the water supply.

6. Go Back to Basics with Cleaning

Many household cleaners are full of harsh chemicals. Instead, try natural alternatives like vinegar, baking soda, and lemon for your cleaning needs. These old-fashioned methods work just as well without the toxic overload. Or use less. Also, avoid things that mix in the air, such as air fresheners. It smells nice, but we just breathe the chemical and get it into our lungs. Is it worth it?

Can overuse of chemicals reduce immunity?

Overuse of synthetic chemicals, such as those found in cleaning products, cosmetics, and even food packaging, has been increasingly linked to weakened immune systems and a rise in allergies. Studies have shown that chemicals like phthalates, bisphenol A (BPA), and various pesticides disrupt the body's natural hormone balance, which in turn affects immune response. Over-sanitization and constant avoidance of microbes, often fueled by chemical-laden products, can reduce the immune system's exposure to natural microbes, preventing it from building strong defenses. Interestingly, living a bit more naturally—exposing the body to benign microbes—can actually help strengthen immunity and reduce allergies. This is sometimes referred to as the "hygiene hypothesis," supported by research from the Journal of Allergy and Clinical Immunology, which suggests that a bit of dirt and microbial exposure can enhance immune resilience.

Conclusion: Awareness, Not Fear

Living in a world filled with chemicals doesn't mean you need to be afraid of everything you touch or use. The goal isn't to eliminate all synthetic materials or chemicals from your life—that would be nearly impossible. Instead, the aim is to become more aware of what you're using and how it might affect your health.

It's about finding that middle ground. Yes, modern life has conveniences we didn't have 100 years ago, but with those conveniences comes responsibility. We can enjoy the benefits of technology and progress while also protecting our health by being smart and selective in what we use every day.

So, which one chemical will you stop using or reduce using from tomorrow onwards? (But don't start smelling bad, though!

CHAPTER 2

Building a Stronger You

Have you ever thought about why some days you feel like you can conquer the world, while other days it feels like the smallest thing can knock you off balance? It's almost like your mind and heart have their workout routines, except they don't come with a manual or a coach. But here's the thing—just like you can train your body to run faster or lift heavier, you can train your mind and emotions, too. The trick? Understanding what makes them tick and giving them the right fuel.

Every day, whether we realize it or not, we're feeding our minds a "mental diet." It's not all about positive vibes and motivational quotes (though they can help). It's about what we choose to focus on, how we handle our emotions, and how we talk to ourselves when things don't go according to plan. And let's face it—life rarely follows our plans, right? The question is: How do we stay mentally strong without burning out or losing ourselves in the process?

Part of this inner workout is about figuring out what makes you *you*. It's learning to be okay with your quirks, the things that make you different, and realizing that these aren't flaws—they're your superpowers. We often think we need to fit into a certain mold to be "normal." But what if normal is just a myth? What if being ordinary is actually pretty extraordinary?

Then there's the big stuff—those deep values you hold onto even when things get messy. They're like the compass that keeps you steady when life throws curveballs. Combine that with the power of slowing down and being present, and you've got a toolkit for navigating the chaos without losing yourself.

By the time you finish this chapter, you'll see that mental and emotional strength isn't about being perfect or never having a bad day. It's about building a strong foundation, knowing when to push yourself, and when to take a break. It's about understanding that you're not broken, even on the tough days. A bad day doesn't mean that you have a bad life.

And most importantly, it's about realizing that *you* are enough, just as you are.

1. Mental and Emotional Health: The Real Pandemic

COVID-19 changed the world, shutting down cities and making masks as common as sneakers. But there's another pandemic that's been around for a while, quietly growing, and it's affecting millions—maybe even you. It's the

pandemic of mental and emotional health issues. Unlike COVID-19, you can't see this pandemic spreading, but its impact is just as real, if not more.

Let's face it: being a teenager today is like being a juggler in a circus. But instead of juggling balls, you're juggling school, friends, family expectations, social media, and your future—all while trying not to drop anything. And here's the kicker: the balls are on fire.

If we compare today's world with the past, we notice that the pressure has cranked up to eleven. Social media didn't even exist for your parents when they were teens. Now, it's a double-edged sword. On the one hand, it keeps you connected, but on the other, it's like living in a fishbowl where everyone's watching, judging, and comparing. Exhausting, isn't it?

Then there's the academic pressure. Getting good grades, getting into a good college, getting a good job—it's like a never-ending staircase, and each step seems higher than the last. Not to mention the fact that the world feels like it's on the brink of disaster with climate change, wars, and political chaos. No wonder anxiety and depression rates are skyrocketing.

The Science Behind the Storm

Your brain is this incredibly complex organ made up of billions of neurons firing like a billion tiny lightning bolts every second. But here's the thing: your brain isn't fully developed until you're about 25 years old. The part that controls decision-making, the prefrontal cortex, is still under construction during your teen years. This is why you might act impulsively or feel like your emotions are all over the place—because they kind of are.

When you're stressed, your body releases a hormone called cortisol. It's like your body's alarm system, telling you to fight, flee, or freeze in the face of danger. This was super helpful when we had to outrun saber-toothed tigers. But in today's world, the "danger" might be an exam or a nasty comment on Instagram. Your brain doesn't know the difference, so it pumps out cortisol anyway. Too much cortisol over time can lead to anxiety, depression, and even physical health problems like headaches and weakened immune systems.

Then there's dopamine, the "feel-good" hormone. Every time you get a like on social media, your brain gives you a little hit of dopamine. It feels good, but it's also addictive. You start craving more likes more validation, and when you don't get it, your mood crashes. It's like being on a rollercoaster that you didn't even buy a ticket for.

Let's talk about some real people. Take Simone Biles, the most decorated gymnast of all time. In the 2020 Tokyo Olympics, she made headlines not for winning medals but for pulling out of the competition to focus on her mental health. Biles admitted that she was struggling with the "twisties," a mental block that can cause gymnasts to lose control of their bodies in mid-air. The pressure to perform at the highest level while the whole world was watching became too much. She chose her mental health over potential gold medals,  sending a powerful message that it's okay not to be okay.

Then there's Naomi Osaka, a tennis superstar who withdrew from the French Open, citing anxiety and the pressure of dealing with the media. Osaka's decision sparked a global conversation about the mental health of athletes, who are often seen as invincible. These athletes are at the top of their game, yet they're struggling with the same mental health issues that millions of other people face.

But it's not just celebrities. A very large number of the world's population is going through Anxiety and Depression right now, and it is increasing year by year. Google and see the stats yourselves.

Nothing is more important than mental and emotional health, and we must recognize it, accept it, and address it!

The Social Media Trap

Social media can be a great way to stay connected with friends and share your life with others. But it can also be a trap. Spending too much time on social media can lead to feelings of loneliness, depression, and anxiety. Why? Because social media is like a highlight reel of everyone's life. You see your friend's vacation photos or their perfect selfie and think, "Why isn't my life that awesome?" But what you don't see are the filters, the multiple takes, and the moments of doubt and insecurity that everyone experiences.

There's even something called "social media envy." It's when you see someone else's life on Instagram or TikTok and feel jealous or inadequate. This can spiral into a cycle of negative self-esteem where you start to believe that you're not good enough, not smart enough, or not attractive enough. But here's the truth: no one's life is as perfect as it looks online.

The Power of Connection

One of the most powerful ways to combat mental health issues is through connection. Humans are social creatures; we're wired to connect with others. When you're feeling down, talking to someone—a friend, a family member, or a counselor—can make a huge difference. It's like shining a light into the darkness. Sometimes, just saying your worries out loud can make them feel less overwhelming.

During the COVID-19 pandemic, people were forced into isolation, and this had a huge impact on mental health. In some places, rates of anxiety and depression doubled. But people found ways to stay connected. Virtual hangouts, online games, and even drive-by birthday parties became the new normal. These connections, even though they were virtual, helped people get through one of the toughest times in recent history.

How to Take Care of Your Mental and Emotional Health

Taking care of your mental health is just as important as taking care of your physical health. In fact, the two are deeply connected. Here are some practical steps you can take:

1. Talk About It

If you're feeling overwhelmed, the first and most important step is to talk about it. Picture this: You're carrying a heavy backpack full of rocks, and each rock represents a worry or fear. Over time, that backpack gets heavier, and you start to feel like you're being crushed under the weight. But what if you could take out some of those rocks by simply talking to someone? When you talk to a friend, a parent, a teacher, or a counselor, you're sharing the load. They may not be able to remove all the rocks, but they can help you carry the weight or even find ways to lighten the load.

Talking about your feelings isn't a sign of weakness; it's a sign of strength. It takes courage to be vulnerable, but it's also incredibly freeing. Bottling up your emotions doesn't make them go away. In fact, it can make things worse.

Talking to someone can also give you a new perspective. Sometimes, when you're in the middle of a problem, it's hard to see a way out. But a fresh set of eyes can help you see things differently and find solutions you hadn't thought of. So, whether it's a quick chat with a friend or a deeper conversation with a counselor, remember that you don't have to go through tough times alone. There's always someone willing to listen and help.

2. Get Moving

When you exercise, your brain releases endorphins. These are like tiny happiness boosters that flood your brain and make you feel good. It's like your brain's way of giving you a high-five for taking care of yourself.

Even a simple walk around the block can make a big difference. Moving your body helps reduce stress, improve your mood, and increase your energy levels.

3. Unplug

Social media is a double-edged sword. On one hand, it keeps you connected to friends and the world around you. On the other hand, it can be a source of stress, anxiety, and FOMO (fear of missing out). Have you ever found yourself mindlessly scrolling through Instagram or TikTok, only to feel worse afterward?

Taking a break from social media is like stepping out of the noise and into a quiet room. It gives you a chance to breathe, think, and focus on the real world around you. Unplugging doesn't mean you have to delete your accounts or go offline forever. It just means taking some time each day to disconnect from the virtual world and reconnect with yourself.

4. Mindfulness

Mindfulness is a fancy word for being fully present in the moment. It's about paying attention to what's happening right now without getting lost in thoughts about the past or worries about the future. Think of mindfulness as a mental workout. Just like you exercise your body to stay fit, you can exercise your mind to stay calm and focused.

One simple way to practice mindfulness is through deep breathing. When you're feeling stressed or anxious, take a few slow, deep breaths. Focus on the sensation of the air entering and leaving your lungs. This helps calm your nervous system and brings your attention back to the present moment.

Another way to practice mindfulness is by paying attention to your surroundings. Notice the colors, sounds, and textures around you. What do you see? What do you hear? How does the ground feel beneath your feet? Engaging your senses in this way can help you feel more grounded and less overwhelmed by your thoughts.

Mindfulness isn't about clearing your mind of all thoughts—it's about observing your thoughts without judgment. It's okay to have worries or distractions; the key is to acknowledge them and gently bring your focus back to the present. Over time, mindfulness can help reduce stress, improve concentration, and increase your overall sense of well-being.

5. Seek Professional Help

Sometimes, despite your best efforts, you might find that your mental and emotional health is still struggling. If you're dealing with anxiety, depression, or any other mental health issue, it's important to seek help from a professional. Therapists and counselors are trained to help you navigate these challenges and provide you with the tools you need to feel better.

Seeking professional help is not a sign of weakness; it's a sign of strength. It shows that you're taking your mental health seriously and that you're willing to do what it takes to feel better. A therapist can help you understand your feelings, identify patterns in your thinking, and develop coping strategies that work for you.

Medication for Anxiety and Depression

Medication for anxiety and depression can be a valuable tool in managing symptoms and improving quality of life, but it's important to weigh the pros and cons before starting treatment. On the positive side, medication can help stabilize mood, reduce overwhelming feelings, and make day-to-day functioning more manageable, especially for those with severe symptoms. Medications, such as selective serotonin reuptake inhibitors (SSRIs) and benzodiazepines, have been shown to reduce symptoms of anxiety and depression significantly. These medications work by altering the levels of certain chemicals in the brain, like serotonin and dopamine, which are often out of balance in individuals with these conditions. By doing so, they can help improve mood, reduce feelings of anxiety, and enhance overall emotional stability. However, there are also potential downsides, including side effects, the possibility of dependency, and the fact that medication may not address the underlying causes of anxiety and depression. It's crucial to have an open discussion with a healthcare provider to determine whether medication is the right choice and to explore other treatment options, such as therapy or lifestyle changes, that might be used in conjunction with or instead of medication.

Understanding Cognitive Behavioral Therapy (CBT)

Cognitive Behavioral Therapy (CBT) is a type of psychotherapy that helps people understand and change their thought patterns and behaviors. Think of it as a way to tend to your mental health garden by pulling out the weeds of negative thoughts and planting seeds of positive behaviors.

How CBT Works

Identifying Negative Thoughts

The first step in CBT is identifying negative thoughts. These are the weeds in your mental garden that can choke out the healthy plants. Common negative thoughts include:

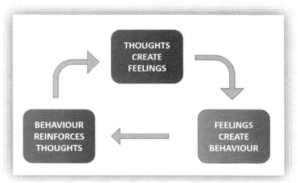

- **Catastrophizing:** Expecting the worst to happen.
- **Overgeneralizing:** Making broad statements based on a single event.
- **Black-and-White Thinking:** Seeing things as all good or all bad.

Challenging Negative Thoughts

Once you've identified negative thoughts, the next step is to challenge them. Ask yourself:

- Is this thought based on facts or assumptions?

- Is there another way to look at this situation?

- What would I say to a friend who had this thought?

Replacing Negative Thoughts

After challenging negative thoughts, replace them with positive, realistic ones. This is like planting healthy flowers in place of weeds. For example:

- **Negative Thought:** "I'll fail this test and ruin my future."
- **Positive Thought:** "I'll do my best on this test. One test doesn't define my future."

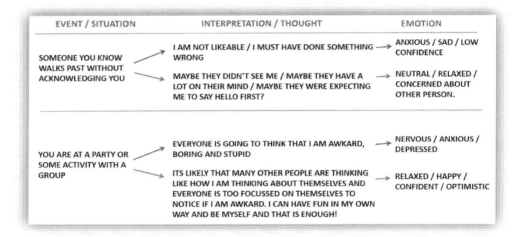

EVENT / SITUATION	INTERPRETATION / THOUGHT	EMOTION
SOMEONE YOU KNOW WALKS PAST WITHOUT ACKNOWLEDGING YOU	I AM NOT LIKEABLE / I MUST HAVE DONE SOMETHING WRONG	ANXIOUS / SAD / LOW CONFIDENCE
	MAYBE THEY DIDN'T SEE ME / MAYBE THEY HAVE A LOT ON THEIR MIND / MAYBE THEY WERE EXPECTING ME TO SAY HELLO FIRST?	NEUTRAL / RELAXED / CONCERNED ABOUT OTHER PERSON.
YOU ARE AT A PARTY OR SOME ACTIVITY WITH A GROUP	EVERYONE IS GOING TO THINK THAT I AM AWKARD, BORING AND STUPID	NERVOUS / ANXIOUS / DEPRESSED
	ITS LIKELY THAT MANY OTHER PEOPLE ARE THINKING LIKE HOW I AM THINKING ABOUT THEMSELVES AND EVERYONE IS TOO FOCUSSED ON THEMSELVES TO NOTICE IF I AM AWKARD. I CAN HAVE FUN IN MY OWN WAY AND BE MYSELF AND THAT IS ENOUGH!	RELAXED / HAPPY / CONFIDENT / OPTIMISTIC

All will be well

Please do not worry at all, my friend, there are solutions for everything! And you know what? You already know those solutions in the corner of your mind! Taking care of your mental health is crucial, and seeking help is a positive step toward feeling better and living a fulfilling life. Don't hesitate to reach out for support and explore the options available to you.

2. Psychology of Emotions and Feelings: Understanding Our Inner World

We all use emojis on WhatsApp, Facebook, Instagram, etc. every day. Have you ever wondered why we have so many types of emotions, and can you even name them? When you go through your day, do you notice when you experience varying emotions? Do you attach yourself to those emotions, or do you observe those emotions, remaining detached, like an observer?

Emotions are powerful and complex. They drive us, hold us back, and color every experience. But what exactly are emotions, and why do we have them?

Emotions are our body's way of communicating with us. They're like an internal GPS, guiding us through life's ups and downs. They're not just random feelings that happen to us; they're deeply rooted in our biology and evolution. Emotions are thought to have evolved because they serve adaptive functions. They help organisms respond to environmental challenges and opportunities in ways that enhance survival and reproductive success.

Why Do We Have Emotions in the First Place?

Emotions might seem like they're just there to make life more complicated, but they actually serve important purposes.

1. **Survival:** Emotions like fear helped our ancestors survive. Even today, fear can keep you safe by warning you of danger.

2. **Communication:** Emotions are a form of communication. When you smile, you're telling others that you're happy. When you cry, you're signaling that you need help or comfort.

3. **Decision-Making:** Believe it or not, emotions play a big role in decision-making. They help you weigh the pros and cons and guide you toward the best choice.

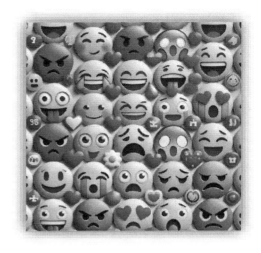

4. **Memory:** Emotions are tightly linked to memory. You're more likely to remember events that had a strong emotional impact, whether it was a joyful celebration or a frightening experience.

5. **Learning:** Emotions also help us learn. If you touch a hot stove and feel pain, you'll remember not to do that again. Similarly, positive emotions reinforce good behavior, encouraging you to repeat it.

How to Manage Your Emotions

Now that you know a bit more about emotions, let's talk about how to manage them. Because, let's face it, emotions can sometimes feel overwhelming. Here are a few tips:

1. **Acknowledge Your Emotions:** The first step in managing your emotions is acknowledging them. Don't try to ignore or suppress them. If you're feeling sad, admit that you're feeling sad.

2. **Understand Your Triggers:** Pay attention to what triggers your emotions. Is it certain people, situations, or thoughts? Understanding your triggers can

help you anticipate and manage your emotions better.

3. **Express Your Emotions:** Don't keep your emotions bottled up. Find healthy ways to express them, whether it's talking to a friend, writing in a journal, or even creating art.

Understanding the 6 Basic Emotions

1. Happiness

- Happiness releases dopamine and serotonin in the brain, creating a sense of well-being.
- **Example:** Eating your favorite ice cream triggers dopamine, making you feel good.

THIS IS WHAT PURE JOY LOOKS LIKE.

2. Sadness

- Sadness can activate the brain's limbic system, which processes emotions.
- **Example:** Losing a pet can cause a deep sense of loss and activate these emotional centers.

3. Fear

- Fear triggers the amygdala, preparing the body for a fight-or-flight response by releasing adrenaline.
- **Example:** Seeing a spider can cause an immediate fear response.

4. Disgust

- Disgust activates the insula, a part of the brain involved in processing aversive stimuli.
- **Example:** A bad smell can trigger a feeling of disgust to protect you from potential harm.

5. Anger

- Anger involves the amygdala and prefrontal cortex, leading to increased heart rate and adrenaline.
- **Example:** Feeling angry when someone cuts you off in traffic.
- *"Holding on to anger is like grasping a hot coal with the intent of throwing it at someone else; you are the one who gets burned"* - *Buddha.*

6. Surprise

- Surprise activates the brain's dopamine system, helping to focus attention and process unexpected events.
- **Example:** A surprise party can cause an immediate, joyful reaction.

Understanding Complex Emotions

1. **Confusion**
   Confusion occurs when the brain struggles to make sense of conflicting or unclear information, engaging the prefrontal cortex to resolve the uncertainty.

   Example: When you're given complicated instructions for a task, you might feel confused as your brain works to process and understand the details.

2. **Excitement**
   Excitement involves a surge of dopamine and adrenaline, creating a heightened state of arousal and anticipation.
   Example: Hearing that your favorite band is coming to town can cause a rush of excitement as you eagerly await the concert.

3. **Embarrassment**
   Embarrassment activates the prefrontal cortex and the limbic system,

often leading to physical reactions like blushing due to increased blood flow.

Example: Tripping in front of a group of people can trigger embarrassment, making you feel self-conscious and physically uncomfortable.

4. **Nervousness**
   Nervousness is driven by the release of stress hormones like cortisol, which prepares the body for potential challenges by increasing alertness.
   Example: Speaking in front of a large audience can make you nervous, causing your heart to race and your palms to sweat.

5. **Loneliness**
   Loneliness activates the same brain regions associated with physical pain, such as the anterior cingulate cortex, highlighting the deep emotional impact of social isolation.

6. **Example:** Moving to a new city where you don't know anyone can lead to feelings of loneliness as you miss familiar connections.

7. **Guilt**
   Guilt involves the activation of the prefrontal cortex, which is responsible for self-reflection and moral reasoning, often leading to feelings of regret.
   Example: Forgetting a friend's birthday might make you feel guilty as you reflect on the missed opportunity to show you care.

8. **Shame**
   Shame is a self-conscious emotion that involves the insula and anterior cingulate cortex, often resulting in a desire to hide or withdraw from others.
   Example: Being caught in a lie can cause intense shame, making you want to avoid facing those you've deceived.

9. **Pride**
   Pride activates the ventromedial prefrontal cortex, which is associated with self-reflection and a positive evaluation of one's actions or

achievements.

Example: Completing a challenging project at school can make you feel proud, boosting your self-esteem and sense of accomplishment.

10. **Jealousy**

Jealousy involves the anterior cingulate cortex and the ventral striatum, areas linked to social comparison and reward processing, often leading to feelings of inadequacy or resentment.

Example: Seeing a friend receive an award you wanted might make you feel jealous, questioning your worth.

11. **Relief**

Relief occurs when the brain shifts from a state of stress or anxiety to one of relaxation, often involving the parasympathetic nervous system, which calms the body.

Example: Finding out you passed a difficult exam can bring a deep sense of relief, releasing the tension you had been carrying.

These complex emotions often blend basic emotional responses with more intricate cognitive processes, making them nuanced and unique to each situation. Understanding them helps us navigate the complexities of our inner world.

Think of emotions as the weather. Sometimes it's sunny, sometimes it's stormy, but each type of weather has its purpose in the grand scheme of things. Remember the Inside Out movie?

Emotional intelligence, the ability to understand and manage our own emotions and the emotions of others, is crucial for personal and professional success. It involves skills such as self-awareness, empathy, and emotional regulation.

Imagine if you could name and understand each emotion as it arises instead of being overwhelmed by it. That's what emotional intelligence helps us achieve. It's like being the captain of your ship, navigating through calm and stormy seas with confidence and control.

The Power of Reaction: How Our Responses Fuel Stress

Stress is often perceived as something that happens to us—a looming deadline, a demanding person, or an unexpected financial burden. While these situations can indeed be stressful, it's not the situations themselves that directly cause stress. Rather, it's how we react to these situations that determine our stress levels. Our reactions—whether they are immediate and emotional or measured and thoughtful—shape our experience of stress.

Our perception of a situation significantly influences our reaction to it. Two people can face the same stressor but react differently based on their perception of the event. For instance:

Example: The Overwhelming Project

- **Scenario:** Sarah and John both receive a new project with a tight deadline.

- **Sarah's Reaction:** Sarah views the project as a personal challenge. She feels overwhelmed, sees the deadline as impossible, and begins to panic. Her stress levels rise, leading to anxiety and a decrease in productivity.

- **John's Reaction:** John sees the project as an opportunity to showcase his skills and advance in his career. He feels a bit pressured but chooses to break down the task into manageable steps and prioritize effectively. His stress levels are lower, and he manages his workload efficiently.

In this example, Sarah's reaction—characterized by panic and overwhelm—intensifies her stress. John's reaction, on the other hand, is proactive and solution-oriented, leading to a more manageable stress level.

Our reactions to stressors can be automatic or mindful. Automatic reactions are often immediate and driven by our emotional responses. Mindful reactions involve a more deliberate and thoughtful approach. Key tips:

1. **Pause and Reflect:** When faced with a stressor, take a moment to pause and reflect before reacting. This brief moment can help you choose a more thoughtful response rather than a knee-jerk reaction.

2. **Reframe the Situation:** Try to reframe the situation in a more positive or manageable light. Viewing challenges as opportunities for growth can alter your reaction and reduce stress.

Do You Attach Yourself to Your Emotions or Observe Them?

When you feel angry or sad, do you become that emotion, or do you notice it from a distance? It might sound a bit strange, but there's a big difference between being your emotion and observing it.

Let's say you're feeling angry because your friend didn't invite you to a party. If you attach yourself to that anger, you might start thinking things like, "They don't care about me" or "I'm not good enough." This can spiral into more negative thoughts and feelings, and before you know it, you're stuck in a cycle of anger and sadness.

But what if you tried observing your anger instead? You might think, "I'm feeling angry right now. That's interesting. Why am I feeling this way?" This approach allows you to step back and see your emotion as just that—an emotion, not a reflection of who you are.

Observing your emotions rather than

attaching yourself to them can be incredibly powerful. It's like being the captain of a ship during a storm. The waves are rough, and the wind is howling, but you know it's just a storm. It will pass, and you'll come out the other side.

Remember, Ships don't sink because of the water around them. Ships sink because of the water that gets in them! Similarly, you will be surrounded by negativity, challenges, and difficulties, but don't let anything get inside your head and weigh you down. Sail like a confident ship, unafraid, aware but unbothered by what's around!

3. Mental Diet: The Information We Consume

A mental diet isn't about calories or carbs. It's about the information and experiences you consume daily. Are you feeding your brain junk, or are you giving it the nutrients it needs to thrive?

Feeding your brain positive, enriching content is like eating a superfood smoothie for breakfast. You feel energized, sharp, and ready to tackle anything. But feed it negativity, endless doom-scrolling, or toxic gossip, and it's like downing a gallon of soda—you might feel a rush at first, but a hard crash follows it.

Media often manipulates emotions by triggering fear and hate. They amplify frightening news stories or overstate threats, making people feel constantly anxious. Sensational headlines and selective reporting keep fear alive, as people are drawn to negative news more than positive. By focusing on crime, conflict, or disasters, media outlets keep audiences engaged, triggering the "fear button."

Similarly, hate is stoked by emphasizing divisions. Highlighting political, racial, or cultural differences inflames anger and reinforces "us vs. them" mentalities. Social media platforms, in particular, thrive on heated debates, creating echo chambers where hate is amplified. Both fear and hate fuel engagement, keeping people hooked to the content. STAY AWAY! Consuming hate-filled information is like drinking poison!

Your brain is still more powerful than the latest AI or quantum computer. It's constantly rewiring itself, creating new connections, and strengthening old ones based on what you think, feel, and experience. This process is called **neuroplasticity**, and it's the reason why your habits—good or bad—are so hard to break.

When you focus on positive thoughts, you're literally building mental highways that make it easier to think positively in the future. It's like upgrading your brain's operating system. The more you use these "roads," the more efficient and automatic they become.

But beware: the same is true for negative thoughts. Let's say you're constantly worrying about what others think of you. Each time you worry, you reinforce that neural pathway, making it easier to worry the next time. It's like creating a shortcut to stress and anxiety.

Athletes, CEOs, and You

Take athletes like Simone Biles or Michael Phelps. Their physical training is only part of the equation. They also have a strict mental diet. Simone Biles isn't just doing flips and spins—she's also visualizing her routines, focusing on every move with laser-like precision. Michael Phelps didn't just swim laps; he mentally rehearsed every stroke, every turn, every breath. This mental conditioning was as crucial as their physical training.

Or look at any successful CEO or Entrepreneur. They don't waste their time watching funny cat videos or binge-watching new web series on criminal investigations.

This does not mean that successful people don't do any entertainment or always watch positive stuff. It is about how much and the discipline of using your brain for more important work first and, say, for more than 95% of the time you have.

The Digital Junk Food Trap

We live in a world where our attention is constantly under siege. Social media, news, memes, YouTube rabbit holes—they're like the fast food of the mental world. They're engineered to be addictive, giving you quick hits of dopamine but often leaving you feeling empty and craving more.

Spending hours scrolling through negative news or comparing your life to filtered Instagram photos is like eating an entire bag of chips. Sure, it feels good at the moment, but later, you're bloated with self-doubt and anxiety.

Feeding Your Brain Right

So, what does a healthy mental diet look like? It's about balance, variety, and being mindful of what you consume. Here's how to feed your brain the good stuff:

1. **Curate Your Media Feed**: Follow accounts and consume content that uplifts, educates, and inspires. Unfollow or mute those that drain your energy or promote negativity.

2. **Hang Out with Positive People**: Your vibe attracts your tribe. Surround yourself with people who encourage, support, and bring out the best in you.

3. **Learn New Skills**: Just like your body needs exercise, your brain thrives on challenges. Learn to code, pick up a new language, or master a musical instrument. This keeps your neural pathways flexible and strong.

4. **Limit Your Screen Time**: Set boundaries for your digital consumption. Use tools like app timers to ensure you're not mindlessly scrolling for hours.

Why We Can't Focus Anymore – And How to Get Some of It Back

Another issue with non-stop mindless consumption of information is that we have lost the ability to focus. Ever notice how hard it is to finish even a single Chapter of a book or even a long YouTube video without drifting to something else? Or how do you start reading an article, but after three tabs and a TikTok, you barely remember what you came for? **Our attention spans are shrinking**, and it's not just you—this is happening to everyone.

But it's not because we're lazy. The way we consume information today—through quick, flashy bursts of content—is rewiring our brains. This is especially true with smartphones, social media, and apps designed to keep you scrolling. So why can't we focus like we used to? And more importantly, is there a way to fix it?

Information Overload: What Happened to Our Attention?

Our brains haven't evolved to handle the amount of information thrown at us every day. A hundred years ago, life moved a lot slower. People read books, had long conversations, and engaged in one task at a time. They weren't interrupted by constant notifications, feeds, and video suggestions trying to capture their attention.

The Real Cost of Constant Distraction

This shrinking attention span has bigger consequences than just getting distracted during a Netflix show. It affects how we think, learn, and interact with each other.

1. Shallow Learning

When we're constantly distracted, we lose the ability to dive deep into topics. Deep learning—where you actually understand and retain information—takes time and focus. The more our brains get used to fast, shallow content, the less we can handle slower, deeper material.

2. Shorter Conversations

Think about the last time you had a conversation that wasn't interrupted by a phone. It's become normal to check our devices while we talk to people. We're not even fully present with others anymore. We skim through conversations as we skim through social media. This hurts our relationships because deep conversations require time and full attention to build trust and understanding.

3. Mental Fatigue

The more we multitask—scrolling through Instagram while watching Netflix or texting while listening to a podcast—the more tired our brains become. Your brain isn't great at doing multiple things at once, even if it feels like it is. Constantly switching between tasks takes more energy than you think, leaving you mentally drained without much to show for it.

So, What Can You Do About It?

Here's the good news: you can train your brain to get some of that focus back. It won't happen overnight, but with a few small changes, you can improve your ability to concentrate and stay present. Limit the screen time, be mindful, be aware, calm down time, and **GET BORED - it is good for your brain** - all the creative ideas and solutions to complex problems come when you let your brain wander.

Remember, attention is like a muscle—the more you work at it, the stronger it gets. So start with small steps. Put your phone away for 30 minutes, have a conversation without checking texts, or read a book for longer than a chapter. You'll be surprised how much more present—and less exhausted— you feel.

So, what 1 change would you make starting tomorrow to help your brain consume better information and give it some space to think?

4. Self-Acceptance and Gratitude: Accepting Who We Are Without Comparison to Others

Have you ever stood in front of a mirror and picked yourself apart? Maybe it's your hair, your skin, or the way your smile looks. This critical habit isn't just limited to appearances. We often compare our skills, achievements, and even our personalities to others. The result? A constant feeling of not being good enough.

Why does this happen? Why is it so hard to just like ourselves the way we are? It's partly because we're surrounded by fake images of "perfection" all the time. Everywhere you look—social media, TV, ads—people seem to have perfect skin, perfect hair, perfect lives.

Self-acceptance means recognizing and embracing all parts of yourself—your strengths, your weaknesses, and everything in between. It's about understanding that you are enough just as you are. It doesn't mean you don't strive for improvement. It means you **love yourself during every step** of that journey.

Let's take a step back and look at the

science behind why we struggle with self-acceptance. Our brains are wired to focus on the negative. This is an evolutionary trait that helped our ancestors survive by paying attention to dangers and problems. Back in the day, if you didn't notice the lion sneaking up behind you, that was the end of your story. Today, instead of lions, we're surrounded by a different kind of danger: the constant pressure to be perfect.

Psychologists call this the "**negativity bias**." It means that we tend to remember the bad things more than the good. If ten people compliment your outfit and one person says something mean, it's that one mean comment that sticks with you. This bias makes it hard to accept ourselves because our brains are always on the lookout for flaws.

But here's the good news: just because our brains are wired this way doesn't mean we can't change the way we think. We can train our minds to focus on the positive and practice self-acceptance.

What Does Self-Acceptance Really Mean?

Self-acceptance isn't about ignoring your flaws or pretending they don't exist. It's about recognizing that everyone has flaws and that they don't make you any less valuable as a person. It's saying, "**Yeah, I'm not perfect, but I'm still pretty awesome in my way**."

Think about someone you really admire. Maybe it's a friend, a teacher, or a family member. Do you think they're perfect? Probably not. You like them because of who they are, not because they have perfect skin or always say the right thing. The same goes for you. The people who care about you don't expect you to be perfect—they love you for who you are.

Why Comparison is Harmful

Comparison is often called the thief of joy, and for good reason. When we compare ourselves to others, we focus on what we lack rather than what we have. This mindset creates a cycle of negativity and dissatisfaction. Here's why it's harmful:

- **Unique Journeys**: Everyone has their path. What works for someone else might not work for you.

- **Incomplete Picture**: We often compare our behind-the-scenes with someone else's highlight reel.
- **Self-Esteem**: Constant comparison erodes self-esteem and breeds insecurity.

I forgive you, I accept you, I love you.

Self-acceptance practices can rewire your brain. Positive affirmations and self-compassion exercises strengthen neural pathways associated with self-worth. It's like building mental muscles that make you more robust against stress.

Imposter Syndrome: Feeling Like a Fraud

Ever felt like you're one step away from being "found out" as a fraud, even when you're actually doing pretty well? That's **imposter syndrome**—the nagging belief that your success is due to luck or trickery rather than your talent, and it can make even high-achievers feel like they don't belong. Don't worry, it is more common than you think!

First coined by psychologists Pauline Clance and Suzanne Imes in 1978, imposter syndrome refers to the psychological pattern where people doubt their accomplishments and have a persistent fear of being exposed as a "fraud" despite evidence of their competence. You could win an award, get praised at work, or ace an exam, but you still feel like you didn't really earn it.

There are a few types of imposter syndrome:

- **The Perfectionist:** Never satisfied with their work, even when it's objectively excellent.

- **The Superhuman:** It feels like they have to juggle all tasks perfectly, or they'll be "caught" as not really qualified.

- **The Natural Genius:** If something doesn't come easily, they feel like they're failing, even when success takes practice.

- **The Soloist:** Prefers to do everything alone because asking for help makes them feel like a fraud.

- **The Expert:** They always feel they need to know more and fear being seen as inexperienced or incompetent.

The Effects of Imposter Syndrome

This constant self-doubt can be exhausting. It makes people work harder, not out of passion but out of fear of being unmasked. You might overprepare for every task, avoid asking for help, or even downplay your achievements. The mental toll can lead to burnout, anxiety, or depression. It also undermines your confidence, making you hesitant to take risks or aim higher in your career.

Famous Faces Who Felt Like Frauds

Here's the kicker: even some of the most successful people on the planet have dealt with imposter syndrome. **Michelle Obama** admitted that she struggled with feeling like she didn't belong at Princeton, thinking she wasn't "smart enough." **Tom Hanks**, one of Hollywood's most accomplished actors, also said he often feels like he's still trying to prove himself. And **Maya Angelou**, despite being an acclaimed writer, once confessed that she feared her success was undeserved and that she'd be exposed as a "fraud."

How to Overcome It

1. **Recognize It for What It Is:** The first step is acknowledging that imposter syndrome exists, and it's common—far more common than you'd think.

2. **Keep Track of Your Wins:** Create a list or a "success journal" where you note your achievements, big or small. This serves as tangible

evidence when your brain tries to convince you that you aren't worthy of your success.

3. **Shift Your Perspective:** Instead of striving for perfection, focus on progress. Understand that failure is part of learning and growth. No one expects you to be perfect all the time, and you shouldn't expect that from yourself.

4. **Talk About It:** Discuss your feelings with a mentor, friend, or counselor. Sometimes, just hearing that others—especially those you admire—have felt the same way can be incredibly validating. You're not alone in this.

5. **Embrace Vulnerability:** Asking for help or admitting that you don't know something doesn't make you any less capable. In fact, vulnerability is a strength, and being open to learning is how you grow.

6. **Reframe Comparison:** It's easy to compare yourself to others but remember, you're only seeing the highlights of their life, not the struggles. Focus on your path, and measure your success against your personal goals, not someone else's.

Imposter syndrome doesn't just fade away as you become more successful. It takes active work to change how you think about yourself and your achievements. Remember, you're not "tricking" anyone. If you've earned praise, recognition, or accomplishments, it's because of your hard work, talent, and effort.

Stop being harsh on yourself!

Stop beating yourself!

Be gentle, kind, and compassionate to yourself!

The Role of Gratitude

Gratitude doesn't have to be about the big stuff. Sometimes, it's about the simple things we usually forget, like waking up to sunlight. We don't think much about it, but there are places where the sun doesn't shine for months.

Or even something as basic as breathing. Every single breath is a gift we don't pay much attention to, yet we depend on it every second.

Then there's clean water. Millions of people around the world walk miles just to fill up a bucket. And here we are, leaving the tap running as we brush our teeth. How wild is that? The next time you take a sip of cold water on a hot day, think about how that's a privilege, not a given.

Even Wi-Fi. We joke about how the internet goes down and the world ends. But imagine going without it for a week. Some people can't even access it, ever. What about Family? It's easy to get irritated when your mom nags you about homework or your sibling steals your charger. But the truth is, having a family is something not everyone gets. You've got people who care enough to ask where you're going, even when it feels like they're just trying to annoy you. That's something special. Whether it's parents, siblings, or even friends who feel like family, just having someone to text, argue with, or share a meal means you've got people in your corner. That's something to be grateful for, even on the bad days.

We complain when the pizza arrives late or when dinner isn't what we wanted, but the fact that you have food at all is huge. In some parts of the world, people wake up wondering if they'll eat at all that day. Meanwhile, we're scrolling through delivery apps and deciding what sounds good. Next time you sit down for a meal, even if it's just a sandwich or last night's leftovers, take a second to appreciate that it's there. You've got access to food—something millions of people struggle to find every day.

And if you're reading this right now, it's a pretty clear sign that you're better off than many. It means you've got access to books, education, and technology. Some kids dream of going to school to learn to read, but they can't. The fact that you can read these words means you have opportunities. You're not stuck in survival mode, and that's something to be grateful for. It's easy to overlook the fact that education is a gift, not a guarantee.

Gratitude is about paying attention to the stuff we take for granted every day. When we stop and notice these small things, life feels a lot more full than we think.

Your Body Loves Gratitude

Gratitude activates several key areas of the brain, each contributing to the overall feeling of well-being. Also, do you know about the **Vagus nerve,** the longest cranial nerve in the body, which extends from the brainstem to the abdomen, touching multiple major organs? This nerve is a critical component of the parasympathetic nervous system, which controls the body's rest-and-digest functions. When we practice gratitude, we stimulate the vagus nerve, which can lead to a reduction in heart rate and blood pressure, promoting a

state of calm and relaxation. The endocrine system, responsible for hormone production, also responds positively to gratitude, increasing Oxytocin and reducing Cortisol.

How to Practice Gratitude

1. **Gratitude Journaling**: Write down three things you're grateful for each day.

2. **Express Gratitude**: Tell someone why you're thankful for them.

3. **Mindfulness**: Take a moment each day to appreciate something simple, like the warmth of the sun or a delicious meal.

Combining Self-Acceptance and Gratitude

When self-acceptance and gratitude are practiced together, they create a powerful synergy. Self-acceptance helps you recognize your inherent worth, while gratitude ensures you appreciate your life's blessings.

Quick Test: How Self-Accepting Are You?

Instructions:

For each statement, rate yourself on a scale from 1 to 5:

- 1 = Strongly Disagree
- 2 = Disagree
- 3 = Neutral
- 4 = Agree
- 5 = Strongly Agree

Statements:

1. I feel comfortable in my skin.
2. I accept my flaws and imperfections.
3. I treat myself with kindness and compassion, even when I make mistakes.
4. I do not compare myself to others frequently.
5. I am proud of my achievements, no matter how small.
6. I acknowledge my strengths and use them to my advantage.
7. I allow myself to feel emotions without judgment.
8. I believe I am worthy of love and respect.
9. I forgive myself for past mistakes.
10. I do not need external validation to feel good about myself.
11. I embrace my unique qualities and talents.
12. I set realistic goals for myself and celebrate progress.
13. I have a positive self-image.
14. I take care of my mental and physical well-being.
15. I accept that not everyone will like me, and that's okay.

Scoring:

- **15-30**: You may struggle with self-acceptance. Consider practicing self-compassion and focusing on your strengths.

- **31-45**: You have a moderate level of self-acceptance. There's room for improvement, but you're on the right track.

- **46-60**: You have a high level of self-acceptance. You understand and appreciate your worth.

5. Resilience and Grit: The Keys to Overcoming Challenges

What sets successful people apart? Is it talent, luck, or something else? It's resilience and grit – the ability to bounce back from setbacks and keep pushing forward. These qualities can make all the difference in achieving your goals and living a fulfilling life. Do you want to achieve your dreams in real life by giving all you have, OR do you want to let the valuable time slip by while you sleep and snooze and do nothing in particular?

I NEVER GIVE UP ON MY DREAMS, I KEEP SLEEPING.

Resilience is the ability to recover from difficulties and adapt to challenging situations. It's like a rubber band that stretches but doesn't break. Grit, on the other hand, is the passion and perseverance to pursue long-term goals. It's the determination to keep going, even when things get tough.

Facing challenges often feels overwhelming at first, like you're standing at the bottom of a giant staircase. You start by doubting yourself, unsure if you can even make the climb. But once you take the first step and begin asking how things shift. With each bit of effort,

96

your confidence builds, and suddenly, what seemed impossible starts feeling doable. The more you try, the closer you get. Before long, doubt turns into determination, and determination turns into achievement. By the end, you realize that the hardest part was simply starting. The rest? Just one step at a time.

Quiz: How Resilient Are You?

1. When something doesn't go your way, what do you do?
   - a) Give up
   - b) Keep trying but feel discouraged
   - c) Learn from it and try again

2. How do you react to criticism?
   - a) Take it personally
   - b) Feel upset, but think about it
   - c) Use it to improve

3. When you set a goal, how likely are you to stick with it?
   - a) Not likely
   - b) Sometimes I do, sometimes I don't
   - c) Very likely

4. How often do you push yourself to do hard things?
   - a) Rarely
   - b) Sometimes
   - c) Often

5. When faced with a difficult situation, what's your first thought?
   - a) "I can't do this."
   - b) "This is hard, but I'll try."
   - c) "I've got this!"

1. Answer: c) Learn from it and try again
   Resilient people see setbacks as opportunities to learn and grow rather than reasons to quit.

2. Answer: c) Use it to improve
   Those with grit use criticism as a tool for self-improvement, seeing it as feedback rather than a personal attack.

3. Answer: c) Very likely
   People with grit are committed to their goals and will stick with them, even when progress is slow.

4. Answer: c) Often
   Resilient individuals often push themselves outside their comfort zones, knowing that growth happens through challenges.

5. Answer: c) "I've got this!"
   Having a positive mindset when faced with difficulty is a key trait of resilience.

Resilience and Grit - The Superpowers of Success

In life, you'll face obstacles that seem insurmountable, moments that make you question whether you can keep going. But remember, every challenge is an opportunity to grow stronger. Resilience and grit are the forces that push you forward when everything else tells you to stop. They are the quiet determination that whispers, "Just one more step." With these traits in your arsenal, there's no mountain too high no storm too fierce. Keep going because on the other side of the struggle lies the success you've been striving for all along.

Your journey is not defined by the challenges you face but by the strength you show in overcoming them.

6. Strengths and Weaknesses: What Are Mine and How Do I Find Them?

As a teenager, you're in the middle of figuring out who you are, and a big part of that process is understanding your strengths and weaknesses. But let's be real—this isn't always easy, and it's not always fun. You might feel like you're supposed to have a bunch of strengths, but what if you don't see any? Or maybe your weaknesses feel overwhelming. The truth is, it's okay to have strengths, it's okay to have weaknesses, and it's  even okay if you don't know what your strengths are yet. This chapter is about being honest with yourself, embracing where you are right now, and figuring out how to move forward.

What if Your Weakness is Actually Your Strength?

Have you ever wondered if your biggest weakness might just be your greatest strength in disguise? It's like in a superhero movie when the hero discovers their power isn't a curse but a gift. Imagine this: you're the last person picked for a sports team because you're "too slow." But guess what? That same slowness makes you super observant, noticing details that others miss. You become the strategist, the person who sees the game in slow motion and can predict moves. Suddenly, that "weakness" is your secret weapon.

In life, people love to label things. "Good" or "bad." "Weak" or "strong." But what if those labels are totally wrong? What if your supposed flaw is just a misunderstood strength waiting for the right moment to shine?

The Strength Trap: When Being Strong Becomes a Problem

Let's flip it around. Imagine being known for a strength—like always being the smartest person in the room. You're that kid who always has the answers in class. Sounds great, right? But soon, you get so used to being right that you stop trying. You stop asking questions because you don't want to look foolish. You stop learning because you're afraid of not knowing. Suddenly, your strength is holding you back. You've built a trap for yourself, and it's a nice, comfy one with a sign that says, "You're too smart to fail."

But what happens when something comes along that you can't solve with smarts alone? Maybe it's a real-life problem, like making friends or managing your time. Or maybe it's something emotional, like dealing with failure. That's when the strength trap slams shut.

Here's the truth: Every strength, when overused, can become a weakness. And every weakness, when understood, can become a strength.

The Biology of Strengths and Weaknesses: Adapt or Die (Not Really, But Kinda)

Did you know that the giraffe's long neck—its greatest strength—is also a huge liability? Sure, it helps the giraffe reach the tastiest leaves high up in the trees. But it also makes the giraffe super slow at drinking water. Why? Because it has to spread its legs awkwardly and bend that long neck down to reach the water, making it vulnerable to predators. Nature is full of these kinds of trade-offs. What makes you awesome in one situation can be a total disaster in another.

Humans are the same. Our strengths and weaknesses are shaped by the environments we grow up in. Take someone who grew up in a chaotic home. They might be super good at staying calm under pressure because they had to learn how to survive in unpredictable situations. But maybe they also struggle to relax, always waiting for something to go wrong. The very thing that helped them survive now makes it hard for them to thrive in calmer, safer environments.

Evolution: The Ultimate Balancing Act

From an evolutionary perspective, every strength we have comes with a cost. Humans developed big brains that allowed us to outsmart predators, but we lost the speed and physical strength of many other animals. We traded brute strength for brainpower. But our intelligence also made us anxious creatures—always worried about the future, always planning. It's like having an overactive mind is both our greatest gift and our biggest curse.

Real-Life Examples: When Weakness Turns Into Strength

Let's look at some real-world examples to drive this home.

1. Nick Vujicic: The Man Without Limbs Who Found His Wings

Nick Vujicic was born without arms or legs. Most people would call that a "weakness." But Nick didn't see it that way. He turned what others saw as his biggest limitation into his greatest strength. Today, Nick is a motivational speaker who travels the world, inspiring millions of people. He doesn't hide his so-called "weakness"—he embraces it. He's living proof that your greatest challenges can fuel your greatest triumphs.

2. Albert Einstein: The "Slow" Genius

Einstein, one of the greatest minds in history, struggled in school. His teachers thought he was slow because he didn't learn the same way as other kids. Today, we might say he had a learning disability. But that "weakness" was actually his strength. Because he thought differently, he questioned the things other people took for granted. And in doing so, he rewrote the rules of physics.

3. Temple Grandin: Turning Autism into an Advantage

Temple Grandin, a scientist and advocate for people with autism, has said that her autism is both her greatest strength and her greatest challenge. Her brain processes information in pictures, not words. This made social interactions difficult for her, but it also gave her a unique perspective on animal behavior, which she used to revolutionize the livestock industry. She turned what many saw as a disability into a superpower.

How to Hack Your Strengths and Weaknesses

Now, let's get practical. How do you figure out what your strengths and weaknesses are? And how do you turn your weaknesses into strengths? Here's a step-by-step guide:

Step 1: Take an Honest Look

This might sound easy, but it's not. Most people avoid looking at their weaknesses because it's uncomfortable. But this is the first step. Ask yourself: What are the things I struggle with? What do I avoid doing because I think I'm bad at it?

Step 2: Get Feedback

Sometimes, we're too close to ourselves to see things clearly. Ask your friends, family, or teachers for feedback. You might be surprised by what they see as your strengths or weaknesses. They might notice strengths in you that you didn't even realize you had.

Step 3: Play to Your Strengths

Once you've identified your strengths, find ways to use them more. This doesn't mean ignoring your weaknesses, but it does mean focusing on what you're naturally good at and leveraging those strengths to succeed.

Step 4: Reframe Your Weaknesses

This is the most important step. Instead of seeing your weaknesses as problems, see them as areas for growth. Ask yourself: How could this weakness actually help me? How could I turn it into a strength? Maybe you're bad at organizing things, but that makes you more creative and flexible. Or maybe you're shy, but that makes you a great listener.

Step 5: Balance, Balance, Balance

Remember the giraffe? Its long neck is both a blessing and a curse, depending on the situation. The key to thriving in life is balance. Know when to use your strengths and when to let them take a backseat. Know when your weaknesses can actually work in your favor.

Fun Facts About Strengths and Weaknesses

- **Owls can't move their eyes**, but they can turn their heads almost all the way around. Their "weak" vision becomes a strength when combined with their incredible neck flexibility.

- **Sharks can't swim backward**, but they don't need to because they're so fast and powerful moving forward.

- **Koalas sleep for up to 22 hours a day**! What seems like laziness is actually a survival strategy. They conserve energy because their food (eucalyptus leaves) doesn't provide much nutrition.

- **Dolphins sleep with one eye open** to stay alert to predators. Being half-awake is their strength!

Here are five tools and websites that you can include in your chapter on finding strengths and weaknesses:

1. **VIA Character Strengths Survey**

   This free test helps individuals discover their top 24 character strengths. Developed by psychologists, it provides insights into how these strengths can enhance personal and professional well-being. It's especially useful for building self-awareness around character-based strengths.

2. **CliftonStrengths (formerly StrengthsFinder)**

   One of the most widely researched tools, this assessment identifies your top strengths out of 34 possible categories. While the test is paid, it offers an in-depth analysis of your strengths and provides actionable advice on how to leverage them in life and work.

3. **HIGH5 Strengths Test**

   This is a free, accessible tool for identifying your top five strengths.

The test is designed based on positive psychology principles, making it ideal for those looking for a practical, quick snapshot of their strengths.

4. **Personal SWOT Analysis (MindTools)**

   MindTools offers a free worksheet for conducting a personal SWOT analysis. This tool is commonly used in professional development to assess strengths, weaknesses, opportunities, and threats, making it highly effective for career growth.

5. **Berkeley   Well-Being   Institute's   Strengths   Exercises**
   Berkeley's platform offers various strength-finding activities and questions that help individuals reflect on their strengths and weaknesses and how they can use them effectively in their daily lives.

7. Mindfulness and Meditation: Calming the Mind in a Busy World

Can you hear yourself think? Have you ever felt like your brain is too noisy? Like there's a rock concert happening in your head, but nobody invited you? Between school, social media, friends, family, and all the other stuff life throws at you, it's easy to get overwhelmed. But what if I told you there's a way to turn the volume down? What if you could find a quiet place in your mind, even when everything around you is chaotic? Welcome to the world of mindfulness and meditation—a kind of mental chill-out zone where you can catch your breath, even when the world feels like it's spinning out of control.

Mindfulness and meditation might sound like something only monks do while sitting on a mountain. But the truth is, these practices are as accessible as checking your phone for the hundredth time today. And the best part? They come with no side effects—unless you count feeling more relaxed, focused, and ready to handle life like a pro.

What Exactly Is Mindfulness?

We briefly talked about Mindfulness earlier in the book as a great tool to calm yourself down.

Have you ever eaten a bag of chips while watching TV, only to realize you've polished off the entire thing without even tasting it? Or walked to school and suddenly found yourself there with no memory of the journey? That's your brain on autopilot— your body's moving, but your mind is somewhere else entirely.

Mindfulness is the opposite of that. It's about paying attention—really paying attention—to what's happening right now. It's like switching off autopilot and grabbing the controls yourself.

Mindfulness in Everyday Life

Mindfulness isn't something you only do while sitting cross-legged on the floor. It's something you can weave into your daily life. Brushing your teeth? Try focusing on the feel of the toothbrush against your teeth, the taste of the toothpaste, and the sound of the bristles. Walking to school? Notice the way your feet hit the ground, the colors around you, the sounds you usually ignore.

The idea is to engage fully with what you're doing right now rather than worrying about that text you haven't responded to or the homework you still need to finish.

Meditation: The Workout for Your Mind

When you think of meditation, you might imagine someone sitting still with their eyes closed, possibly chanting "om." And yeah, that's one way to do it, but meditation is much more than that. At its core, meditation is about training your mind to focus and redirect your thoughts. It's like doing mental push-ups to make your brain stronger, more flexible, and more resilient.

Our brains can sometimes feel like that tipsy monkey, jumping from one thought to another, always swinging between worries, ideas, and distractions. One moment, we're thinking about school; the next, we're stressing over the future or daydreaming about the weekend—just like the monkey leaping from branch to branch without a plan. But meditation is like giving that wild monkey a little rest. It helps calm the constant jumping, bringing focus and peace. When we meditate, we give our mind the chance to slow down and breathe, helping us stay grounded no matter how many "branches" our thoughts try to swing between.

There are many different types of meditation, but most of them share some basic elements: a quiet place, a comfortable position, a focus of attention (like your breath or a specific word), and an open attitude toward whatever thoughts pop into your head.

The Science of Meditation

Meditation is like a spa day for your brain. Studies show that regular meditation can reduce anxiety, improve concentration, and even make you happier. How? By changing the way your brain works.

When you meditate, you're not just zoning out; you're actively engaging your brain's "default mode network"—the part of your brain that's active when your mind is wandering. Meditation helps to calm this network down, which is why you feel more focused and less stressed afterward.

In fact, researchers have found that people who meditate regularly have more gray matter in certain areas of the brain. Gray matter is like your brain's power source—it's involved in muscle control, sensory perception, decision-making, and self-control. More gray matter means a better ability to handle whatever life throws your way.

Different Types of Meditation

Meditation isn't one-size-fits-all. There are tons of different types to choose from, depending on what you need:

1. **Mindfulness Meditation:** This is the big one. You focus on your breath and let thoughts pass by without getting tangled up in them. It's like watching clouds drift across the sky.

2. **Loving-Kindness Meditation:** In this practice, you focus on sending good vibes to yourself and others. You repeat phrases like "May I be happy" or "May you be safe" to cultivate a sense of kindness and compassion.

3. **Body Scan Meditation:** This involves focusing on different parts of your body, from your toes to your head, to release tension and become more aware of how your body feels.

4. **Guided Meditation:** If you find it hard to sit in silence, guided meditations can help. These involve listening to someone (or an app) walk you through the meditation step by step.

5. **Transcendental Meditation:** This involves repeating a specific word or phrase (called a mantra) to help you settle into a deep state of relaxation.

How to Start Meditating

Starting a meditation practice doesn't mean you need to sit for hours on end. In fact, just five to ten minutes a day can make a big difference. Here's how to get started:

1. **Find a Quiet Spot:** You don't need a fancy meditation room. Any quiet place will do. It could be your bedroom, a corner of the library, or even a quiet park.

2. **Get Comfortable:** Sit or lie down in a position that feels comfortable.

You don't need to sit cross-legged unless that's comfortable for you.

3. **Focus on Your Breath:** Close your eyes and start by taking a few deep breaths. Then, let your breathing return to normal. Pay attention to the sensation of your breath moving in and out of your body.

4. **Let Thoughts Pass By:** When thoughts pop up (and they will), don't try to fight them. Just notice them and let them go, like leaves floating down a stream.

5. **Start Small:** Aim for just five minutes at first. As you get more comfortable, you can gradually increase the time.

Latest Trends in Mindfulness and Meditation

Technology isn't just about distractions—it can also help you chill out. Meditation apps have become super popular and for a good reason. They're like having a meditation teacher in your pocket, guiding you through different practices whenever and wherever you need them.

Some of the most popular meditation apps include:

1. **Headspace:** Offers guided meditations, mindfulness exercises, and even sleep sounds.

2. **Calm:** Known for its soothing background sounds and "Sleep Stories," which are like bedtime stories for grown-ups.

3. **Insight Timer:** Offers a massive library of free guided meditations from various teachers around the world.

4. **Simple Habit:** Provides quick, 5-minute meditations designed to fit into your busy day.

And who says meditation has to involve sitting still? Mindful movement practices like yoga and Tai Chi combine physical exercise with mindfulness. These practices encourage you to focus on your breath and body as you move, making them a great way to release stress while staying active.

Steve Jobs, the co-founder of Apple, practiced meditation to boost his creativity and focus. He believed that a calm mind was essential for innovation. So meditation can take a bit of credit for those iPhones! After all, a calm brain works best with focus and creativity. If you fill it with Insta reels or mundane, trivial matters of daily life and struggles, there will be no space in the brain to create something wonderful.

Brain Waves and Binaural Beats

This is another method to calm yourself down. You know how your brain feels different when you're cramming for a test versus when you're chilling with a book? That's because your brain is firing off different waves depending on what you're doing. There are five main types of brain waves: Delta, Theta, Alpha, Beta, and Gamma. Each has a different frequency and is linked to a specific mental state.

Delta Waves (1-4 Hz) show up during deep sleep. **Theta Waves** (4-8 Hz) are linked to daydreaming or meditation. **Alpha Waves** (8-12 Hz) are present when you're relaxed but alert, like when you're daydreaming. **Beta Waves** (12-30 Hz) dominate when you're problem-solving or focused, and **Gamma Waves** (30-100 Hz) are associated with peak concentration and learning.

How Binaural Beats Work

Binaural beats are a kind of brainwave therapy. Here's when you play two slightly different frequencies in each ear—say, 300 Hz on the left and 310 Hz on the right—your brain detects the 10 Hz difference and creates a third "phantom" beat at that frequency. This encourages your brain to sync up with that frequency. If you want to chill, you might listen to Theta binaural beats; if you need to focus, Beta waves could be your go-to. Try it out and see if it works for you. There are dozens of apps available on Apple and

Android stores. But be careful and consult an adult before using.

If you Google, you will see dozens of more relaxing or meditating techniques. You need to try and see what works for you. E.g., if counting upwards doesn't work for you (1,2,3,4...), try counting backward (..4,3,2,1). Or if closing your eyes brings back all negative thoughts, keep the eyes open and focus on an object. If nothing works, just work out by listening to rhythmic music or mantra or heavy metal, whatever.

Meditation is hard. Overall, see what methods work for you, but by incorporating mindfulness and meditation into your daily routine and making it something you enjoy, you can transform your mind from a chaotic city into a peaceful sanctuary. A stable, relaxed mind will give you the foundation to do amazing things in life. So, do you want to try it, or do you think you are already peaceful inside? If you want to try, what will you start tomorrow to get that inner peace that Master Shifu talked about in the Kung Fu Panda movie?

8. The Beauty of an Ordinary Life

When you're growing up, it can feel like the world is constantly telling you to stand out. Be special. Be extraordinary. Be the best at something—whether it's becoming a famous artist, earning millions, or inventing the next big thing. It's like there's a race happening all around you, and the prize is some version of success that means everyone knows your name, you're rich, and you've "made it."

But here's the thing: *not everyone has to be special* in the way the world defines it. And that's okay. In fact, it's more than okay. It's wonderful. The idea that life is only valuable if you're extraordinary is a trap that sets you up for a lot of unnecessary pressure. And while money and fame can be goals to work toward if that's what drives you, they aren't the only things that give life meaning.

Ordinary, But Not Less

Let's start with something simple: most people live what the world would call "ordinary" lives. They aren't super famous, they don't have millions of dollars, and they won't be remembered in history books. But that doesn't mean they're unimportant. It doesn't mean their lives lack value. Think

 about your family, your friends, your neighbors. They go to work, they take care of their kids, and they contribute to their communities in quiet, meaningful ways. And yet, they love, they laugh, and they find joy in small moments—a good meal, a conversation, a peaceful weekend.

Ordinary moments often carry the most weight. What's more important: owning the latest luxury car or having a friend who genuinely cares about you? Is it better to be adored by millions of people who don't really know you or to have a couple of close friends who know your deepest thoughts?

The Myth of "Special"

The truth is, not everyone needs to be special in the way we've been taught to understand it. The pressure to always stand out can be exhausting. It's like running on a treadmill that never stops. Even if you achieve fame or wealth, the world always pushes you to go further. More followers, more money, more success. It's a cycle that rarely leads to lasting happiness.

What if being "ordinary" is actually the key to a good life? What if your value isn't in how you're perceived by others but in how you live each day? *The people who matter most to you—the ones you laugh with, care for, and love—don't care if you're famous or wealthy. They care about you, as you are.*

Finding Meaning in the Everyday

If you take a close look, there's an enormous richness in the simple things that make up our daily lives. Imagine waking up to the smell of fresh tea or coffee, feeling the warmth of the sun on your face during a morning walk, or enjoying a conversation with someone you care about. These moments aren't flashy, but they are filled with meaning. They connect us to ourselves and others.

Research even shows that people who find contentment in life aren't always the ones chasing big dreams or major success. Studies on happiness reveal that strong relationships and a sense of community often matter more than money or fame. It turns out a quiet, simple life can be deeply fulfilling because it's rooted in what makes us human: connection, love, and purpose. No one on their Deathbed ever said, "Oh, I wanted to work harder and earn more money" or "Oh, I wanted to buy that stupid sports car. Below are the things people most regretted, as per the National Institute of Health(ncbi.nlm.nih.gov)

1) "I wish I'd had the courage to live a life true to myself, not the life others expected of me."

2) "I wish I hadn't worked so hard." *(BTW, don't take this as an excuse not to work hard. This doesn't mean you don't work hard - this means you don't work too hard to become sick or lose other important aspects of life, such as your loved ones)*

3) "I wish I'd had the courage to express my feelings."

4) "I wish I had stayed in touch with my friends."

5) "I wish I had let myself be happier"

Well, these things are meant more for adults and not for teens, but you will be one before you even realize it!

It's Okay to Want More

Now, this isn't to say you shouldn't dream big or work hard if your goal is to achieve more. If you have ambitions to be rich or famous, that's absolutely  fine, too. There's nothing wrong with wanting financial freedom or to be recognized for your talents. Go for it, but know that even if you reach those goals, it's the ordinary parts of life that will still bring the most grounding joy.

Working toward your goals—whether it's building a business, becoming an artist, or traveling the world—can be exciting and rewarding. But just remember that the destination isn't the only thing that matters. It's the journey along the way. Whether you hit the top or not, it's the people you meet, the lessons you learn, and the experiences you gather that will ultimately shape your life.

The Freedom to Choose

Here's the most important part: *you get to choose.* You can live a quiet, fulfilling life and never be famous, and that's a perfectly valid and beautiful choice. Or, if money and recognition are what you want, you can go after them with all you've got. But no matter what you choose, understand that one path isn't better than the other.

Whether you aim for the stars or cherish the quiet, small things, what matters most is that you're living in a way that's meaningful to you.

If your dream is to be rich and famous, pursue it with passion, but know that those things aren't the only markers of success. If your goal is to lead a simple, peaceful life surrounded by people who matter, that's a path worth walking to.

What matters most is that you live on *your* terms, and that's something no measure of fame or money can ever replace.

So, what do you want from your Life?

∾
CHAPTER 3

Skills More Important Than Rote Learning and Memorization

"Education is not the learning of facts, but the training of the mind to think.' -

Albert Einstein

Imagine this: you're in the year 2050. Robots and AI handle most of the routine tasks. With ChatGPT now almost as ubiquitous as Google and so many other AI tools getting launched every week, we can see a glimpse of the future already. In a world where technology can do almost everything, what will make you stand out? The answer is simple: skills that are needed to work with People and skills machines can't replicate or at least not replicate yet —communication, collaboration, creativity, confidence, critical thinking, continuous learning, time management, and leadership. These skills are more important than ever, given that machines can handle other things.

Our current education system, based on a 20th-century model, emphasizes memorization and rote learning. But in the 21st century, we need different skills. Computers can store information and perform repetitive tasks, but they lack the human touch. They can't communicate with empathy, collaborate effectively, think creatively, or lead with vision, at least not yet, though it may change once we have Artificial Super Intelligence; who knows? But till then, machines can't beat people who are dealing with other people.

Do you know how we used to cram for tests by just memorizing facts and figures? Well, that old-school way of learning is becoming less important now. Think about it: with all the information we need just a click away, we don't really need to remember everything.

What really matters these days is how we use that information. Like being able to look at data, question it, and make smart decisions—that's what critical thinking is all about—and solving problems? That's not just about finding the right answer but coming up with creative solutions when things get tough or unpredictable.

Creativity is critical, too. It's what drives new ideas and keeps things exciting, whether you're in business, tech, or any field, really. And you know how work is nowadays—team projects, diverse groups, and all that. Being able to communicate well and work with others is super important.

Plus, the world changes so fast. Being adaptable and flexible means you can roll with the punches and thrive, no matter what gets thrown your way. So yeah, while memorizing stuff might still help in some situations, it's really these broader skills that set us up for success in today's world. They make us better thinkers, collaborators, and innovators, which is what we really need now.

Humans got smarter and better at surviving because we learned to interact with each other. Talking and understanding each other helped us share ideas and solve problems together. Living in groups made us safer and allowed us to split up tasks, so everyone had a role. We developed empathy and cooperation, which kept our communities strong. Sharing knowledge and skills across generations led to new inventions and cultural practices. Social bonds and emotional support improved our mental health. Overall, teamwork and communication were key to evolving into the advanced species we are today.

Let's dive into these essential skills and discover how they can make you not just a better student but a better human being ready for the challenges of the future with these timeless skills!

1. Communication: Making Connections

Think of communication as the Wi-Fi of human interaction. When it's strong, everyone's connected, sharing memes, ideas, and jokes with zero lag. But when it's weak, it's like a bad internet connection—messages get scrambled, and no one really knows what's going on. So, whether you're trying to ask for

extra fries or negotiate that group project, having good communication skills is like having a supercharged Wi-Fi signal: it makes everything run smoother, faster, and a whole lot more fun.

Communication is the process of sharing information, ideas, and feelings. It's how we connect with others, express our thoughts, and build relationships. Communication isn't just about speaking. It involves listening, observing, and understanding non-verbal cues. In fact, research shows that about 55% of communication is non-verbal, 38% is tone of voice, and only 7% is the actual words spoken.

The Basics: Speaking and Listening

Speaking: More Than Words

Think about the words you use every day. Simple stuff, right? "Hi." "Bye." "Please stop stealing my fries." But what if I told you that words have power? Not like magical wizard power, but the kind that can change someone's mood, influence decisions, or even start (or stop) a war. In fact, history is filled with examples of people who used words to change the course of history. Martin Luther King Jr., for

instance, used words to fight for civil rights. Malala Yousafzai used them to stand up for education. And someone like Winston Churchill used words to keep the spirits of an entire nation alive during a war.

When you speak, you're doing more than just using words. You're sharing ideas, emotions, and intentions. Think about a time when you were really excited about something. Did you talk faster? Use your hands more? Maybe your voice got a little higher. That's because communication is also about body language and tone.

1. **Be Clear:** Before you even start talking, make sure you know what you want to say and set the Background or Context first. Imagine trying to tell a story but forgetting the plot halfway through—it leaves everyone confused, including you! Organize your thoughts so that your message is easy to follow.

2. **Be Concise:** Think of speaking like sending a text. You want to get your point across without sending a novel-length message. If you ramble on, people might zone out or forget the main point. Stick to the important stuff and leave out the fluff. It's like a good meme; it's all about impact, with as few words as possible. That doesn't mean you ignore the details where needed - the key is to be punchy.

3. **Use Body Language:** Sometimes, what you're saying isn't nearly as important as how you're saying it. Think of a happy dog wagging its tail with its ears back - isn't that expressive enough to melt your heart without any words? Of course, we don't have tails, but we have our facial expressions and the whole body that participates in conveying the message. Crossing your arms might make you seem closed off, while a genuine smile can make someone feel at ease. So next time you're in a conversation, pay attention to more than just the  words—watch the hands, the posture, the way someone's eyes dart around when they're nervous. There are so many books on body language that you are interested in reading.

4. **Maintain Eye Contact:** Look people in the eye to show you're listening and confident in what you're saying. But don't overdo it—no one likes being stared down like a final boss in a video game!

5. **Adjust Your Tone:** If words are the lyrics, then tone is the music. And just like music, it can completely change the message. Say "I'm fine" in a cheerful voice, and it sounds like everything's good. Say it in a monotone or sarcastic voice, and it suddenly means, "I'm actually not fine, but I don't want to talk about it." Tone is why texting can sometimes get you into trouble. Without tone, it's hard to tell if someone is joking, serious, or mad. It's like trying to watch a movie on mute. You might get the basic idea, but you miss all the emotions that make it real.

6. **The Art of Persuasion: Getting What You Want Without Being Pushy** Let's face it—everyone wants something. Maybe it's to win an argument, convince your parents to let you go out, or just make someone laugh. Persuasion is the art of getting what you want, but it's not about tricking or manipulating people. It's about presenting your case in a way that makes the other person see your point of view. To persuade effectively, you need to know your audience. Are they the kind of person who loves logic and facts, or do they respond better to emotions and stories? Use the right approach, and you'll find it's much easier to get your way. But remember, with great power comes great responsibility. Don't use your persuasive skills to become a manipulative jerk.

Listening: The Unsung Hero

Great listeners are like detectives in a mystery novel—they pick up on the subtle clues in what people say, how they say it, and even what they don't say. By tuning into these details, they can understand the real message behind the words, often uncovering hidden meanings or emotions that aren't immediately obvious. In a way, listening is like solving a puzzle; the more pieces you collect, the clearer the picture becomes.

Tips for Effective Listening

1. **Pay Attention:** In a world full of distractions, paying attention can be a challenge, but it's the first step to being a good listener. Think of it like

watching your favorite show—if you don't pay attention, you'll miss important plot twists.

2. **Show You're Listening:** Listening isn't just a passive activity; it's something you actively engage in. Small actions like nodding, making eye contact, and using verbal acknowledgments like "I see" or "uh-huh" are the equivalent of sending a thumbs-up emoji during a chat. These gestures let the speaker know you're following along and interested in what they have to say.

3. **Don't Interrupt:** Interrupting someone mid-sentence is like trying to skip ahead in a game before completing the current level—it's frustrating and ruins the flow. Let the speaker finish their thought before you jump in.

4. **Ask Questions:** If something isn't clear, don't be afraid to ask questions. Clarifying what you don't understand helps prevent misunderstandings and shows that you're genuinely interested in what the other person is saying. It also encourages the speaker to elaborate, adding more pieces to the puzzle.

5. **Provide Feedback:** Once the speaker has finished, summarizing what they said is a great way to show you've understood. By reflecting on what you heard, you confirm that you're on the same page and give the speaker a chance to correct anything you might have misunderstood. This step solidifies the connection between speaker and listener, making the conversation more meaningful and productive.

Written Communication

Written communication covers everything from emails and texts to letters and social media posts. One of the biggest advantages of writing is that it gives you time to think before you express your thoughts. You can carefully choose your words, structure your message, and ensure that you're communicating exactly what you mean. However, written communication lacks the nuances of verbal and non-verbal cues, like tone of voice or facial expressions, which can lead to misunderstandings if you're not careful. Always consider how the reader might interpret your words, and when in doubt, err on the side of clarity and kindness.

The Brain's Role

Communication is a complex process that involves several parts of the brain, as you can see above. The image above is a rough representation of the brain - not 100% scientifically accurate - Search the web to see the exact structure, how many more areas are there, and what they do. Humans still have a very limited understanding of how their brains work. Can you imagine?

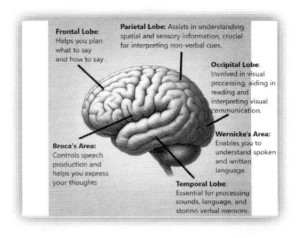

When you speak, your brain's Broca's area helps you form words. When you listen, your brain's Wernicke's area helps you understand them. Mirror neurons in your brain enable you to empathize with others, making communication a shared experience. And so on.

Evolution of Language

Humans have evolved to communicate in sophisticated ways. Early humans used gestures and sounds. Over time, these evolved into complex languages. This ability to communicate has been crucial for survival, helping us to form societies, share knowledge, and build civilizations.

The oldest languages in the world offer a fascinating glimpse into the early stages of human civilization and communication. Among the oldest known languages are Sumerian, Egyptian, Akkadian, and Elamite. Sumerian, used in ancient Mesopotamia, is often regarded as one of the earliest written languages, with evidence dating back to around 3100 BCE. The Sumerians used cuneiform script, which involved pressing wedge-shaped symbols into clay tablets. Egyptian hieroglyphics, another ancient writing system, emerged around the same period, with inscriptions found on monuments and tombs dating to approximately 3000 BCE. These languages played a crucial role in the administration, literature, and culture of their respective societies.

Another significant ancient language is Sanskrit, which originated in the

Indian subcontinent and is considered the liturgical language of Hinduism, Buddhism, and Jainism. Sanskrit texts, such as the Vedas, are among the oldest known religious texts, with roots tracing back to around 1500 BCE. Meanwhile, the Chinese language, with its earliest forms seen in the Oracle Bone Script, dates back to the Shang dynasty around 1200 BCE. These languages have evolved over millennia, influencing modern languages and preserving the cultural heritage of their regions. They provide invaluable insights into the development of human thought, social structures, and early literary achievements.

Sign Language

Beyond spoken languages, the world is also home to hundreds of different sign languages, each with its grammar, syntax, and lexicon. Amazing, isn't it? These visual languages are fully developed and sophisticated means of communication used primarily by the Deaf and hard-of-hearing communities. American Sign Language (ASL), British Sign Language (BSL), and French Sign Language (LSF) are just a few examples, each differing from

one another as much as spoken languages do. Sign languages are not universal; they evolve naturally within communities, influenced by their unique cultural contexts.

Emojis

What would we do without emojis? Aren't they so cool? The history of emojis dates back to the late 1990s. Shigetaka Kurita, a Japanese designer, created the first set of 176 emojis for NTT DoCoMo, a Japanese mobile operator. These early emojis were designed to facilitate quick and concise communication on mobile phones, reflecting common emotions and concepts. Don't we love all those cute emojis! Also very handy when we have nothing to say, isn't it?

Mastering communication is probably the most important thing you should learn. It helps you connect, understand, and influence the world around you. Whether you're speaking, listening, writing, or using digital platforms, good communication skills will open doors and create opportunities.

2. Collaboration: Working Together

Collaboration is one of the reasons humans have dominated the planet. Early humans had to work together to survive. They hunted in groups, protected each other from predators, and shared resources. Those who cooperated had a better chance of survival, and their genes got passed down. Over time, collaboration became a fundamental part of what it means to be human.

Even today, studies show that teams outperform individuals when solving

complex problems. Whether it's in business, sports, or science, collaborative efforts lead to more creative solutions, higher productivity, and better outcomes.

When you work with others, you combine strengths, compensate for weaknesses, and share the workload. Think of it like the Avengers coming together to defeat Thanos. Each hero has unique abilities, but it's their collaboration that saves the day.

Our brains are wired for collaboration. There's this thing called mirror neurons, which fire not just when you do something but when you see someone else do it. This means that when you see your friend solve a problem, your brain lights up as if you're solving it, too. It's like you're borrowing their brainpower for a moment.

This isn't just a random quirk; it's deeply rooted in our evolution. Early humans who cooperated and formed strong social bonds had a better chance of surviving and thriving. So, our brains evolved to reward social interactions with feel-good hormones.

When you work with others, you don't just add your skills together—you multiply them. It's like 3 + 3 = 9 or more. When you collaborate, your ideas bounce off each other. You see things from different angles, learn new things, and come up with solutions you'd never have thought of on your own.

The Construction of the Great Wall of China

The Great Wall of China, one of the most iconic structures in the world, wasn't built by one emperor or a single architect. It took centuries and millions of workers to construct. They had to collaborate across generations, with different teams handling different sections, each building on the work of those who came before. The Great Wall is a testament to what humans can accomplish when they work together. It stretches over 13,000 miles,  and it's still standing after more than 2,000 years. That's the power of collaboration—creating something that lasts.

Modern Marvel: The International Space Station

Zoom forward to today, and you've got the International Space Station (ISS). The ISS is like the ultimate group project, except this one is actually cool. It's a joint effort by 15 countries, including the USA, Russia, Japan, and several European nations. Scientists and engineers from all over the world collaborated to build it, and astronauts from different countries lived and worked there together.

Animal Collaboration

Humans aren't the only ones who collaborate. Take ants, for example. Humans aren't the only ones who've mastered the art of collaboration. Take

ants, for example. These little guys are incredible! Did you know a single ant can carry up to 50 times its body weight? Ants live in colonies that can number in the millions, and their teamwork is out of this world. They can build intricate underground nests with tunnels and chambers that would make an architect proud. These nests are not just random dirt piles; they're complex structures designed to support the entire colony. Each ant has a role—some are workers, others are soldiers, and some take care of the queen and her brood.

When it comes to gathering food, ants are super organized. They form long lines and work together to transport food back to the nest. And if they come across a large piece of food, they'll join forces to move it. It's like watching a well-oiled machine in action. Each ant knows exactly what to do, and they communicate with each other using chemical signals called pheromones. These signals tell other ants where to go and what to do, ensuring everyone is on the same page.

Defense is another area where ants truly shine. When a predator threatens the colony, soldier ants spring into action. They work together to fend off the intruder, using their mandibles and stingers to protect their home. It's like having a tiny but mighty army ready to defend the fort.

And have you ever heard of ant bridges? Some ant species can link their bodies together to form bridges over gaps or water. They literally use themselves as building materials to help their fellow ants cross obstacles. It's like the ultimate display of teamwork and sacrifice.

These tiny creatures are masters of collaboration, and their ability to work together is a big part of why they've been so successful for millions of years.

Or take bees, for example. These little insects are some of nature's most incredible collaborators. When you think about bees, you probably picture them buzzing around flowers, but there's so much more to their story.

First off, bees live in highly organized colonies, often numbering in the tens of thousands. At the heart of each hive is the queen bee. Her job is to lay eggs, and she can lay up to 2,000 eggs a day! The rest of the bees fall into different roles. One of the most fascinating things about bees is how they find food. When a worker bee discovers a good source of nectar, she doesn't just keep it to herself. Instead, she returns to the hive and performs what's known as a "waggle dance." This dance is a complex series of movements that tells the other bees exactly where to find the flowers. The angle and duration of the dance convey precise information about the distance and direction of the nectar source. It's like having a GPS built right into their behavior!

When it comes to defense, bees are ready to protect their hive at all costs. Guard bees stand watch at the entrance, and if a threat is detected, they release an alarm pheromone to alert the other bees. In no time, the hive can mobilize a swarm of defenders to fend off predators or invaders. It's a coordinated and effective defense system that keeps the colony safe.

Next time you see a bee buzzing around, remember there's an entire world of collaboration and hard work behind that little insect.

Cognitive Load Theory

There's a concept in psychology called cognitive load theory. It suggests that our brains can only handle so much information at once. When we collaborate, we distribute the cognitive load. Instead of one person being overwhelmed, the team can share the mental effort, making it easier to solve complex problems.

Challenges of Collaboration

Working with others isn't always easy. There are disagreements, egos, and miscommunications. Sometimes, people don't pull their weight, and you end up doing most of the work. Other times, everyone has a different idea of how things should be done, and it feels like you're going in circles. But these challenges are part of the process. Collaboration requires patience, compromise, and the ability to listen. It's about finding a balance between standing your ground and being flexible. When you overcome these challenges, the results are often worth it.

How to Be a Great Collaborator

Active Listening

One of the most important skills in collaboration is active listening. This means truly hearing what others are saying, not just waiting for your turn to speak. It involves asking questions, summarizing what you've heard, and showing empathy.

Flexibility and Adaptability

Good collaborators are flexible and adaptable. They're open to new ideas and willing to change their approach. This adaptability is key to navigating the dynamic nature of teamwork. How do you handle conflicts when working with others? Do you voice your opinion if you don't agree with something? Do you lose your temper?

A Sense of Humor

Never underestimate the power of humor. It can lighten the mood, reduce stress, and strengthen bonds. A good laugh can make even the toughest tasks more manageable.

Collaboration is at the heart of human progress. From ancient tribes to modern teams, working together allows us to achieve more than we ever could alone. It builds connections, fosters innovation, and, when done right, makes the journey enjoyable. So, the next time you're faced with a big task, remember: you don't have to do it alone. Find your team, share your ideas, and see how much further you can go together.

3. Creativity: Unleashing Your Inner Artist

Where does creativity come from? Is it a bolt of lightning that strikes you in the shower? Or maybe it's a magical power only some people have, like Harry Potter's wand. Nope. Creativity isn't magic. It's more like a muscle. The more you use it, the stronger it gets.

Think about a blank page or an empty canvas. It can be intimidating. What do you put on it? Where do you even start? Creativity is about taking that blank space and filling it with something new, something that's never existed before. It's about seeing the world differently, finding connections others don't see, and expressing ideas in a way that makes people stop and think. It's something we all have, whether we're designing a poster for school, solving a math problem, or coming up with a new way to organize our room. Creativity isn't a gift for a select few. It's part of being human!

The Art of Problem-Solving

When we talk about creativity, people usually think of art—painting, music, writing. But creativity shows up in more places than you might realize. Have you ever had to come up with a clever way to finish a school project at the last minute? Or have you figured out how to sneak a snack without getting caught by your parents? That's creativity in action.

Creativity is problem-solving with flair. It's the ability to look at a problem and say, "How can I solve this in a new way?" It doesn't always involve painting or writing a song. Sometimes, it's about coming up with an original idea to solve a practical problem. The world's greatest inventors, like Thomas Edison or Marie Curie, were creative not because they were artists but because they saw problems and found new ways to fix them.

Imagination is key

One of the best things about being creative is that it has no rules. You can imagine anything you want, no matter how wild or impossible it seems. The best part? Imagination doesn't care if your idea is realistic or practical. In fact, the crazier your idea, the more creative it might be. Some of the greatest inventions and ideas started as things people thought were impossible. Imagine if the Wright brothers had decided that flying was just a dream. They wouldn't have invented the airplane. Einstein mostly imagined the mind-boggling theories of relativities and proved those later.

When you come up with an idea, your brain lights up like a Christmas tree. There's a constant exchange of information between different parts of the brain, especially the left (logic) and right (creativity) hemispheres. Studies have shown that creativity isn't just about using the "right side" of the brain. It's about using both sides in new ways. The logical side organizes thoughts and processes information, while the creative side helps you think outside the box. When they work together, that's when the magic happens.

Creativity in Everyday Life

1. School Projects

Creativity doesn't just live in art class. It shows up in math, science, history, and even sports. Think about a school project. Sure, you could do the bare minimum: slap some text on a poster, print a few pictures, and call it a day. But what if you wanted to make it stand out? That's where creativity comes in. Maybe you can add a 3D model or a funny skit, or you can use animation to explain your point. Creativity makes your work not just good but memorable.

2. Social Media and Memes

Memes, TikTok trends, and Instagram stories are all forms of modern creativity. Memes, especially, are like the digital version of storytelling. People take a basic format and remix it to fit a new situation. Some of the funniest memes come from taking two completely unrelated ideas and smashing them together. This kind of creativity isn't about making art for a museum. It's about quick thinking, being funny, and capturing a moment in a way that makes people laugh or think.

3. Everyday Problem-Solving

Remember that time you couldn't find a screwdriver, so you used a butter knife to fix something? That's everyday creativity. It's about using what you have to solve a problem in a new way. Whether you're organizing your messy desk, figuring out a faster way to get your homework done, or inventing a new snack combination, creativity is always at work.

How to Be More Creative

1. Try New Things

The easiest way to spark creativity is to try something new. Take a class on a subject you know nothing about, watch a movie in a different language, or read a book from a genre you've never explored. When you expose yourself to new experiences, your brain makes new connections. These connections can lead to fresh ideas.

2. Embrace Mistakes

Creativity isn't about getting everything right on the first try. In fact, it's the opposite. Mistakes are where creativity thrives. Some of the best ideas come from experiments that didn't go as planned. Think about it—Velcro was invented because a guy noticed burrs sticking to his dog's fur. Penicillin was also discovered because a scientist left a petri dish out overnight.

3. Brainstorm with Others

Creativity doesn't always happen in isolation. In fact, bouncing ideas off other people can make your ideas even better. The next time you're stuck on something, talk it out with a friend. They might suggest something you hadn't thought of, or their idea could spark a new direction for you.

4. Get Bored!

When you're not constantly busy or distracted, your mind has a chance to wander, which is when the best ideas can pop up. Boredom gives your brain some breathing room to think deeply and come up with new, exciting ideas. It's in those quiet moments that you can daydream, imagine different possibilities, and connect ideas in ways you wouldn't normally. So next time you're bored, don't rush to fill the time—let your mind roam, and you might come up with something awesome! Don't do it all day, though, mate - you have work to do!

Creativity in History: From the Wheel to the Web

The Invention of the Wheel

One of the earliest and most impactful inventions in human history is the wheel. Its invention revolutionized transportation and machinery. While the exact origin of the wheel is unknown, it is believed to have been invented around 3500 B.C. in Mesopotamia. The idea to use circular objects to facilitate movement required creative thinking and problem-solving, leading to advancements that shaped civilization.

The Printing Press by Johannes Gutenberg

Before the printing press, books were copied by hand, a painstaking and time-consuming process. In the mid-15th century, Johannes Gutenberg's invention of the printing press transformed the dissemination of information. This breakthrough made books more accessible, fueling the spread of knowledge and ideas during the Renaissance.

The Theory of Relativity by Albert Einstein

Albert Einstein's theory of relativity changed our understanding of space, time, and gravity. His creative thought experiments, like imagining riding alongside a beam of light, led him to insights that revolutionized physics. Einstein's ability to think beyond

conventional wisdom exemplifies how creativity can lead to profound scientific discoveries.

The Creation of the Internet

The internet as we know it today is the result of numerous creative minds building on each other's ideas. From the initial concept of a global network to the development of protocols like TCP/IP, the internet is a testament to collaborative creativity. Tim Berners-Lee's invention of the World Wide Web in 1989 transformed the internet into a user-friendly platform, enabling the digital age we live in today.

The Human Genome Project

Mapping the entire human genome was a colossal creative and scientific endeavor. Initiated in 1990 and completed in 2003, the Human Genome Project aimed to identify all the genes in human DNA. This project required innovative techniques and international collaboration, leading to breakthroughs in medicine, genetics, and our understanding of human biology.

African Storytelling Traditions: Creativity in Words

One of the most fascinating aspects of African storytelling is that much of it exists in the form of oral tradition. Unlike in many parts of the world where stories were written down on paper or carved into stone, African stories were primarily told aloud. These tales weren't recorded in books or tablets but carried in the minds and hearts of people. They were passed down from elders to children, from one generation to the next, like precious heirlooms.

Takeaway Challenges for you ▢

1. Try a new hobby this week, something you've never done before.

2. Spend 15 minutes each day letting your mind wander and write down any random thoughts.

3. Solve a real-world problem using a creative approach, like redesigning your study space.

4. Partner with a friend on a creative project, like making a short film or starting a blog.

5. Read about a topic you know nothing about and see what ideas it sparks.

Creativity is not just for the select few; it's for everyone. It's about exploring the world with a curious mind, taking risks, and allowing yourself the freedom to think differently. The human brain has about 86 billion neurons, creating countless connections and possibilities. Now, go out there and unleash your inner artist!

4. Confidence: Cultivating Self-Belief

Confidence isn't magic. You don't wake up one day and have it. It's not some exclusive membership you're born into. Real confidence is a skill, and, like all skills, you can build it over time.

First off, confidence isn't about always feeling like you're right or thinking you're better than everyone else. That's arrogance. Confidence is more like trusting yourself—believing that you can handle whatever life throws at you, even if you don't have all the answers right away. It's the voice in your head that says, "Okay, I may not know how to do this yet, but I can

134

figure it out."

Picture this: You're on a hike, standing at the bottom of a huge mountain. Some people might look up and think, "No way. I can't do this." That's a lack of confidence. But someone else who's equally unsure might say, "I have no idea how I'm going to reach the top, but I'll take one step at a time." That's confidence. It's not about knowing you'll succeed but about trusting you'll be okay if you try.

The Science of Confidence

Your brain is constantly taking in information from the world around you, scanning for threats and rewards. The more successful experiences you have, the more your brain builds a "confidence circuit," making it easier to believe in yourself the next time you face a challenge. But here's the catch: You won't always succeed right away, and that's okay. The key is to try, fail, learn, and try again. The brain actually grows when you make mistakes and learn from them. It's like a muscle getting stronger with each repetition at the gym. The more you challenge yourself, the more your brain adapts.

Building Your Confidence Toolbox

So, how can you build your confidence, brick by brick? Here are a few tools:

1. **Face Your Fears, Little by Little**

   You don't have to dive headfirst into your biggest fears. Start small. If you're scared of public speaking, maybe start by talking in front of one or two friends. Then, work your way up to a small group and, eventually, a larger crowd. Each time you push your comfort zone, it grows a little bigger.

2. **Set Small, Achievable Goals**

   Confidence comes from success, but you don't need to land on the moon to feel successful. Break big goals into smaller steps. Each time you complete one, you'll feel a little boost in confidence, which motivates you to keep going.

3. **Positive Self-Talk (But Keep It Real)**

   You've probably heard about affirmations, where people say things like, "I am amazing. I am unstoppable." Instead of going overboard with positive self-talk, try something realistic: "This is tough, but I've done hard things before, and I can figure it out." Your brain will believe that way more than "I'm the best," and it'll give you the boost you need. Although some studies tell that you can fool your brain as well as it can not always differentiate between the Real and Fake - interesting, isn't it? Try it.

4. **Embrace Failure**

This one's hard, but it's crucial. The more comfortable you get with failure, the more confident you become. Every time you fail and get back up, you're telling yourself, "I can handle this." It's not about never failing; it's about how quickly you recover and learn.

Why Confidence Matters

Let's zoom out for a second. Why should you care about confidence in the first place? Because confidence affects every part of your life. It influences how you approach challenges, how you interact with people, and even how you see yourself. Confident people are more likely to take risks, which leads to more opportunities. They're also more resilient when things go wrong, bouncing back faster than those who are paralyzed by self-doubt.

Confidence in Action

Michael Jordan, one of the greatest basketball players of all time, didn't make his high school varsity team at first. Instead of giving up, he used this setback as motivation to work harder. His confidence grew with every practice session, turning him into a legend.

Or consider Malala Yousafzai, who, despite being attacked for advocating for girls' education, continues to speak out with unwavering confidence. Her belief in her cause has inspired millions worldwide. Where did her confidence come from? It wasn't that she never felt fear. **A brave person is not someone who does not have fear or gets scared. A brave person is someone who does the right thing despite being scared.** Going against your fear is what takes courage and bravery. Malala has said many times that she was scared. But she believed in her cause, and that belief gave her the strength to keep going. Her confidence wasn't about being fearless; it was about being determined.

Power Posing!

Did you ever notice how your body kind of takes over when you're nervous? Your shoulders hunch, your arms cross, and suddenly, you're making yourself as small as possible. That's body language working against you. But here's the cool part: you can flip that script. The way you hold yourself doesn't just reflect how you feel— it actually changes how you feel. Think of it like a loop. **Your brain and body are always in conversation, sending signals back and forth.** When you slouch or cross your arms, your brain thinks, "Okay, we're in a defensive, nervous state." But when you stand tall, you tell your brain, "I've got this."

This brings us to the idea of *power posing*, which social psychologist Amy Cuddy popularized. She discovered something mind-blowing: by adopting "high-power" poses, you can trick your brain into thinking you're more confident than you actually feel. It sounds almost too simple to be true but studies back this up. Your body can literally *hack* your brain.

Power poses are big, open, expansive postures. Think about the way a superhero stands—legs wide apart, hands on hips, chin slightly raised, owning the space around them. They don't shrink. They don't slouch. They take up space unapologetically. These poses signal dominance, control, and—most importantly—confidence.

Here's what Amy Cuddy found: When you adopt a power pose for just two minutes, your body chemistry starts to change. Specifically, levels of cortisol (the stress hormone) decrease, and testosterone (the hormone linked to dominance and confidence) increases. You're not just *pretending* to be confident—you're actually altering the hormone levels in your body, shifting yourself into a more confident state.

Reflection Time: Boosting Your Confidence

Think of confidence as your cheerleader, always encouraging you to go for it, no matter what! Now, take a moment to think about your confidence levels.

1. What's one thing you're really good at? How did you get so good?

2. What's one area of your life where you don't feel confident? Why?

3. When was the last time you took a risk? How did it feel afterward?

4. Think of a time you failed at something. What did you learn from that experience?

5. What's one small step you can take today to build confidence in a new area?

5. Critical Thinking: Analyzing and Evaluating

You're scrolling through social media, and you see a post that says, "Cows produce more milk when they listen to classical music." Huh. Sounds weird, right? You could just shrug, believe it is true, like the post, and move on. Or you could ask yourself: "Wait, is that even true? And what could be the reason behind it?"

That's where critical thinking comes in. It's the ability to question what you're being told, dig deeper, and find the truth. We tend to believe what we see, especially if it's on the internet or if our friends say it.

But the world is full of half-truths, illusions, and outright lies. And if you don't question things, you'll be lost in the noise, like trying to find a needle in a haystack... with a blindfold on.

Imagine you're sitting at lunch with your friends, and one of them says, "Did you know the Great Wall of China is the only man-made object visible from space?" Now, this might sound legit. You've probably heard it before, maybe in school, maybe from a documentary. But ask yourself: "How do they know?"

This question — "How do you know?" — is the ultimate weapon for critical thinkers. It cuts through opinions, guesses, and misinformation like a lightsaber through butter. It forces people to back up their claims with evidence. And, more importantly, it makes YOU think. Where did that fact come from? Is it based on real science? Did someone actually test it?

In fact, astronauts have repeatedly said that the Great Wall is NOT visible from space with the naked eye. Myth busted! By the way, did you know that the International Space Station is actually visible from the Great Wall or from anywhere with the naked eye due to those giant solar panels?

Why Your Brain Loves Shortcuts

Now, why don't we question things more often? Why do we believe stuff so easily? Well, the human brain is lazy! Our brains love shortcuts. They look for the quickest path to the easiest answer. It's called **cognitive bias**, and we all have it.

Take the **confirmation bias** — it's like that friend who only listens to what they want to hear. If you believe something is true, you'll look for evidence

that supports it and ignore anything that doesn't. It's why conspiracy theories spread like wildfire. People find one piece of shaky evidence, and they cling to it like a life raft in a storm.

Thousands of people across the world still believe that the Earth is flat. I asked one of them, and they said, "Scientists just don't want us to know the truth." At first, I laughed it off. But then I asked, "How do you know?"

He pulled up a YouTube video with grainy footage and dramatic music and someone speaking confidently and passionately, with no solid evidence or science.

This skepticism mirrors a concept called **Cartesian doubt**, which comes from philosopher René Descartes. He proposed that we should doubt everything we can't be certain of, stripping away all assumptions until we reach an undeniable truth. While Descartes used this method to establish a foundation for scientific knowledge, Flat Earth believers take a more selective approach, doubting specific scientific claims while accepting others without the same level of scrutiny.

The Milk and the Music

Remember the cow thing? Turns out, there's a grain of truth in it. In a study published by the University of Leicester, researchers found that cows exposed to slow, calming music produced more milk than cows listening to fast-paced tunes. Classical music, in particular, seemed to work best.

The Paradox of Experts

Now, here's something tricky about critical thinking: sometimes, even experts get it wrong. It doesn't mean you shouldn't listen to them — experts are experts for a reason. But it's important to remember that they're human too. They can make mistakes, they can be biased, and sometimes, they can be just plain wrong.

Take the story of **Dr. Ignaz Semmelweis**. He was a doctor in the 1800s who discovered that washing hands dramatically reduced the spread of infection in hospitals. It seems obvious now, right? But at the time, most doctors ignored him. Some even mocked him. They didn't believe him because they thought they already knew everything. Sadly, it took decades for the medical community to catch up. Meanwhile, people died because they didn't question the experts.

So, here's the takeaway: even when you're dealing with experts, don't just take their word for it. Ask, "How do you know?" and check the evidence for yourself.

What's the Harm of Being Gullible?

And it's not just about trivia or internet rumors. Critical thinking impacts your whole life. Take your future career, for example. If you don't learn how to  think critically, you could end up in a job that promises the world but delivers nothing. Or you might fall for a get-rich-quick scheme, investing your savings into something that turns out to be a scam. Or, even more seriously, you could vote for policies or leaders that sound great on the surface but are actually based on lies and misinformation. In a world where everyone is trying to convince you of something — advertisers, politicians, influencers — critical thinking is the only thing that can protect you.

Building Critical Thinking Skills: A Step-by-Step Guide

1. Ask Questions

Start by asking questions about everything. Why did this happen? What is the evidence? Who is providing this information? Asking questions helps to uncover deeper understanding and exposes assumptions that might not hold up to scrutiny.

Example:

Imagine you read a news article claiming that a certain diet leads to significant weight loss in a short time. Instead of accepting the claim at face value, you start asking questions: What kind of diet is it? How was the study conducted? Who funded the research? Is there a peer-reviewed study backing these claims? By asking these questions, you might discover that the study was funded by a company that sells diet supplements, which could introduce bias into the results.

2. Gather Information

Collect data and information from multiple sources before forming an opinion. Look for reputable sources and check the credibility of the information. Gathering diverse perspectives can provide a more rounded view of the topic.

Example:

If you're researching climate change, don't rely solely on a single website or a couple of articles. Look for information from scientific journals, government publications, and international organizations like the Intergovernmental Panel on Climate Change (IPCC). Check the authors' credentials and the publication dates to ensure the information is current and credible. This comprehensive approach helps you build a well-informed understanding of the topic.

3. Evaluate the Evidence

Examine the evidence critically. Is it strong or weak? Is it based on facts or opinions? Look for logical consistency and be aware of any biases that might affect the interpretation of the evidence.

Example:

Suppose you're evaluating the effectiveness of a new drug. Look at the clinical trial data: How many participants were involved? Was there a control group? What were the measured outcomes, and how significant were they? Distinguish between anecdotal evidence (e.g., testimonials) and scientifically rigorous data (e.g., randomized controlled trials). A critical evaluation might reveal that while some testimonials are positive, the scientific data shows minimal improvement over a placebo.

4. Consider Different Viewpoints

Think about alternative perspectives and consider how they might impact your understanding of the issue. Being open to different viewpoints can help prevent tunnel vision and lead to more balanced conclusions.

Example:

When discussing economic policies, consider viewpoints from different schools of thought, such as Keynesian economics, classical economics, and modern monetary theory. Each perspective provides unique insights and solutions. By considering these different viewpoints, you can better understand the potential impacts of a policy on various aspects of the economy, such as inflation, unemployment, and income distribution.

5. Reflect on Your Thinking

Take time to reflect on your thought processes. Are you being objective? Are there any biases affecting your judgment? Reflecting on your thinking can help you improve and refine your critical thinking skills over time.

Example:

After a heated debate on social media, take a step back and reflect on your arguments. Were your points based on solid evidence, or were they influenced by emotional responses or preconceived notions? Did you dismiss opposing viewpoints too quickly? Reflecting on these aspects can help you recognize areas where your critical thinking could be improved and guide you toward more reasoned and balanced discussions in the future.

6. **Give your brain some breathing space.**

Thank God we didn't have phones back then, and some great minds were at work - thinking deeply! Imagine Isaac Newton sitting under that famous apple tree, but instead of a ripe apple falling on his head, he's scrolling through his phone. He's deep into a feed filled with random memes, conspiracy theories, and hot takes on gravity. Would Newton have discovered the laws of motion if he were busy liking cat videos?

Well, maybe. Newton had a razor-sharp mind, but the key to his genius was his curiosity and his ability to question everything. If he'd been glued to his phone, he might have missed the apple falling, but his critical thinking skills would kick in. He'd pause mid-scroll and ask, "Wait a second...

why do things fall at all?" Instead of believing whatever he saw on social media, Newton would probably have started researching, cross-checking sources, and doing experiments (maybe even using his phone to Google the math).

The Role of Cognitive Bias

Cognitive biases are mental shortcuts our brains use to process information quickly. While they can be helpful, they often lead to errors in thinking. Understanding common biases can help us recognize and mitigate their effects. Here are some common categories and examples of thinking biases:

1. Heuristics

- **Availability Heuristic**: This is when you think something is more likely to happen just because you can remember examples of it easily.
  - ○ **Example**: If you hear a lot about shark attacks on the news, you might think they're really common, even though they're super rare.

- **Representativeness Heuristic**: This is when you judge something based on how much it resembles your idea of a typical example.
  - ○ **Example**: If you meet someone who loves computers and is a bit quiet, you might automatically think they're a nerd, even though they could be into all sorts of things.

2. Social Biases

- **Ingroup Bias**: This is when you prefer people who are part of your group over those who aren't.
  - ○ **Example**: If you're on a sports team, you might think your team members are cooler and nicer than people from other teams just because they're "your" people.

- **Halo Effect**: This is when you let one good quality about someone affect your whole opinion of them.

- o **Example**: If someone is really good-looking, you might also think they're smart and funny, even if you don't know much else about them.

3. Memory Biases

- **Hindsight Bias**: This is when you think you knew something was going to happen all along after it already happened.
  - o **Example**: After your favorite team wins a game, you might say, "I knew they were going to win!" even if you weren't sure before.
- **Self-Serving Bias**: This is when you take credit for good things but blame outside factors for bad things.
  - o **Example**: If you get a good grade, you might think it's because you're smart, but if you get a bad grade, you might blame the teacher for not explaining things well.

4. Decision-Making Biases

- **Confirmation Bias**: This is when you look for information that supports what you already believe and ignore info that doesn't.
  - o **Example**: If you believe a certain celebrity is awesome, you'll focus on good news about them and ignore any bad press.
- **Anchoring Bias**: This is when the first piece of information you get influences your decisions too much.
  - o **Example**: If a store says a jacket was originally $200, but now it's $100, you might think $100 is a great deal, even if the jacket's not worth that much.

5. Belief Biases

- **Belief Bias**: This is when you judge an argument based on how believable you think the conclusion is rather than the actual evidence.
  - o **Example**: If someone says eating chocolate makes you smarter and you love chocolate, you might believe them without

checking the facts.

- **Attentional Bias**: This is when you focus more on certain things and ignore others, affecting your decisions.

    o **Example**: If you're really focused on your new crush, you might not notice how your best friend is feeling left out.

Critical thinking is like a mental workout that keeps your brain in top shape. By honing your ability to analyze and evaluate information, you'll be better equipped to navigate the complexities of life with confidence and clarity. So, gear up and start thinking critically!

To warm you up, here is a riddle: You find yourself in a room with four colored boxes: red, blue, green, and yellow. Inside one of these boxes is a treasure. Each box has a label, but only one label is true. The labels read:

- **Red box:** The treasure is not in the blue box.
- **Blue box:** The treasure is in the red box.
- **Green box:** The treasure is not in this box.
- **Yellow box:** The treasure is in this box.

Which box contains the treasure, and how do you determine it?

No, I won't tell you how to solve it, but let me give you a hint about which color box it is. That color is the one that Night Vision Goggles use!

6. Continuous Learning: Lifelong Curiosity

Learning doesn't end when the school bell rings for the last time. In fact, that's when the real learning begins. Life is an endless classroom, and the only way to survive, let alone thrive, is to keep asking questions, stay curious, and embrace the fact that continuous learning is not just a choice — it's a

necessity. Some of the most brilliant minds in history never stopped learning. Take Leonardo da Vinci, for example. The guy was an artist, sure, but he was also an inventor, scientist, engineer, and mathematician. He never settled for what he knew. He constantly experimented and studied new things, from the human body to how birds fly. Why? Because he was endlessly curious, and he knew that the more he learned, the more connections he could make between seemingly unrelated topics.

Albert Einstein was the same. After developing the theory of relativity, he didn't just sit back and call it a day. He kept working, trying to understand the universe at deeper levels, asking new questions, and challenging even his ideas. And you know what he said? "The more I learn, the more I realize how much I don't know." That's the mindset of a continuous learner: They're never satisfied, and they never think they've learned it all.

The Curiosity of a Five-Year-Old: Why It Matters More Than You Think

You've probably heard the phrase "curiosity killed the cat," implying that curiosity can lead to trouble. But in the context of continuous learning, curiosity is less of a danger and more of a superpower. Instead of killing the cat, curiosity actually drives growth. Without curiosity, we'd never ask the questions that spark innovation or pursue knowledge that

expands our horizons.

In fact, it's often the most curious individuals — those who challenge the status quo and ask "why" — who come up with breakthroughs in science, technology, and even in everyday life.

Think back to when you were five years old. Everything was a question. Why is the sky blue? Why does the moon follow me? Why can't I eat cookies for breakfast? Five-year-olds are relentless question-asking machines. They are mini-philosophers, constantly trying to make sense of the world around them. And guess what? That's the kind of mindset you need to keep if you want to become a lifelong learner.

Now, adults don't ask questions because they think they should already know the answers. If you're afraid to ask, you stop learning.

The World is Changing Faster Than You Think

In today's world, staying in one place intellectually is like standing on a conveyor belt that's moving backward. If you're not constantly learning, you're falling behind. That's why continuous learning is more important now

than ever before. The skills that are in demand today might be obsolete in a decade, and new technologies will require people to be adaptable.

Here's a real-world example: Kodak, the company that practically invented the camera, failed to embrace digital photography when it first emerged. They stuck to what they knew — film. Now, when was the last time you saw someone use a

Kodak film camera? Right. Because Kodak didn't keep learning and adapting, they fell behind, while companies that embraced new tech, like Canon and Nikon, moved ahead.

On the flip side, companies like Amazon and Netflix thrived because they didn't stop evolving. Netflix started by mailing DVDs to people's homes, and now they're one of the biggest streaming services in the world because they kept learning, adjusting, and anticipating what their customers wanted next.

Note these are not black-and-white examples, and there is so much that goes into making a company successful or bankrupt, including the timing and luck to some extent. Who knows, Kodak will be successful again, and the new age companies fall behind if they don't catch up with the AI revolution! What I intend to convey here is that both companies and individuals need to learn and adapt all the time.

Real Learning Means Getting Uncomfortable

Marie Curie, the famous scientist, was one of the first women to win a Nobel Prize. She didn't have a lot of formal education growing up. Still, she was so eager to learn that she moved to Paris and enrolled at the Sorbonne University, where she had to study physics and chemistry in French — a language she didn't fully understand. That's a whole new level of discomfort! Yet, her drive to learn ultimately led her to discover radioactivity, changing science forever.

The Learning is in the Doing

One of the best ways to keep learning is by doing. You can read all the books and watch all the TED Talks in the world, but if you don't apply what you've learned, it's just knowledge without experience. It's like learning how to ride a bike by reading the instruction manual — you'll never know if you can actually balance until you get on the thing and start pedaling.

Platforms for Learning

There are countless platforms out there to help you keep learning. Here are some examples; I'm pretty sure you would already know some, as these are very common. I hope you find at least one of these interesting and it becomes your go-to destination for whatever you want to learn. Remember, sometimes, the first baby step to open a website is enough to get you started. I have given QR codes for quick access to their websites so that you don't have an excuse to do this 'later' ⏾.

1. Coursera

Coursera offers online courses from top universities and companies worldwide. You can learn about anything from data science to personal development. Coursera partners with universities like Stanford and Yale, allowing you to take courses from these prestigious institutions without leaving your home.

2. Khan Academy

Khan Academy is a free educational platform offering courses primarily in math and science but also in humanities, economics, and more. Khan Academy started when Salman Khan began tutoring his cousin online. His videos were so helpful that he decided to make them public. Today, millions use Khan Academy to learn.

3. LinkedIn Learning

LinkedIn Learning offers video courses taught by industry experts in software, creative, and business skills. Many professionals use LinkedIn Learning to stay updated with the latest skills required in their fields, from programming languages to management techniques.

4. edX

Like Coursera, edX offers courses from top universities and institutions. You can learn subjects ranging from computer science to languages.edX was founded by Harvard and MIT in 2012. It's a nonprofit platform with a mission to increase global access to high-quality education.

5. Skillshare

Skillshare is an online learning community with thousands of classes in design, business, tech, and more. It's great for creatives looking to improve their skills. Skillshare classes are project-based, so you'll be doing hands-on work rather than just watching videos.

6. Udacity

Udacity offers courses with a focus on tech, like programming, data science, and artificial intelligence. Many companies recognize Udacity's "Nanodegree" programs, making them valuable for career advancement.

7. Duolingo

Duolingo is a language-learning platform that turns learning a new language into a game. Studies have shown that using Duolingo is as effective as a university semester of language education.

8. YouTube

YouTube isn't just for cat videos. It's a treasure trove of educational content. You can find tutorials on just about anything. Channels like TED-Ed and CrashCourse offer high-quality educational videos that make learning fun and accessible.

9. TED Talks

TED Talks are short, powerful talks (18 minutes or less) from experts on various subjects.TED stands for Technology, Entertainment, and Design. Talks cover everything from science to business to global issues.

10. MasterClass

MasterClass offers online classes taught by famous experts. Want to learn filmmaking from Martin Scorsese or cooking from Gordon Ramsay? MasterClass brings you lessons from the world's best, allowing you to learn from people who have truly mastered their crafts.

Learning is a lifelong journey.

The only way to thrive in this fast-changing world is to commit to lifelong learning. It's the only option that keeps you adaptable and open to new possibilities, ensuring that you stay relevant no matter how the world changes. If you think you've learned enough, the world will quickly prove you wrong.

7. Time Management: Mastering the Clock

Imagine you've got 24 hours to finish a school project, clean your room, hang out with friends, scroll through TikTok, and maybe—just maybe—sleep. You tell yourself, "I'll start in an hour." But guess what? An hour turns into two, then five, and suddenly it's 11 PM, and you're wondering where your day went. It didn't go anywhere; you just didn't manage it.

Everyone has the same 24 hours a day. Elon Musk or Beyoncé? Same 24 hours. The kid next door who somehow finishes all their homework and has a social life? Same 24 hours. You? The trick isn't to have more time but to use it smarter. And yes, I know, this sounds like one of those cheesy motivational posters, but hang with me here.

Why Your Brain is Terrible at Time

Let's start with the hard truth: Your brain is a liar. I'm not kidding. It **underestimates** how long things take and **overestimates** how much free time you have. You start playing a video game thinking, "I'll play for 30 minutes"? Then, three hours later, you're still there, wondering why you're hungry and can't feel your legs. That's called **time distortion**, and it's your brain's way of convincing you that "just one more round" is a reasonable life choice.

Scientists say our brains aren't great at time management because they evolved to deal with more immediate concerns. Back when humans were hunting mammoths (or trying not to get eaten by one), you didn't need to plan your week or think about deadlines. You just had to make sure you didn't become lunch. Fast forward a few thousand years—now, instead of outrunning wild animals, you've got to outrun homework assignments, exams, and maybe even a part-time job.

The Pizza Analogy: Slicing Up Your Day

Think of your day like a pizza. You get 24 slices (hours), and every slice goes somewhere—sleep, school, social media, whatever. You can't add extra slices (sorry, no bonus hours). The problem is most people aren't great at deciding what toppings (tasks) should go on their pizza.

Ever heard of Parkinson's Law? It says that "work expands to fill the time available for its completion." So, if you give yourself three days to finish a project, guess what? You'll probably take all three days, even if you could've knocked it out in five hours.

Time Vampires: What's Sucking Your Hours Away?

Now, let's talk about time vampires—those sneaky little things that suck up your hours without you noticing. You know the culprits: scrolling through Instagram, binge-watching shows, and "just checking" your messages for the 100th time. It's like your time disappears into some black hole. Here's a wild stat: The average person spends 2.5 hours a day on social media. That's like spending over 37 full days a year just scrolling. Imagine what you could do with an extra month!

Battle Plan: The Three Golden Rules of Time Management

So, how do you fight back and reclaim your time? Here are **three golden rules**:

1. **Set Priorities**: Not all tasks are created equal. Some things are "must-do" (like finishing that essay), and others are "nice-to-do" (like organizing your sock drawer). Focus on the big stuff first, or you'll end up wasting time on small things and then panic about the important ones later.

2. **The Pomodoro Technique**: This is a simple method where you work for **25 minutes**, take a 5-minute break, and repeat. It helps you focus by breaking the day into manageable chunks so you're not overwhelmed by a mountain of tasks.

3. **Time Blocking**: Plan your day by blocking out chunks of time for different tasks. It's like setting a meeting with yourself. And let's be honest—you're more likely to follow through if it's scheduled. You can even block time for doing nothing. Yes, "relax" can be a task too!

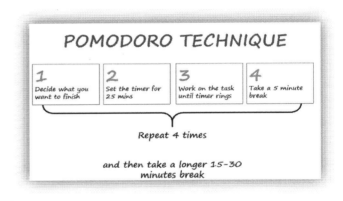

The Myth of Multitasking

Studies show that multitasking doesn't actually save time; it makes you less efficient. Your brain isn't wired to juggle multiple tasks at once, so trying to do five things at the same time just means you're doing five things badly. Think of it like trying to ride a unicycle while juggling flaming swords. Sure, you can try, but it's going to end in disaster.

Are you 'PRO' in Procrastination?

Here's a weird fact: You procrastinate because your brain wants to **avoid pain**. And no, I'm not talking about physical pain. The pain, in this case, is the discomfort of doing something boring, hard, or stressful. So, your brain goes, "Hey, let's just watch funny videos for a bit and deal with this later." The problem is that "later" comes, and now you've got a mountain of work and zero motivation.

There's even a name for this cycle: the **Procrastination Doom Loop**. You procrastinate, feel guilty about it, and then procrastinate more to avoid the guilt. The good news? You can break the loop by tackling tasks in small, bite-sized pieces. Start with just 5 minutes, and once you get rolling, it won't feel so bad.

The Eisenhower Matrix

Meet Dwight D. Eisenhower, a former U.S. President and a genius at time management. He created a simple tool called the Eisenhower Matrix. It helps you decide what to do now, what to schedule for later, what to delegate, and what to drop. Here's how it works:

1. **Urgent and Important**: Do it now! (e.g., studying for tomorrow's test)

2. **Important but Not Urgent**: Schedule it. (e.g., working on a long-term project)

3. **Urgent but Not Important**: Delegate it. (e.g., replying to a non-critical text)

4. **Not Urgent and Not Important**: Drop it. (e.g., mindlessly scrolling through social media)

The Power of a To-Do List

You might think to-do lists are for forgetful people. But here's the thing: they're for anyone who wants to get stuff done. Write down everything you need to do and check off tasks as you complete them. It's satisfying and keeps you on track.

1. **Be Specific**: Instead of writing "study," write "study biology chapter 4."

2. **Break It Down**: Big tasks can be overwhelming. Break them into smaller, manageable steps.

3. **Set Deadlines**: Give yourself a time frame for each task. It adds a sense of urgency.

4. **Prioritize**: Use the Eisenhower Matrix to decide what comes first.

5. **Schedule your Fun:** You won't feel guilty if that's part of your planned day.

See a comparison table below on 2 choices we all can make, either by doing hundreds of small irrelevant things, constantly switching from one to another, OR focusing on a few important goals of our lives. I know this table will sound too preachy and idealistic, but I am sure you will get the message. **There is always a sweet spot between being a slave of the clock or a slave of temptations/distractions**. Find yours!

7:00 AM – Snoozes the alarm multiple times, finally gets up at 7:30.	7:00 AM – Gets up on time, stretches, and drinks water to wake up fully.
8:00 AM – Scrolls through social media, mindlessly watching TikToks and YouTube shorts for an hour.	8:00 AM – Reviews tasks for the day, sets up a to-do list, and checks any homework deadlines.
9:00 AM – Eats a quick breakfast while texting friends about memes and the latest trends.	9:00 AM – Has breakfast, reads a chapter of a book for school, or works on a personal project.
10:00 AM – Starts a homework assignment, but gets distracted by phone notifications and starts chatting on Snapchat.	10:00 AM – Starts homework or school project and puts the phone in "Do Not Disturb" mode. Works uninterrupted for 45 minutes.
11:00 AM – Plays video games or browses Reddit, thinking "I'll get to my homework later."	11:00 AM – Takes a 15-minute break, stretches, and checks messages before getting back to work.
12:00 PM – Eats lunch while binge-watching a Netflix show, loses track of time, and watches "just one more episode."	12:00 PM – Eats lunch while listening to a podcast or watching an educational YouTube video related to an interest or hobby.
1:00 PM – Feels unmotivated, spends another hour on Instagram or Snapchat, checking notifications.	1:00 PM – Gets back to homework or practice for a hobby (like coding, music, or art).
2:00 PM – Plans to start homework but watches more TikToks or gets lost in a gaming livestream on Twitch.	2:00 PM – Finishes homework or tasks, then spends some time learning something new (like coding, learning an instrument, or working on a side project).
3:00 PM – Joins a friend group call but doesn't do anything productive, just gossiping or talking about random stuff.	3:00 PM – Takes a break with friends but keeps it short, maybe catching up on fun stuff or relaxing with a hobby.
4:00 PM – Decides to go to the gym or exercise but gets distracted by Netflix again. Workout plan forgotten.	4:00 PM – Goes for a workout, run, or skateboarding session, staying active and clear-headed.
5:00 PM – Realizes a homework deadline is coming up, panics, and tries to cram last minute.	5:00 PM – Finishes up any last tasks, revisits goals for the day, and checks if there's anything left to do.
6:00 PM – Half-heartedly attempts some homework, but motivation is gone. Browses Reddit and Discord instead.	6:00 PM – Takes some chill time, guilt-free, playing a video game or hanging out with friends.
7:00 PM – Eats dinner while watching YouTube or binging shows. Homework still incomplete.	7:00 PM – Eats dinner while talking with family or doing something fun like watching a good movie or playing a game.
8:00 PM – Decides to start homework, but distracted again by social media, more Netflix, or chatting with friends.	8:00 PM – Finishes off remaining tasks or uses this time for personal growth (like a hobby or reading).
9:00 PM – Procrastinates more, feeling guilty but keeps wasting time on random distractions.	9:00 PM – Winds down with a book or a creative activity, reflecting on the day, preparing for the next.
10:00 PM – Regrets wasting the day, stresses about homework, stays up late doing half-finished work.	10:00 PM – Gets ready for bed on time, feeling satisfied with the progress made throughout the day.
11:00 PM – Finally tries to sleep but is on the phone until midnight, feeling restless and overwhelmed.	11:00 PM – Falls asleep peacefully, feeling accomplished and ready for the next day.

Mind-boggling Scientific Fact - Time is Relative!

Do you know time moves slower on the 1st floor of a building than on the 8th floor? This is because gravity slows down time, so the closer you are to the center of the earth, the slower time gets. Of course, there is a very small difference, but it can be very significant if you are near a black hole! According to Einstein's theory of relativity, time is relative and can vary depending on speed and gravity—astronauts on the International Space Station age slightly slower than people on Earth.

If you watched the **Interstellar movie,** there was a scene when 3 crew members left behind 1 of the crew on the mother spaceship and traveled to a Black Hole called 'Gargantua'. Because of the effect of the immense gravity of the black hole, just a few hours near the black hole were equivalent to a few years for the person who did not travel. So when the crew came back in a few hours, several years had passed for the person who was waiting for them on the mother spaceship. Unimaginable but true and scientifically proven!

Time is the one thing we can never get back. But with the right strategies, you can make every second count. Now, go out there and conquer your day!

8. Leadership: Everyone Can Be a Leader

When you think of a leader, you might picture someone giving orders, making big decisions, or standing in front of a crowd. But here's the truth: being a leader isn't about bossing people around or having all the answers. In fact, the best leaders don't focus on being in charge. They focus on bringing the best out of others.

Imagine this: You're on a team project at school. Everyone's arguing, the project is falling apart, and deadlines are looming. But instead of panicking, you take a deep breath, step in, and calmly help everyone figure out what needs to get done. You're not bossy; you're solution-focused. That's what a real leader does—helps the team move forward.

Leadership Isn't Just for Presidents and CEOs

You don't have to be the class president, team captain, or CEO to be a leader. You can show leadership in the smallest ways every day. Maybe you're the person who encourages others when they're down or the one who listens when no one else does. Or maybe you're just the kid who quietly gets things done without making a big fuss about it. That's leadership, too. It's not about the title—it's about your actions.

Leaders Listen More Than They Speak

Most people think leaders need to be the loudest voice in the room. But here's the twist: great leaders listen more than they talk. They don't interrupt others or hog the spotlight. Instead, they pay attention to what people are saying, especially when those people feel unheard.

Leaders Take Responsibility—Even When Things Go Wrong

Everyone loves being the leader when things are going smoothly. But what about when things go wrong? That's when true leadership kicks in. Great leaders don't point fingers or make excuses when the going gets tough. Instead, they step up and take responsibility, even when it's not their fault.

Think of Captain Sully, the pilot who safely landed a plane on the Hudson River. When his plane had an engine failure after takeoff, he didn't panic or blame the situation. He took control, assessed the risks, and made a quick decision that saved everyone's lives. He didn't sit around waiting for someone else to fix the problem. That's leadership in action— staying calm, taking charge, and owning the situation, no matter how tough it is.

Leaders have high EQ

EQ means understanding not only your feelings but also the feelings of others. And trust me; people would rather follow someone who gets them emotionally than someone who's just smart but disconnected. Leaders with high EQ know how to read the room. They can tell when someone's struggling, when morale is low, or when someone needs a boost of confidence. Imagine you're on a soccer team, and one of your teammates has been missing shots all game. Instead of criticizing them, a good leader might offer encouragement: "Hey, you've got this. Let's get the next one." That small boost can change everything.

The Myth of the "Born Leader"

A lot of people think you're either born a leader, or you're not. That's a myth. Leadership is a skill, not a personality trait. Sure, some people might be more outgoing or naturally confident, but real leadership is something anyone can learn and develop. It's about growth, not genetics.

Take Mahatma Gandhi, for example. He wasn't born into a position of power, nor was he some towering figure with a commanding presence. In fact, he was quiet and reserved. But through his actions—like leading peaceful protests and advocating for nonviolence—he inspired millions to follow him. Leadership is about your impact, not your natural personality.

Why Leading by Example is a Game-Changer

If you want to lead, you've got to lead by example. Want your friends to stay focused on a project? You better be the first one working hard. Do you want people to treat each other with respect? You better show kindness and respect in everything you do.

A leader doesn't say, "Go do this," and sits back. A leader says, "Let's do this," and gets involved.

The Power of Positivity

You don't have to be a cheerleader, but having a positive attitude can make all the difference as a leader. When things go wrong—and they will, because life is messy—people look to the leader for how to react. If you panic, get negative, or start blaming people, the whole team will fall apart. But if you stay positive, keep things in perspective, and encourage others, you can help turn a bad situation around.

Leadership Is About Growth—Yours and Others

The best leaders don't just focus on winning or being the best. They focus on growing—both themselves and their team. Leaders are always learning, always listening, and always improving. If you're not open to feedback or afraid to fail, you're not leading; you're just

managing.

Types of Leadership

Leadership has roots in our evolutionary history. Early humans survived because they had leaders who could navigate dangers, find food, and resolve conflicts. These leaders weren't always the strongest but often the smartest and most resourceful. Let's look at some types of leadership:

1. Autocratic Leadership: Iron Fist

Autocratic leaders make decisions without consulting others. Think of a drill sergeant or a strict boss. They expect obedience and rely on control. This style can be effective in situations where quick decisions are needed or where the leader has the most knowledge.

During World War II, Winston Churchill's autocratic leadership style was crucial in making swift, decisive actions to counter the Nazi threat.

2. Democratic Leadership: Power to the People

Democratic leaders value input from their team. They encourage discussion and consider everyone's opinion before making decisions. This style fosters collaboration and creativity.

Nelson Mandela used democratic leadership to dismantle apartheid in South Africa. He listened to various viewpoints and built a consensus.

3. Transformational Leadership: Inspiring Change

Transformational leaders inspire and motivate their teams to exceed their limits. They focus on the big picture and encourage personal growth and innovation.

4. Transactional Leadership: The Reward System

Transactional leaders focus on structure, rules, and rewards. They set clear goals and provide rewards for achieving them. This style is effective in organizations where performance is closely monitored and rewarded. Typical corporate leadership could be termed transactional leadership.

5. Servant Leadership: Leading by Serving

Servant leaders prioritize the needs of their team. They lead by example and focus on the well-being and development of their followers. This style builds strong, loyal teams. Mahatma Gandhi exemplified servant leadership by leading India's non-violent independence movement and putting the needs of his people first.

6. Laissez-Faire Leadership: Hands-Off Approach

Laissez-faire leaders take a hands-off approach, giving their team members the freedom to make decisions and solve problems on their own. This style can be effective with highly skilled and motivated teams. Warren Buffett is known for his laissez-faire leadership style. He trusts his managers to run the companies he invests in without much interference.

Leadership isn't a far-off dream or a trait reserved for a chosen few. It's something everyone can develop and practice in their daily lives. Whether you're leading a group project at school, standing up for a friend, or starting a new initiative, you have the potential to be a leader. So step up, speak out, and lead the way.

Selling Skills - It's Not About Being Pushy, It's about Being Persuasive

Selling skills are needed everywhere, and it's not just about money. When you hear the word "sales," you might picture a sleazy car dealer trying to convince you to buy something you don't need. But selling is a life skill, and you're doing it all the time—even if you don't realize it. Every time you convince your friends to watch a movie, persuade your parents to extend your curfew, or even try to get someone to like your idea in a group project, you're selling.

Selling skills are about getting people on board with your way of thinking. It's not about being pushy or manipulative. It's about **building relationships, understanding what people want**, and communicating in a way that makes them say, "Yes, I'm in!"

The Key to Selling? Understanding People

Here's a little secret: **selling is mostly psychology**. It's about understanding how people think, what motivates them, and how to tap into those feelings. You can't sell effectively if you don't understand what the other person wants or needs. Imagine trying to sell ice cream to someone who's lactose intolerant—it's not going to work because you didn't take the time to understand their needs.

The most successful salespeople aren't the ones who talk the most; they're the ones who listen the best. They pay attention to what the other person is really saying, ask smart questions, and figure out how to meet their needs. It's kind of like being a detective, but instead of solving crimes, you're solving people's problems.

People Buy With Emotions, Not Logic

People don't buy things because of logic—they buy because of emotions. Sure, you might think you're making a logical choice when buying something, but most of the time, it's how you feel that drives the decision. Think about the last time you bought something you didn't really need. Was it because you weighed all the logical pros and cons, or was it because it made you feel good?

In selling, it's the same way. If you're trying to sell an idea, a product, or even yourself, you have to **connect emotionally**. People want to feel understood, appreciated, and valued. If you can make them feel like what you're offering solves their problem or makes their life better, they'll be more likely to say yes.

The Power of Storytelling

One of the best ways to sell anything is through storytelling. Why? Because **stories create emotional connections**. People are more likely to remember a story than a list of facts. Think about the commercials that stick in your head. They're usually the ones that tell a story— maybe it's about a family coming together at the dinner table or a hero overcoming obstacles to achieve their dreams. Those stories don't just inform; they move you.

The Art of Asking Questions

Want to know one of the best-selling techniques? It's simple: **ask good questions.** Not just any questions—questions that get the other person talking about themselves, their needs, and their problems. When you ask the right questions, you're not only showing that you care about what they think, but you're also gathering valuable information that can help you figure out how to offer a solution.

Handle Rejection Gracefully

Rejection is a part of life, and it's definitely a part of selling. But here's the trick: **don't take it personally**. Rejection doesn't mean you're a bad salesperson or that your idea is terrible. It just means that person wasn't ready, or maybe it wasn't the right fit for them.

The best salespeople see rejection as an opportunity to learn. Every "no" brings you closer to a "yes" because you're learning what works and what doesn't. It's all about resilience—the ability to bounce back, try again, and improve each time.

The "Win-Win" Mindset

In sales, you don't want to "win" at someone else's expense. You want to create a **win-win situation**. That means both sides walk away feeling like they got something valuable. If you push someone into agreeing with you or buying something they don't need, they'll feel like they lost—and that's not good for a long-term relationship.

Think of selling like planting seeds. You're not just trying to score a quick win. You're building relationships and trust that will grow over time. When you focus on creating value for the other person, you build loyalty and long-term success.

The Value of Authenticity

The best salespeople are the ones who are authentic—they genuinely believe in what they're selling, and they care about the people they're selling to. Being authentic means being yourself, not some smooth-talking robot trying to close a deal.

When you're real with people, they're more likely to trust you. And trust is the foundation of any successful relationship, whether it's in sales or life.

The Elevator Pitch: Selling in 60 Seconds

Sometimes, you only have a short window to get your point across. That's where the **elevator pitch** comes in. An elevator pitch is a **quick, persuasive summary** of what you're selling—whether it's an idea, a product, or even yourself. The goal is to hook the other person's attention in 30 to 60 seconds, just like if you were riding an elevator together.

Here's a quick formula: Start with a problem or need, then offer your solution, and end with why it's valuable. For example, if you're pitching an idea for a school fundraiser, your elevator pitch might sound like: "Our school needs new sports equipment, but we don't have the funds. I've come up with a fun run that will raise money while getting the whole community involved. It's a win-win for everyone!"

In the end, selling is more about relationships than it is about transactions. When you focus on understanding people, listening to their needs, and being authentic, you're not just selling—you're building trust, creating value, and helping others. And that's a skill that will take you far in life!

So, where will you apply some sales techniques in your life going forward?

10. Public Speaking - OMG

You're sweating, your voice cracks and your brain is screaming, "Abort mission!" But here's the thing: everyone feels this way at some point. Even the best speakers in the world—yes, even those TED Talk pros—started out nervous, fumbling through words and wondering why they ever agreed to speak in public.

Public speaking is often cited as one of the most common and intense fears. Surveys and studies frequently rank it above other fears, including heights, spiders, and even death. The fear of public speaking, also known as

glossophobia, affects many people due to the potential for social judgment, embarrassment, or making mistakes in front of others. The intensity of this fear can be attributed to the social anxiety it provokes.

Humans have evolved to be social beings, and being judged or rejected by a group can trigger a fight-or-flight response. In ancient times, standing out or being singled out could mean danger or exclusion from the group, which could be life-threatening. Although those stakes no longer apply, the brain can still react to public speaking as if it's a high-risk situation.

The good news is that public speaking is a skill you can learn. It's not something you're born with. It's not magic, and it doesn't require you to have some mythical level of confidence. It's just like learning to ride a bike. At first, you'll wobble, maybe even fall. But once you get the hang of it, you'll cruise.

In fact, science shows that most people in the audience are rooting for you, not sharpening their pitchforks. **Your brain is just overreacting** because it hasn't caught up with the fact that messing up a speech doesn't equal social death anymore. So, next time you feel stage fright kicking in, just remind yourself: there's no tiger, and even if you flop, you'll still have lunch friends!

Demosthenes: From a Stuttering Orphan to Ancient Greece's Greatest Orator

Demosthenes was born in ancient Athens, and if you had met him as a young man, you'd probably never have guessed he would one day become Greece's most powerful public speaker. He was an orphan, physically frail, and had a terrible stutter. In a culture that valued eloquence and oratory, Demosthenes was far from being a natural talent. When he first tried speaking in public, he was mocked and humiliated for his weak voice, awkward pauses, and speech impediment.

Demosthenes wasn't born with the confidence or skills to speak publicly, but he refused to let his failures define him. Instead of giving up, he **developed a strict training regimen** to overcome his weaknesses. He practiced speaking with pebbles in his mouth to strengthen his voice and improve clarity. He trained his lungs by delivering speeches while running uphill or shouting over the ocean waves to build stamina and projection. He even practiced in front of a mirror to correct his awkward gestures and body language.

His methodical approach to improving his voice, gestures, and delivery style made him stronger with every practice. Eventually, he became Athens' most respected orator, delivering speeches that moved people to action and cemented his legacy as one of history's greatest speakers.

Speaking Is More Than Talking: It's Connecting

Here's a secret: **Public speaking isn't really about speaking**. It's about connecting. Think of it like this: When you talk to your friends, you're not just throwing words at them. You're sharing ideas, making them laugh, maybe telling a story they'll remember. That's what great public speaking is—it's not just about dumping information on people; it's about creating a connection with them.

So, when you're speaking to an audience, whether it's 5 people or 500, focus on **making them feel something**. It could be excitement, inspiration, curiosity, or even laughter. If you make your audience feel something, they'll listen—and more importantly, they'll remember what you said.

Fear Is Normal: You're Not Alone

That feeling of your stomach flipping, palms sweating, and heart racing? It's totally normal. In fact, some of the best public speakers in the world still feel nervous before stepping onto the stage. The trick isn't to eliminate fear—it's to **use it**. Your body is giving you energy when you're nervous. It's preparing you for action. So instead of thinking, "I'm scared, this is going to go horribly," try flipping the narrative to: "I'm excited. I've got this!" Nervousness and excitement feel almost identical to your body; it's your brain that decides which one to focus on.

Preparation Is Your Best Friend

Imagine trying to bake a cake without reading the recipe or measuring the ingredients. That's what it's like to give a speech without preparing. You might pull it off, but it's probably going to be messy, chaotic, and undercooked. Preparation is the key to public speaking.

Start by understanding your topic inside and out. Know what you want to say, but don't just memorize every word. Instead, focus on the key points you want to make. Write down your main ideas on index cards or create a simple outline. This will help you stay on track without sounding like a robot.

Next, **practice, practice, practice**. Practice in front of a mirror, practice in front of your dog, practice in front of your little brother (who will probably laugh at you, but hey, at least you're getting feedback). The more you practice, the more comfortable you'll feel with your material.

Your Audience Wants You to Succeed

Here's a myth that people often believe: *The audience is judging you*. In reality, most people in the audience want you to succeed. No one is sitting there hoping you'll mess up. If you stumble over a word or forget a point, they're not going to boo you offstage. They're just glad they're not the ones speaking!

In fact, if you show that you're human—by smiling, laughing at yourself, or even pausing to collect your thoughts—it makes you more relatable. The audience will root for you even more.

The Power of a Story

People love stories. It's how we've passed down information since humans were sitting around campfires. When you include a story in your speech, you **draw your audience in**. A good story can make your point stick in people's minds long after you've finished speaking.

Let's say you're giving a speech about climate change. You could throw out a bunch of statistics (which people will probably forget), or you could tell a story about how people of a town were affected by a flood. A personal, relatable story will have far more impact than cold, hard facts. **Stories create emotional connections**, and that's what makes them powerful.

And remember: smile! A smile can instantly make you more approachable and help break the ice with your audience.

The Art of Pausing

Most people think public speaking is about filling every second with words. But here's the truth: **Silence can be powerful**. When you pause, it gives your audience time to absorb what you just said. It also gives you a moment to collect your thoughts and breathe.

Pausing also makes you sound more confident. Instead of rushing through your words, a well-timed pause shows that you're in control. So, don't be afraid of silence. Use it to your advantage.

Handling Mistakes Like a Human

Here's the thing: No one expects you to be perfect. If you mess up, stumble over a word, or forget what you are going to say, it's not the end of the world. **Everyone makes mistakes**. The key is how you handle them.

If you forget your next point, take a breath, smile, and glance at your notes. If you stumble over a word, laugh it off and keep going. The audience will forget about the mistake as long as you move on confidently. It's only awkward if you make it awkward!

The Power of the Voice

Your voice is your most powerful tool when it comes to public speaking. But it's not just about what you say—it's about **how** you say it. Vary your tone, volume, and pace to keep your audience engaged. No one wants to listen to a speaker who drones on in a monotone voice.

Use your voice to create emphasis. For example, if you're delivering an important point, slow down and lower your voice. If you're telling an exciting part of your story, speed up slightly and raise your voice to match the energy.

Reflection Time: Journal Prompts

- What's your biggest fear about public speaking, and how can you start to overcome it?
- What's the best speech or presentation you've ever seen, and what made it so memorable?

11. Failures - How to Fall Flat, Get Up, and Keep Going

Let's be honest—failing sucks. Whether it's flunking a test, losing a game, or messing up in front of a crowd, failure can feel like someone hit the "Game Over" button on your life. But here's the twist: **it's not the end**. In fact, failure is more like hitting the reset button. It's a chance to restart, learn, and come back stronger.

Think about it. **Every successful person has failed**—probably more than you know. Michael Jordan was cut from his high school basketball team. Twelve publishers rejected J.K. Rowling before someone took a chance on *Harry Potter*. And Albert Einstein? He couldn't speak fluently until he was nine years old. They didn't stop at failure. They kept going, learned from their mistakes, and used their setbacks as fuel to succeed.

Failure Is Feedback in Disguise

Here's the deal: **failure is feedback**. It's the universe's way of saying, "Hey, that didn't work. Let's try something different." Instead of seeing failure as a giant stop sign, think of it as a detour—an opportunity to figure out what went wrong and how to fix it.

Picture this: You're baking a cake, and it comes out flat as a pancake. It's tempting to toss the whole thing in the trash and never bake again. But what if you tweak the recipe and try again? Maybe next time, you can add more baking powder or mix the batter longer. The point is **each failure teaches**

you something new. It's like having a cheat code for the next round.

"Failure is a bruise, not a tattoo." — *Jon Sinclair*

"Success is not final, failure is not fatal: it is the courage to continue that counts." — *Winston Churchill*

"The only real mistake is the one from which we learn nothing." — *Henry Ford*

"Our greatest glory is not in never failing, but in rising every time we fail." — *Confucius*

"Failure is success in progress." — *Albert Einstein*

Why Failing Is Actually Good for Your Brain

Believe it or not, **science is on your side** when it comes to failure. Studies show that when you fail and then try again, your brain literally rewires itself to learn from the mistake. It's called neuroplasticity, and it's your brain's way of getting smarter through trial and error. Every time you stumble and get back up, your brain gets stronger, more resilient, and more capable of tackling the next challenge.

Think of it like leveling up in a video game. Each failure gives you **experience points** that make you better equipped for the next round. So, while failure may sting at the moment, it's actually helping your brain get tougher for the long haul.

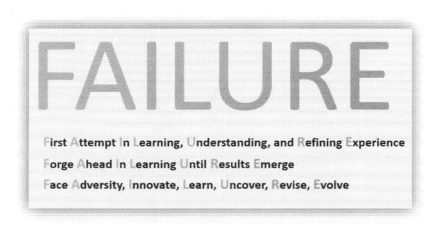

Embrace the Mess: Perfection Is Overrated

You know what's overrated and actually doesn't even exist? Perfection. When you're constantly chasing perfection, you're setting yourself up for disappointment. Nobody's perfect, and trying to be is like trying to catch smoke with your bare hands.

Instead of aiming for perfection, aim for progress. Progress means you're moving forward, learning, and improving. It means you're okay with the messiness of life and the fact that sometimes you'll trip along the way. Think of failure as a necessary pit stop on the road to success. It's not a dead end; it's part of the journey.

The Art of Failing Gracefully

Let's get one thing straight: **failing doesn't mean you're a failure**. There's a big difference between failing at something and labeling yourself as a failure. When you fail, it's just one moment, one experience—not your entire identity. So, how do you handle failure like a pro?

1. **Own it**: First, accept that it happened. Pretending you didn't fail doesn't help anyone. In fact, ignoring failure only makes it worse. Own up to it, and be honest with yourself.

2. **Laugh at it**: Failure is a lot less scary when you can laugh at it—messed up in front of the whole class? Laugh it off. Sent an embarrassing text to the wrong person? Shake it off. When you don't take yourself too seriously, failure loses its power.

3. **Learn from it**: After you've owned it and laughed at it, dig into it. What can you learn from this failure? What went wrong, and how can you fix it next time? Reflect on the experience, take notes, and use it as a stepping stone.

Failure Builds Resilience

Resilience isn't something you're born with. It's something you build over time by **facing challenges head-on**. The more you push through tough situations, the stronger your resilience muscle gets.

Artist Sylvia Duckworth created the iceberg illusion theory of success to illustrate the amount of work that goes into something great, particularly writing. The iceberg illusion is a visual representation of the stages of learning that someone with a growth mindset goes through to be successful. The iceberg illusion theory of success shows that people only see the tip of the iceberg or the success, but not the stages of mistakes, failures, and persistence that led to that success

The Marshmallow Challenge

The Marshmallow Challenge is a popular team-building exercise where participants have to build the tallest structure possible using spaghetti, tape, string, and a marshmallow. Studies show that kindergartners often outperform business school graduates in this challenge. Why? Because kids are not afraid to fail. They experiment, learn from their mistakes, and try again. This embodies experiential learning—testing, failing, reflecting, and improving.

Moving On: Don't Let Failure Define You

One of the hardest parts about failure is moving on. It's easy to get stuck in a loop of regret, replaying the failure over and over in your mind like a bad movie. But here's the truth: **you can't change the past**. You can only learn from it and keep moving forward.

Let's say you failed an exam. It's tempting to dwell on what went wrong and beat yourself up about it. But will that change the grade? Nope. Instead, focus on what you can do next. Can you study differently? Ask for help? Retake the test? **Keep your eyes forward**, not backward.

How to Fail Well

There's an art to failing well, and it goes like this:

1. **Accept it**: Failure is a normal part of life. The sooner you accept that the easier it becomes to deal with.

2. **Break it down**: Look at your failure in pieces. Was it a lack of preparation? A wrong approach? Break it down so you can figure out what to fix.

3. **Take action**: Don't let failure paralyze you. Use it as motivation to take action. Try again with a new strategy, or tackle a different challenge with the lessons you've learned.

4. **Move on**: Don't let failure stick to you like gum on your shoe. Once you've learned from it, **let it go** and move on. There's more ahead of you than behind you.

Failure Is Just One Chapter in Your Story

Remember, **failure isn't your whole story**—it's just one chapter. And every good story has a few plot twists, right? The key is to keep writing, to keep going, and to understand that failure is just part of the adventure.

It's like falling off a bike. The more you fall, the better you get at balancing, and pretty soon, you're riding smoothly. Life works the same way. The more you fail, the better you get at navigating challenges, and pretty soon, you're handling things like a pro.

Failure isn't something to fear. It's something to embrace, learn from, and use as fuel to keep going. So, the next time you fall flat, remember: **it's not the end—it's just the beginning of your comeback story**.

CHAPTER 4

Understanding Money and Finance

Imagine you're on a ship sailing through uncharted waters. Without a map or a compass, you'd be lost at sea, drifting aimlessly. The world of money and finance is much like that vast ocean, and understanding how it works is like having that all-important map and compass. If you don't manage your money, your money will manage you. It dictates your lifestyle, future aspirations, and even your sense of security.

We live in an era where financial literacy is more critical than ever. Technology, globalization, and the ever-evolving economic landscape mean that understanding money isn't just for adults; it's a crucial life skill for everyone. Think of money as the blood that keeps the world's economy alive. Without it, nothing functions properly. But don't worry, you won't need a PhD in economics to get a handle on your finances. Just a bit of knowledge and some smart habits can set you on the right path.

In this chapter, we'll dive deep into the world of finance. We'll explore the basics of banking, the variety of financial products available, the importance of credit scores, and the power of saving and investing. We'll also look at the exciting (and sometimes wild) world of cryptocurrency, learn how to protect ourselves from fraud and scams, etc. Let's set sail on this financial journey!

1. Banks - The Vaults That Keep the World Running

Why do people trust their hard-earned money to some institution instead of keeping it hidden under their mattress? Or why do your parents go to a bank to get money instead of printing it themselves? Welcome to the fascinating world of banks, a place where money takes on a life of its own. Let's dive in and uncover the mystery behind banks, their roles, and why they are crucial in our lives.

Banks are like the engine behind the scenes that keeps everything moving. When you think of banks, you might just picture a place to stash your cash, but they're much more than that. They are the **heart of the global economy**. Imagine a world where everyone hides their money under their mattress. That would mean no loans, no businesses expanding, no one buying houses, and no one going to college on a student loan. Basically, nothing would grow. Banks help **circulate money**, allowing it to flow where it's needed most and helping people achieve their goals.

A Place for Money to Hang Out

Imagine a bank as a giant piggy bank but much more sophisticated. It's a place where people store their money safely. However, unlike your piggy bank at home, which just holds your coins and notes, a bank uses your money to make even more money. Sounds a bit magical, right? In medieval times, money changers or lenders conducted their business on benches or counters in marketplaces. The bench or table on which they worked was referred to as a "banca," and that's where the word Bank comes from.

The Basics: Deposits and Withdrawals

At its core, a bank is a place where you can deposit (put in) and withdraw (take out) money. When you deposit money, the bank keeps it safe and gives you a record of how much you have. This record is known as a bank statement. When you need money, you can go to the bank, use an ATM, or go online to withdraw it. It's like having a secure vault, but with easy access whenever you need cash.

How Do Banks Make Money?

You might wonder, how do banks stay in business when they're paying you interest on your savings? Banks make money mainly by **charging interest on loans**. When someone takes out a loan to buy a house, start a business, or pay for college, they have to pay that money back—with interest. The interest is a percentage of the loan that serves as the bank's profit.

Banks also make money through **fees**—for example, they charge you for withdrawing money from a different bank's ATM, for not maintaining a minimum balance, or for overdrafting your account. These little fees add up to a significant income source for banks.

Why You Should Care About Interest Rates

Interest rates are a major factor when dealing with banks. Whether you're saving money or borrowing it, interest rates determine how much you'll earn or owe.

- **For savings**: The higher the interest rate, the more money you'll make on your savings. But these rates are often very low, so don't expect to get rich just from saving money in the bank.

- **For loans**: The lower the interest rate, the better. This means you'll pay less over time for big purchases like a home or a car.

Central banks (like the Federal Reserve in the U.S. or the European Central Bank in Europe) set a **base interest rate**, which influences how much banks charge for loans or offer for savings. These rates fluctuate based on the health of the economy—when times are tough, rates tend to drop to encourage borrowing and spending; when the economy is doing well, rates rise to avoid inflation.

How Do Loans Work?

When you take out a loan, you're borrowing money from the bank, but it's not free. You have to **pay it back with interest**, which is essentially a fee for borrowing.

- **Personal Loans**: These are usually taken out for things like medical expenses, weddings, or emergencies. The loan is paid back over a fixed period with regular installments.

- **Home Loans (Mortgages)**: One of the biggest loans you can take out. A mortgage is a loan to buy a house. You borrow a large sum and pay it back over many years—usually 15 to 30.

- **Student Loans**: Many students around the world rely on loans to pay for their education. Like other loans, you have to pay them back, but they often come with lower interest rates and a longer repayment period.

Getting a loan requires a credit check to see if you're trustworthy with borrowed money. This is where your credit score becomes really important.

Digital Banking – The New Normal

Gone are the days when you had to visit a bank branch for everything. Now, with digital banking, you can manage almost everything from your phone or computer. Whether it's transferring money, paying bills, or depositing checks, you can do it all through an app.

Many banks today also offer **online-only accounts** with better features or perks because they don't have the overhead costs of maintaining physical branches. Some examples of online-only banks are **N26** (Europe), **Monzo** (UK), and **Chime** (US).

The convenience of digital banking means you can manage your money anytime, anywhere. But it's also important to be aware of **online security risks** like fraud or phishing. Always be cautious and make sure your bank uses secure encryption for transactions.

What About Investments?

Banks aren't just for holding and lending money—they also help you grow it through **investment products**. Some common investment tools banks offer are:

- **Mutual Funds**: Pools of money from various investors used to buy stocks, bonds, and other securities.

- **Fixed Deposits**: As mentioned earlier, these offer higher returns than regular savings accounts but require you to lock your money in for a set period.

- **Retirement Accounts**: Many banks offer **retirement savings plans** (like a 401(k) in the U.S.) where you can invest your money for the long term.

The Different Types of Banks

Commercial Banks

These are the banks you see on every street corner. They handle day-to-day banking needs like deposits, withdrawals, and loans. Examples include Chase, Bank of America, and Wells Fargo.

Investment Banks

These banks deal with big businesses and investments. They help companies go public, merge with other companies, or buy large assets. Goldman Sachs and Morgan Stanley are examples of investment banks.

Central Banks

Every country has a central bank that manages monetary policy, controls the money supply, and oversees the banking system. In the United States, it's the Federal Reserve. The European Central Bank (ECB) manages monetary policy for the Eurozone. The Bank of England serves as the central bank for the United Kingdom. In Japan, the Bank of Japan oversees financial stability, while the People's Bank of China does the same in China. These central banks are crucial for maintaining economic stability and regulating the financial sector.

15 Fascinating Facts About Banks

1. The First Bank

The first modern bank, the Taula de la Ciutat, was established in 1401 in

Barcelona, Spain. It was created to manage and lend public funds, serving as a precursor to modern banking systems.

2. ATMs in the 1960s

ATMs revolutionized banking by providing 24/7 access to cash. The first ATM was installed by Barclays Bank in Enfield, London, in 1967. Invented by John Shepherd-Barron, this machine changed the way people accessed their money.

3. Swiss Banking Secrecy

Switzerland's banking system is renowned for its confidentiality. Swiss banks, governed by strict privacy laws established in 1934, have historically offered clients anonymity and protection from prying eyes, although recent international pressure has led to increased transparency.

4. Largest Bank by Assets

The Industrial and Commercial Bank of China (ICBC) is the largest bank in the world by assets, with over $4 trillion. It serves more than 400 million retail customers and has a significant global presence.

5. Robots and AI in Banking

Banks are increasingly utilizing robots and AI to enhance customer service and streamline operations. For example, HSBC uses Pepper, a humanoid robot, in some of its branches to assist customers and provide information.

6. Mobile Banking Pioneers

Kenya's Equity Bank is a pioneer in mobile banking, using the M-Pesa platform to provide financial services to millions of people who previously had no access to banking. This innovation has significantly boosted financial inclusion in Africa. People can now store and transfer money straight from their mobile phones, with no need for a bank. This simple idea revolutionized the way Kenyans handled money. In 2020, about 75% of adults in Kenya used M-Pesa regularly for payments, saving money, and borrowing. It shows how banking isn't just about fancy buildings or vaults—sometimes, all you need is a phone to be part of the financial system.

7. Banking Without a Bank

With the rise of neobanks, digital-only banks such as Chime, Monzo, and N26 offer banking services without any physical branches. These banks provide convenient mobile-first experiences and have gained popularity among younger, tech-savvy users.

8. Contactless Payment Explosion

The use of contactless payments has surged globally, accelerated by the COVID-19 pandemic. In countries like the UK, contactless payments now account for more than half of all in-person transactions, offering a quick and hygienic way to pay.

9. Banking Apps and Super Apps

In countries like China, super apps such as WeChat and Alipay integrate a multitude of services, including banking, into a single platform. These apps allow users to pay bills, transfer money, book tickets, and even invest, all within one app, making banking incredibly convenient.

These facts highlight the diverse and evolving nature of banks, showcasing how they adapt to technological advancements, regulatory changes, and shifting consumer needs.

Challenge - Open a Bank account if you don't have one!

Go and try opening a bank account. Find out what the minimum age is to open an account. If you are over that age, find out what documents are needed and what the process is. If you are eligible, open an account right away and learn hands-on! Here are typical steps to open an account:

Step 1: Research Local Bank Options for Teen Accounts

Start by exploring banks in your country that offer **teen or youth accounts**. These accounts are usually designed for minors and may require a **joint account** with a parent or guardian. Look for banks with:

- **Low or no fees**
- **No minimum balance**
- **Interest on savings**
- **Online or mobile banking** availability (if that's important to you)

Make sure to check local regulations, as some countries might require specific documentation or age limits.

Step 2: Gather Required Documents

Although the required documents might vary slightly from country to country, here's a general list of what you may need:

- **Identification**: A **passport**, **national ID card**, **student ID**, or **birth certificate** may be required depending on your location.

- **Tax Identification Number**: In some countries, like the U.S., you'll need a **Social Security Number**; in others, you'll need a **National Insurance Number** (UK) or **Tax File Number** (Australia).

- **Proof of Address**: You might need to provide a **utility bill**, **school letter**, or **residence certificate** that proves where you live.

- **Parent or Guardian's ID**: Your parent or guardian will also need to provide identification since this will likely be a joint account.

- **Parental Consent**: In some countries, a **written consent** from your parent or guardian is necessary.

Step 3: Decide on a Savings or Checking/Current Account

Choose whether you want:

- **Savings Account**: This is ideal for building savings and earning interest on deposits.

- **Current Account (Checking Account in some countries)**: Perfect for daily transactions, such as spending money or receiving allowances. Many banks offer **combo accounts** for teenagers, which allow you to hold both types of accounts under one plan.

Step 4: Visit the Bank With a Parent or Guardian

Depending on your country, some banks will require you to visit a physical branch with your parent or guardian to complete the application. However, some banks allow you to open an account online. Always check the **specific rules in your region**.

Step 5: Complete the Application

Whether you're applying in person or online, you'll need to fill out an application form. This will include:

- **Personal information** (name, date of birth, address)
- **Parent/guardian details**
- **Services** you want (debit card, online banking, etc.)

You may need to sign documents alongside your parent or guardian. In some countries, digital signatures may be accepted for online applications.

Step 6: Make the Initial Deposit

Most banks require a small initial deposit to open the account. This could vary:

- **No deposit** (some banks might not need an initial deposit, especially for youth accounts)
- A small deposit such as **$5, £10, €15, or equivalent** in your currency. You can deposit this money by bringing cash, transferring it from another account, or even using mobile money services if they are available in your country.

Step 7: Set Up Online and Mobile Banking

Access to **online banking** or a **mobile app** is crucial for teens today. Make sure to set this up to check balances, transfer money, and manage the account easily from your smartphone or computer. In some countries, mobile banking apps are the primary way to manage finances, so look for banks that offer good digital experiences.

Step 8: Understand the Fees and Rules

Fees and regulations vary by country. Ask about any fees, including:

- **ATM fees**: Some countries may have higher fees for using ATMs outside your bank's network.
- **Overdraft fees**: Learn if your account allows overdrafts and what the penalties might be.
- **Foreign transaction fees**: If you're using the account internationally, ask about any charges for currency conversion or using your card abroad.

Also, understand the **age rules**: many banks automatically transfer a teen account to a standard adult account when you turn 18 or 21.

Step 9: Obtain a Debit Card (Optional)

If your bank offers a **debit card** for teen accounts, they will issue it after your account is set up. In some regions, debit cards may be mailed to you, while in others, you may get them directly from the bank branch. You can use the debit card to:

- **Withdraw cash from ATMs**
- **Make purchases** at stores or online (depending on your country's regulations)

Step 10: Monitor and Manage Your Account

Now that your account is set up make sure to monitor your spending and saving habits. You can check your account balance regularly via:

- **Bank apps** or **online banking** platforms

- **Monthly statements** are sent by your bank (digitally or via mail). Be sure to keep an eye on any new fees or changes in terms as your account grows.

Banks might seem complicated, but they are crucial for the economy and our daily lives. Understanding how they work can help you manage your money better and appreciate the role they play in society. Banks don't just keep your money safe. They allow the economy to grow by lending money to people and businesses. Think of them as the **bridge between people who have extra money and people who need it.** Without banks, it would be hard for anyone to buy a house, start a business, or even go to school.

2. Financial Products: Exploring the Options

Imagine walking into a financial marketplace that's as diverse as the world itself. You've got people buying, selling, and investing in all sorts of things. Some are saving for the future, others are building businesses, and a few are hedging against risks. The key to navigating this complex system is understanding the many financial products available. Think of these products like the tools you'd find in a toolbox — each designed for a specific purpose. Let's dive into this toolbox and explore what's inside.

Savings Accounts – The Global Piggy Bank

A savings account is the simplest financial product. It's like a piggy bank but safer and with a little bit of interest. Whether you're in Canada or Kenya, banks offer these accounts so you can stash your money securely and earn a small return.

Examples:

- **Ally Bank (USA)** offers high-interest online savings accounts.

- **National Australia Bank (Australia)** has simple savings accounts that reward consistent savers.

- **Barclays (UK)** has an instant access savings account for flexibility.

Fun Fact: In Japan, people often open savings accounts not just to save but also to manage their payments since they deal with fewer credit cards compared to countries like the U.S.

Checking Accounts – Daily Financial Fuel

Checking accounts (or current accounts outside the U.S.) are your financial fuel for daily spending. You deposit money, write checks, and make payments. It's like the kitchen of your financial house, where things are always moving.

Examples:

- **DBS Bank (Singapore)** offers multi-currency checking accounts, which are perfect for business people working internationally.
- **ICICI Bank (India)** provides zero-balance accounts for those who need flexibility in maintaining minimum funds.

Certificates of Deposit (CDs) – Lock and Earn

Think of a **Certificate of Deposit (CD)** as a financial locker. You place your money inside for a fixed time, and in exchange, the bank gives you higher interest than a regular savings account. But there's a catch—you can't touch the money for that period. This is ideal for people who want a secure, no-risk way of earning better interest.

Examples:

- **Santander Bank (Spain)** offers CDs with terms ranging from a few months to several years.
- **HSBC (Hong Kong)** provides fixed deposits in multiple currencies, catering to global savers.

Real World Insight: In Argentina, where inflation is sky-high, people often use CDs to avoid the devaluation of their currency, locking in a safe return while waiting for the economy to stabilize.

Bonds – The Government's IOU

A **bond** is essentially a loan that you give to a government or company. They promise to pay you back with interest. It's like lending money to a friend who promises to return it after a few years, with extra cash as a thank you.

Examples:

- **U.S. Treasury Bonds** are a low-risk investment backed by the U.S. government.
- **Indian Government Bonds** are often used by local investors looking for stability.
- **Euro Bonds** allow investors to buy debt from European countries, even if they live outside Europe.

Fun Fact: Some countries like Greece and Italy have had to issue bonds with very high interest rates during financial crises to attract investors willing to take on the risk of lending to their governments.

Stocks – A Slice of Ownership

When you buy **stocks** (or shares), you're buying a tiny piece of a company. If the company does well, you benefit from their success. But if the company flops, you share in the losses. Stocks are one of the most popular financial products for building wealth.

Examples:

- **Apple (USA)** is one of the world's most valuable companies, and its stock has made many investors rich.
- **Tencent (China)** is a tech giant, and owning shares gives you a piece of the booming tech industry in Asia.
- **Nestlé (Switzerland)** offers stable returns, given its global footprint in food and beverages.

Interesting Tidbit: In Nigeria, retail investors are growing rapidly thanks to online platforms that allow everyday people to trade stocks on their smartphones.

Mutual Funds – Group Investment Power

A **mutual fund** is a pool of money from many investors. It's like going to a buffet — everyone chips in to get more options, and a fund manager decides how to invest it. Mutual funds are great for people who want diversification but don't have the time or expertise to pick individual stocks.

Examples:

- **Vanguard Total World Stock Index Fund** (USA) gives exposure to the global stock market.

- **UTI Equity Fund (India)** is popular among retail investors for its steady long-term performance.

- **Schroders Global Cities Real Estate Fund (UK)** invests in property markets around the world.

Exchange-Traded Funds (ETFs) – Stocks on Autopilot

An **ETF** works like a mutual fund, but it's traded on stock exchanges just like regular stocks. ETFs let you invest in a collection of assets—whether it's stocks, bonds, or commodities—with a single purchase.

Examples:

- **iShares MSCI Emerging Markets ETF (USA)** allows you to invest in growing markets like Brazil, China, and South Africa.

- **Lyxor ETF (France)** tracks the top companies in the European market.

- **Nikko AM Singapore STI ETF** invests in Singapore's largest companies.

Global Note: ETFs are growing fast in countries like Japan and Germany, where investors seek diversified exposure without needing to manage individual stocks.

Credit Cards – Spend Now, Pay Later

A **credit card** allows you to borrow money for purchases, which you can pay off at the end of the month. But if you don't, you'll pay interest, which can stack up fast. Credit cards are convenient but can lead to debt if not used wisely.

Examples:

- **American Express (USA)** is known for premium travel rewards and customer service.
- **SBI Credit Card (India)** offers cash-back on fuel and online purchases, which are perfect for everyday spending.
- **Discover (USA)** is widely accepted in North America, offering good cash-back deals.

Fun Fact: In Scandinavian countries like Sweden, credit cards aren't as popular as in the U.S. Many people prefer using debit cards or mobile payments through apps like Swish.

Mortgages – The Big Loan for Your Home

A **mortgage** is a loan you take out to buy property. You pay back the loan over many years, plus interest. Mortgages make homeownership possible for millions of people around the world.

Examples:

- **Wells Fargo (USA)** is a major provider of home loans.
- **Standard Bank (South Africa)** helps locals buy homes in emerging markets.
- **Bank of Ireland** offers mortgages with fixed or variable interest rates.

Real-Life Situation: In Singapore, the government provides subsidized housing loans for first-time homebuyers, making it easier to own property in one of the world's most expensive cities.

Insurance – Protection from the Unknown

Insurance is a financial product that protects you against risk. Whether it's health, life, car, or home insurance, you pay a small fee (premium) to get financial protection when bad things happen.

Examples:

- **Allianz (Germany)** provides global health insurance policies.

- **AIA (Asia)** offers life insurance and savings plans across Southeast Asia.

- **AXA (France)** is a major player in property and casualty insurance worldwide.

Fun Fact: In some countries like the U.K., you're required by law to have car insurance, while in the U.S., health insurance is a hot political issue.

Cryptocurrencies – The Digital Revolution

Cryptocurrencies are digital or virtual currencies that use cryptography for security. Unlike traditional currencies issued by governments, cryptocurrencies operate on decentralized networks, often powered by **blockchain technology**. This makes them resistant to fraud and central control.

Bitcoin (BTC) was the first cryptocurrency, created in 2009 by an anonymous person (or group) known as **Satoshi Nakamoto**. It's often referred to as "digital gold" because it's limited in supply (only 21 million Bitcoins will ever be mined) and is seen as a store of value. However, its price can be highly volatile.

Examples:

- **Bitcoin (BTC)** is widely regarded as a store of value and the most famous cryptocurrency.

- **Ethereum (ETH)** allows for "smart contracts" and decentralized apps, going beyond simple currency use.

- **Ripple (XRP)** focuses on enabling fast, low-cost international money transfers.

- **Tether (USDT)** is a **stablecoin**, meaning it's pegged to traditional currencies like the U.S. dollar to avoid volatility.

Real-World Usage: In countries with unstable currencies, like Venezuela and Argentina, people use Bitcoin as a hedge against inflation, preserving their savings in a currency that doesn't rapidly lose value.

How Cryptocurrencies Work

Cryptocurrencies function on a decentralized network of computers called nodes. Network participants verify transactions through cryptography, and these transactions are recorded in a public ledger known as the blockchain. It's this decentralization that makes cryptocurrencies so appealing — no central authority, like a bank, controls them.

Why Use Cryptocurrencies?

1. **Decentralization**: No single government or entity controls cryptocurrencies, making them borderless and resistant to censorship.

2. **Low Transaction Costs**: Cryptos like Ripple can process international payments faster and at a fraction of the cost of traditional banks.

3. **Anonymity**: Cryptos offer a level of privacy that traditional banking does not.

Fun Fact: In El Salvador, Bitcoin is now legal tender. This means that businesses must accept Bitcoin for transactions, just like the U.S. dollar.

Risks of Cryptocurrencies

While cryptos offer exciting possibilities, they also come with significant risks:

1. **Volatility**: The value of cryptocurrencies can swing wildly, as seen with Bitcoin's history of sharp rises and drops in price.

2. **Regulatory Uncertainty**: Governments are still figuring out how to regulate cryptos. In countries like China, cryptocurrency transactions are restricted, while in others, like the U.S., they are closely monitored for compliance with financial laws.

3. **Security Risks**: Cryptocurrency exchanges have been targets of hacks.

For example, in 2014, **Mt. Gox**, a major Bitcoin exchange, collapsed after being hacked, leading to the loss of millions of dollars worth of Bitcoin.

We've explored a vast range of financial products, each one serving a unique purpose in our global financial ecosystem. Whether it's the simplicity of a savings account, the ownership potential in stocks, or the cutting-edge innovation of cryptocurrencies, each product offers opportunities and risks. Understanding these products is like mastering tools in a toolbox—you use the right one at the right time, depending on your financial goals.

So, which product did you find most interesting and why?

3. Taxes - The Invisible Shadow in Your Life

Let's talk about something that touches every part of your life, whether you realize it or not: **taxes**. Yep, taxes. It sounds boring at first, right? But taxes are sneaky. You pay them almost every day, and you don't even notice. It's like that one friend who eats your fries all the time without buying their own.

You might think, "But I'm not working. I don't get a paycheck, so no taxes for me!"
Hate to break it to you, but taxes are *everywhere*. Every time you buy something, eat out or even download an app, you might be paying taxes without realizing it. Let's dive into the invisible taxes in your everyday life.

1. Sales Tax: The Sneaky Friend

You buy a soda, a pair of shoes, or a video game. Let's say it costs $10. But when you get to the checkout, suddenly it's $10.60. What happened? You just got hit with **sales tax**. That's the extra charge governments add to almost everything you buy. It's their way of saying, "Hey, thanks for contributing to the roads, schools, and stuff!"

In the U.S., sales tax changes depending on the state. In Oregon, there's no sales tax. But in California, you'll pay around 7.25% extra on most things. Meanwhile, in Europe, most countries have a **value-added tax (VAT)**, which is like sales tax but often even higher—sometimes over 20%!

2. Gasoline Tax: The Hidden Cost of Filling Up

Every time your parents fill up the car with gas, they're paying a tax—**fuel tax**. This tax helps fund road repairs and maintenance, which you appreciate when you're driving and not falling into potholes every five seconds. In the U.S., for every gallon of gas, about 18 cents goes to the federal government, and states add their tax on top. In Germany, taxes make up over half of the price of gas!

3. The "Fun" Tax on Movies, Concerts, and Sports

Love going to the movies? How about concerts or sporting events? Well, there's a tax for that, too, my friend. In many countries, there's an **entertainment tax** on tickets for concerts, movies, and sporting events. In India, there's an entertainment tax of around 28% on movie tickets. You thought you were just paying for popcorn and a seat to watch the latest superhero flick? Think again.

4. Digital Taxes: When Your Apps and Games Get a Cut

Have you ever bought an app a song on iTunes, or made an in-app purchase? There might be a tax attached to that, too. Many countries are now adding **digital taxes** on online purchases like apps, video streaming subscriptions, or video games. In the European Union, digital goods (like apps, e-books, or even an in-app sword for your character) are taxed with VAT, just like physical goods. So, that $5 app might actually cost you $6 after taxes.

5. Sugar Tax: Sweet but Costly

If you love soda or sugary snacks, some countries have something called a **sugar tax**. Governments started adding this tax to sugary drinks and foods to discourage people from eating too much sugar (and to help pay for healthcare costs linked to obesity). In the UK, there's a sugar tax on soft drinks. So, if your favorite soda has too much sugar, you're going to pay more for it.

6. Import Tax: When Your Online Order from Another Country Gets Expensive

Have you ever ordered something from another country and wondered why it costs way more by the time it arrives at your door? That's because of **import taxes**. When products come from other countries, governments charge a fee to let them into the country, and those fees get passed on to you. You order a cool new pair of sneakers from the U.S., but when it arrives in Canada, you have to pay a customs fee. Yep, that's an import tax at work!

7. Phone and Internet Tax: Surfing the Web with a Side of Fees

Even your phone and internet come with taxes. That monthly bill your parents pay? Buried in the fine print, you'll probably find a **telecom tax** that helps fund public services. It's like paying rent for living in the digital world. In the U.S., you might notice a "universal service charge" on your phone bill. This helps fund internet access for rural areas. Similar taxes exist globally to keep the digital world running.

8. Property Taxes: Your House Has a Price Tag Too

If you live in a house, your parents are paying **property taxes**. The government charges a tax based on the value of your home, and this money often funds local schools, parks, and libraries. Even if you're not paying it directly, you're benefiting from it every day. In countries like the UK or Australia, property tax is a key source of local government revenue, ensuring your neighborhood has paved roads, public services, and even streetlights.

9. Carbon Tax: Paying for Pollution

With climate change becoming a bigger issue, some governments have introduced a **carbon tax** on companies that produce a lot of pollution. While this one isn't hitting you directly at the checkout, companies might raise prices to cover this tax, meaning you pay a little more for the same product.

In Sweden, there's a carbon tax on fossil fuels, which helps fund clean energy initiatives. While it's targeted at big companies, consumers may see higher prices on gas or electricity bills.

10. Airport and Travel Taxes: The Cost of Seeing the World

Planning a vacation or dreaming of traveling abroad? Airfare isn't just about paying for the seat and peanuts. Governments add **airport taxes**, **tourism taxes**, and sometimes even **departure taxes**. If you fly from Japan, you might have to pay a "Sayonara Tax," which is a small fee added to international flights as a tourism tax. In many countries, part of your ticket cost goes straight to government taxes for airports and maintenance.

11. Income Tax: The Money You Never Get to See

Here's the tax that most people think of first—**income tax**. You earn money, and then the government takes a portion of it. Simple, right? Well, not really. Depending on where you live, the percentage of your income that gets taxed can vary a lot. Some countries have **progressive taxes**, which means the more you earn, the higher your tax rate. Others have **flat taxes**, which means everyone pays the same percentage no matter how much they make.

The real kicker with income tax? You don't even get to touch that money. It's deducted from your paycheck automatically. In the U.S., someone earning $1,000 might see only $750 in their bank account after federal, state, and local taxes are taken out. In Denmark, taxes can go up to 55%! But in the UAE, there's **no income tax** at all. Lucky, right?

Income tax funds the big stuff: defense, healthcare, education, infrastructure, and much more. If you've ever wondered how your country builds roads or pays teachers, income tax is a big part of it.

12. Payroll Tax: Your Paycheck's Little Sister

Closely related to income tax is **payroll tax**, but this one's a bit different. Payroll taxes are taken out of your paycheck specifically to fund social programs like **Social Security** and **Medicare** in the U.S. In other countries, it funds things like pensions or national healthcare systems. In the U.S., around 7.65% of your paycheck goes to payroll taxes. Your employer also pays the same percentage, so if you earned $100, $7.65 goes to fund Social Security and Medicare, and your employer chips in another $7.65.

Why It Matters: Payroll taxes make sure people have a safety net when they retire or need medical help. So when your grandparents get their retirement checks, that's partly because of payroll taxes.

13. Excise Tax: The Hidden Tax on Special Stuff

Ever heard of a **sin tax**? It's an excise tax but with a dramatic twist. This tax is applied to specific goods that governments either want to control or profit from, like cigarettes, alcohol, or even gasoline. The idea is to make people

think twice about buying these products—or at least pay more for the privilege. If you're in Australia, you'll notice that cigarettes are crazy expensive (which is good, right). That's because of excise taxes that add up to around 60% of the total price. In the U.S., gas also has excise taxes—about 18 cents per gallon at the federal level, with more added by individual states.

14. Inheritance Tax: Death and Taxes, Literally

Ever heard the saying, "Nothing is certain but death and taxes"? Well, **inheritance tax** is the perfect combination of the two. It's a tax you have to pay when you inherit money or property after someone dies. The logic? Governments want a cut of the wealth passed down from generation to generation. In the U.K., inheritance tax can be as high as 40% on anything over £325,000. In Japan, it's even higher—up to 55%. In the U.S., it's called the **estate tax**, and while it only kicks in on very large inheritances, it can still take a significant chunk.

The idea is that this tax prevents wealth from accumulating too much in a single family, spreading it around through public services instead. However, many people argue about how fair or unfair this is, especially for smaller inheritances.

15. Corporate Tax: The Business of Taxes

When companies make money, they also have to pay taxes on their profits. This is called **corporate tax**. It's just like income tax but for businesses instead of individuals. But here's the thing: big corporations often have ways to legally reduce their tax bills by using loopholes deductions or even moving their headquarters to countries with low taxes (hello, Ireland!). In the U.S., the corporate tax rate is 21%, but some companies like Amazon and Apple have been known to pay much less by using various tax strategies. In other countries like Germany, the corporate tax rate is around 30%, while in countries like Hungary, it can be as low as 9%.

16. Capital Gains Tax: When Your Investments Pay Off... and So Does the Government

Ever dream of investing in stocks, real estate, or starting your own business? If you do, and you make money from it, you'll likely face a **capital gains tax**. This tax applies to the profit you make when you sell an investment for more than you bought it.

If you buy $1,000 worth of stock in a company and sell it later for $1,500, that $500 profit is taxed. In the U.S., the capital gains tax rate is anywhere from 0% to 20%, depending on how long you hold the investment and your total income. Some countries, like Belgium, have no capital gains tax on stocks, while in Sweden, it can go as high as 30%.

17. Tariffs: The Price of Crossing Borders

When goods move between countries, governments often impose a tax on those imports or exports called **tariffs**. This is a way for countries to protect local industries by making imported goods more expensive. While companies usually pay tariffs, the cost is often passed on to consumers—you.

If you buy an imported car in India, part of the high price you pay includes tariffs imposed by the government. In the U.S., tariffs on products from China during trade wars made everything from electronics to clothing more expensive.

Tariffs are a way for governments to control trade, but they can also lead to higher prices for everyday goods. This can affect global supply chains and the cost of the things you buy.

18. Luxury Tax: For the Finer Things in Life

If you can afford to buy a yacht, a sports car, or designer clothes, governments often think you should be able to pay a little extra. That's where **luxury tax** comes in. It's a tax on high-end goods that are seen as non-essential, like fancy cars, private jets, or expensive jewelry.

In Canada, if you buy a new car that costs over CAD 100,000, you'll pay a luxury tax of 10% on the amount over that limit. Australia also has a luxury car tax on vehicles that exceed a certain threshold, making them even more expensive.

Luxury taxes are a way for governments to target wealthier individuals who can afford to spend big on non-essential items. It's also a way to fund public services without putting extra pressure on lower-income households.

19. Tourist Tax: Pay to Visit

If you've ever traveled to a foreign country, you might have unknowingly paid a **tourist tax**. This tax is added to hotel stays, flights, or even at the airport when you leave. The idea is that tourists should contribute to the local economy since they use public services like roads, parks, and waste management.

In Italy, visitors have to pay a tourist tax called the **"tassa di soggiorno"** when they stay at a hotel. The rate depends on the city, but it's often a few euros per night. In Bali, Indonesia, tourists pay a small environmental tax when they arrive.

Phewww. Exhausting, isn't it? Now that we've covered 20 different types of taxes, it's time to reflect on the taxes that touch your life— both directly and indirectly.

Next time you buy something or use a

service, notice how much you are paying as tax!

4. Credit Score: The Secret Number That Follows You Around

Let's say you want to borrow a friend's bike, but they're a little worried. Will you return it on time? Will you scratch it up or lose it? If you've always been trustworthy, they'll probably lend it to you without a second thought. If you have a history of wrecking bikes and forgetting to return stuff, well... good luck.

A credit score is just like that trust test, but for borrowing money. It's a three-digit number (usually between 300 and 850) that tells banks, companies, or even landlords whether you can be trusted to borrow money and pay it back. It is like a report card for grown-ups, but instead of grades, you get a number between 300 and 850. This number tells lenders how likely you are to repay a loan. Actual numbers depend on which Credit bureau and which country it is, but see below a <u>rough</u> example:

- **300-579**: Yikes! You've got some work to do.
- **580-669**: Not bad, but room for improvement.
- **670-739**: Good job, you're reliable.
- **740-799**: Great! You're a financial whiz.
- **800-850**: Excellent! You're basically a money superhero.

Different agencies around the world calculate credit scores. For example, in the U.S., the main ones are **Experian**, **Equifax**, and **TransUnion**. In India, it's **CIBIL**, and in the UK, Experian UK and TransUnion UK are available. No matter where you live, there's likely a company calculating your score as soon as you enter the world of credit.

Why Should You Care About Credit as a Teen?

You might be thinking, "I don't have a credit card, and I'm not borrowing money. Why should I care about my credit score?" But here's the catch: your credit history starts earlier than you think.

- **Student Loans:** Planning to go to college? Many students take out loans to cover tuition, and those loans show up on your credit report.

- **Cell Phone Contracts:** If you're on a phone plan, that's technically a form of credit. Missing payments could affect your score.

- **Future Apartment Leases:** Want to move out someday? Landlords often check credit scores before renting to make sure you're good for the rent.

So, building good habits now—like paying bills on time and not taking on more debt than you can handle—will save you a lot of headaches later.

How is Your Credit Score Calculated?

This is where it gets a bit technical, but hang in there. Your credit score is like a formula, and it's based on a few key ingredients:

a. Payment History (35%)

This is the big one. Do you pay your bills on time? Whether it's a car loan or a credit card payment, every missed payment dings your score. Imagine this as the "due date" on your homework. Late work gets a lower grade, right?

- **U.S. Teen:** If you have a credit card and miss your payment by even a day, that could hurt your score.

- **UK Teen:** You miss your monthly phone bill? That's noted, too.

b. Credit Utilization (30%)

How much of your available credit are you using? If your credit limit is $1,000 and you're constantly maxing out your card, it suggests you rely too heavily on borrowed money. Experts recommend using less than 30% of your available credit.

- If you have a credit card with a £500 limit in the UK and you spend

£400, you're using 80% of your available credit—ouch. Keep it below £150 for a better score.

c. Length of Credit History (15%)

The longer you've had credit, the better it looks. Someone who's had a credit card for ten years and always paid on time is a safer bet than someone who just got their first card last month.

Fun Fact: In countries like Japan, many people use credit cards only for small purchases to build a long and stable credit history over time.

d. Types of Credit (10%)

Lenders like to see that you can handle different types of credit. This could be a credit card, student loan, car loan, or even a mortgage. It's like showing off your ability to juggle. Can you handle multiple responsibilities?

e. New Credit (10%)

Every time you apply for new credit, like a loan or credit card, your score is slightly lower. This is called a **hard inquiry**. It's like telling lenders, "I'm looking to borrow more," which might make them nervous.

Why Should You Avoid Credit Card Debt?

Credit cards can be a useful tool or a dangerous trap. Used wisely, they help you build credit. But here's where it gets tricky: **credit card debt grows fast**—and I mean really fast. Credit card companies charge interest, which is like a fee for borrowing money. The longer you take to pay off your balance, the more you owe. It's like a snowball rolling downhill, getting bigger and bigger until it's out of control.

In the U.S., many people fall into the trap of minimum payments. Let's say you owe $1,000, and the credit card company says, "No problem, just pay $25 this month." But here's the catch—they add **interest** to the remaining $975, and that debt keeps growing. By the time you pay it off, you've shelled out way more than the original $1,000.

Global Differences in Credit Systems

Not every country uses credit scores the same way. In some places, credit works behind the scenes, while in others, it's front and center.

Example:

- **Germany:** The SCHUFA system controls creditworthiness, and it's strict. A missed phone bill can damage your credit record for years.

- **France:** People rely more on debit cards, and credit cards aren't as common as they are in the U.S. However, banks still track how well you manage your bank accounts and loans.

- **China:** Credit scores are relatively new. The country is introducing a **social credit system**, which tracks not just financial behavior but social behavior too, like whether you obey traffic rules or recycle.

Building Credit as a Teen: How to Start Early

You don't have to wait until you're 25 to start building your credit score. There are a few ways to start building credit even before you have a job or a credit card.

a. Become an Authorized User

Your parents might add you as an authorized user on their credit card. This lets you use the card (with their permission), and it helps build your credit as long as they pay the bill on time.

b. Get a Student Credit Card

Many banks offer credit cards designed for students. These have low limits and are meant to help you learn responsible borrowing. Just make sure you pay off the full balance each month!

c. Start with a Small Loan

Some people start their credit journey with a small, manageable loan—like for a used car. Just like with a credit card, the key is to make every payment on time.

How Bad Credit Can Affect Your Life

Here's where things get serious. A bad credit score can follow you around like a bad haircut you can't fix.

- **Loans:** Banks won't trust you with money, or they'll charge you super high interest rates.
- **Renting:** Landlords often check credit scores. If yours is low, you might struggle to rent an apartment.
- **Jobs:** In some countries, employers check credit scores to see if you're responsible. If your credit is bad, it could hurt your chances of landing a job.
- **Phone Plans:** Even getting a good phone plan can become difficult with bad credit. Some companies will make you pay a hefty deposit.

The Myth of "No Credit, No Problem"

Some people think that if they don't have any debt or credit history, they're golden. But here's the thing: **no credit history is almost as bad as a bad one.** Lenders have no idea if you're trustworthy, so that they might assume the worst.

Jane's Journey to a Better Credit Score

Meet Jane. She's 25 and just got her first job. She wants to rent an apartment, but the landlord says she needs a good credit score. Jane checks her score and sees it's a sad 580. Here's how she improves it:

Step 1: Pay Bills on Time

Jane sets up automatic payments for her bills. No more missed payments! After a few months, her score starts to climb.

Step 2: Reduce Debt

Jane owes $1,000 on her credit card. She decides to pay off as much as she can asap. As her debt goes down, her credit score goes up.

Step 3: Keep Old Accounts

Jane thinks about closing her first credit card account because she rarely uses it. But she learns that keeping it open can help her credit history. So, she keeps it.

Step 4: Avoid New Credit

Jane resists the urge to open new credit card accounts just for the signup bonuses. Her restraint pays off when her score improves.

Step 5: Mix It Up

Jane takes out a small personal loan and pays it off on time. This adds to her credit mix, boosting her score even more.

Step 6: Register as a voter

In the UK, registering as a voter is good for your credit history. Basically, the more sources the companies have to get the data related to you, the better.

Credit scores aren't just random numbers. They're based on algorithms and statistical models that predict behavior. Here's how it works:

- **Data Collection**: Credit bureaus (like Experian, TransUnion, and Equifax) collect data from banks, credit card companies, and other lenders.

- **Analysis**: This data goes into a complex algorithm that analyzes your financial behavior.

- **Prediction**: The algorithm predicts how likely you are to default on a loan based on your past behavior.

- **Score Generation**: Finally, your score is generated and updated regularly.

And that's a wrap on credit scores! They might seem like a mystery, but with some smart habits, you can master the art of managing your credit.

5. The Power of Compound Interest

Imagine you're at the top of a snowy hill, and you start rolling a small snowball. As it rolls down, it picks up more snow, getting bigger and bigger. By the time it reaches the bottom, it's a giant snow boulder. That's kinda how compound interest works with money.

Let's say you put $100 in a savings account with a 5% interest rate. After the first year, you get $5, making it $105. The next year, you earn interest on $105, not just your original $100. This keeps going, and over time, your money grows like a snowball rolling down a hill.

The Rule of 72

Here's a cool trick: the Rule of 72. It's a quick way to estimate how long it will take for your money to double with compound interest. You divide 72 by your interest rate, and the result is the number of years it will take. For example, with a 6% interest rate, 72 divided by 6 is 12 years. So, your money will double in 12 years. Pretty neat, huh?

The Power of Starting Early

Consider two friends, Alice and Bob. Alice starts saving $100 a month at age 25, and Bob starts saving the same amount at age 35. By the time they're both 65, Alice will have more than double the money than Bob, even though they both saved the same amount each month. That's because Alice gave her money more time to grow with compound interest.

The Coffee Conundrum

Here's another example: the coffee conundrum. Imagine you spend $5 on coffee every day. If you saved that money instead and invested it with a 7% interest rate in 30 years, you'd have over $150,000. That's a lot of money for giving up coffee, right? I mean not giving up as you can have filter coffee, but giving up those expensive ones. Well, life is all about choices.

The Rice and Chessboard Legend:

In ancient times, there was a king who a man approached. The man presented the king with a seemingly modest request: to be rewarded with rice. The wise man proposed that he should receive one grain of rice for the first square of a chessboard, two grains for the second square, four grains for the third square, and so on, doubling the number of grains of rice on each subsequent square of the chessboard. The king, amused by the simplicity of the request, readily agreed. After all, a chessboard has only 64 squares, and

it seemed like a trivial reward. However, as the king began to calculate the amount of rice needed, he soon realized the enormity of the wise man's request. The progression of rice grains on the chessboard squares follows an exponential growth pattern:

- Square 1: 1 grain of rice

- Square 2: 2 grains of rice

- Square 3: 4 grains of rice

- Square 4: 8 grains of rice

- and so on

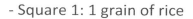

This doubling continued for each of the 64 squares. By the time the grains of rice needed for the 64th square were calculated, the number had become astronomically large. Specifically, the amount of rice required for the 64th square alone was 2^{63} (since the first square is 2^0), which equals 9,223,372,036,854,775,808 grains of rice. When the total amount of rice across all 64 squares was summed, the king found he would need 18,446,744,073,709,551,615 grains of rice.

This number was so enormous that it far exceeded the king's entire rice supply, his kingdom's reserves, and, indeed, likely all the rice in the world at that time. The king, recognizing the wisdom and the lesson in the request, understood the limitations of his knowledge and the vastness of mathematical concepts.

And there you have it! Compound interest isn't just for math nerds or financial experts. It's a concept that, if understood and applied, can lead to amazing growth in various aspects of life. So, what small habit could you start today that would compound into a significant improvement over time?

6. Fraud & Scams: Protecting Your Money

You get an email that says there's been "unusual activity" on your account and asks you to confirm your password and personal information so that it can show the unusual activity. Panic sets in, and you click the link and enter your details. Within minutes, your bank account is drained. You've just fallen victim to phishing!

In 2023, approximately 2.6 to 2.8 million fraud reports were filed in the U.S. alone, highlighting the massive scale of online scams . Globally, about 25.5% of people have experienced some form of online fraud or identity theft, with an estimated $1 trillion in losses in 2023. This means millions of people are likely scammed daily worldwide, given the constant evolution and rise of online fraud tactics.

Types of Scams You Need to Watch Out For

1. Phishing Scams

This is one of the most common types of fraud. In phishing scams, fraudsters send fake emails, text messages, or calls pretending to be from a trustworthy source—like your bank, an online store, or a government agency. The message will often have a sense of urgency ("Your account is locked! Verify now!") to make you react quickly without thinking. Once you hand over your details, they use them to access your accounts.

Example: You receive an email saying, "Your Netflix account has been suspended. Click here to fix it." The link takes you to a fake website that looks just like Netflix's login page. Once you enter your password, the scammer now has access to your account—and possibly much more if you reuse passwords across different sites.

2. Online Shopping Scams

In this scam, you're lured in by unbelievable discounts on a shopping website. You make a purchase, but the product never arrives. Sometimes, the website itself is fake, and other times, it's a legitimate-looking store that vanishes after taking your payment.

Example: A website sells high-end sneakers at 80% off. You think you've hit the jackpot, so you place an order. Days, weeks, and then months go by, and nothing shows up. Even worse, the website is now gone.

3. Investment Scams

These involve getting people to invest money in "can't-miss" opportunities that promise huge returns. Spoiler alert: they don't deliver. Ponzi schemes are classic examples of this, where early investors are paid with money from new investors, creating a cycle of fraud.

Example: You come across an ad about a cryptocurrency investment opportunity that promises to triple your money in three months. Desperate for quick cash, you invest. But after a few weeks, the website disappears, and so does your money.

4. Romance Scams

In romance scams, fraudsters create fake online dating profiles to build romantic relationships with their victims. Once they've gained trust, they ask for money under the guise of needing help with an emergency.

Example: You meet someone online, and after a few weeks of messaging, they claim they need money for a medical emergency. You send them funds to help out, only to realize later that the person wasn't real.

5. Identity Theft

This happens when someone steals your personal information—like your Social Security number or credit card info—to open new accounts, take out loans, or make purchases in your name.

Example: A scammer uses your stolen credit card number to make purchases, or worse, takes out a loan using your name. You're left with a mountain of debt that isn't even yours.

How to Protect Yourself from Scams

1. Be Skeptical

If something seems too good to be true, it probably is. Always question unexpected emails, offers, or messages that ask for personal information.

2. Double-Check the Source

If you receive a suspicious message claiming to be from your bank, don't click on any links. Instead, go directly to your bank's official website or call their customer service number to verify.

3. Keep Your Personal Information Private

Never give out your Social Security number, credit card information, or passwords unless you're sure you're dealing with a legitimate company. Be cautious about what you share on social media—oversharing can make you an easy target for fraudsters.

4. Use Strong Passwords and Two-Factor Authentication

One of the simplest ways to protect yourself is to use strong, unique passwords for different accounts. Adding two-factor authentication gives an extra layer of protection, requiring you to confirm your identity through another device.

5. Monitor Your Accounts Regularly

Check your bank and credit card statements regularly for any suspicious activity. Catching fraud early can prevent bigger problems down the road.

6. Report Suspicious Activity

If you think you've fallen victim to a scam, report it immediately to the relevant authorities, like the Federal Trade Commission (FTC) or your country's equivalent. The sooner you act, the better your authorities can take action. In many cases, quick reporting might allow you to recover lost funds or prevent further damage.

How Scammers Play on Your Emotions

Fraudsters often target emotional responses like fear, greed, or love. They might create a fake crisis (like your bank account being "locked") or a too-good-to-be-true opportunity (a business investment that promises massive returns). These emotional triggers make people act fast without thinking through their decisions.

Famous Scams

1. Bernie Madoff's Ponzi Scheme

One of the most infamous scammers, Bernie Madoff, ran a massive Ponzi scheme where he promised investors consistent returns. In reality, he was using new investors' money to pay off earlier investors. This went on for years before it collapsed in 2008, and he was eventually sentenced to 150 years in prison.

2. The Nigerian Prince Scam

This scam involves receiving a message from someone claiming to be a "Nigerian prince" who needs help transferring money out of the country. In return for your help (and a small payment upfront), they promise you a large reward. Of course, the reward never comes.

3. The 419 Scam

419 scam is an advance-fee scam where the scammer promises the victim a large sum of money (often from an inheritance or lottery) but requires the victim to pay a small fee upfront to release the funds. Once the fee is paid, the scammer disappears, and the victim never sees a penny.

In today's digital world, scams and fraud are an ever-present danger. They're sneaky, sophisticated, and designed to play on your emotions. However, by staying informed, protecting your personal information, and being cautious with unsolicited messages, you can shield yourself from these threats. It's always better to double-check and be skeptical than to lose your hard-earned money.

7. Glossary

Here's a list of financial terms that you might not normally know. These cover everything from digital payments to investments and from business terms to global financial concepts. Understanding these can help you make smarter money decisions as you get older.

- **P&L (Profit and Loss Statement)**
  A financial document that shows the revenues (profits) and expenses (losses) of a company over a specific period is used to see if a business is making or losing money.

- **Overdraft**
  When you spend more than what's in your bank account, the bank covers the extra but charges you a fee for going into "overdraft."

- **Android Pay / Google Pay**
  A mobile payment system that allows you to use your phone to pay for things by linking it to your credit or debit card so that you can pay from the Phone using the card virtually and don't need to carry the

physical card.

- **PayPal**
  An online platform that lets you send and receive money, buy things, or pay for services without sharing your bank details.

- **Venmo**
  A popular app in the U.S. used for sending money to friends or paying for small purchases, commonly used for splitting bills.

- **NFT (Non-Fungible Token)**
  A unique digital asset representing ownership of something like art, music, or virtual goods, which cannot be duplicated.

- **ROE (Return on Equity)**
  A measure of how profitable a company is relative to the shareholders' investment, indicating if an investment is worthwhile.

- **APR (Annual Percentage Rate)**
  The interest rate charged on a loan or credit card over a year, including any fees or extra costs.

- **IPO (Initial Public Offering)**
  When a private company sells shares to the public for the first time, it is publicly traded.

- **Bear Market**
  A period when stock prices fall, usually by a significant amount, signaling a downturn in the market.

- **Liquidity**
  How an asset, like money or property, can be turned into cash without losing its value.

- **Equity**
  Ownership in something, whether it's a company (shares) or a home (the portion of the home you've paid for).

- **Capital Gains**
  The profit made when an investment, like stocks or property, is sold for more than its purchase price.

- **Dividends**
  A share of a company's profits paid out to shareholders, often as cash

or additional shares.

- **Bond**
  A loan to a company or government, where they promise to pay back the money with interest at a later date.

- **Asset**
  Anything valuable that you own, like money, stocks, or property, which can be sold or increase in value.

- **Liability**
  Anything you owe, such as loans, credit card debt, or mortgages, which decreases your overall financial worth.

- **Net Worth**
  The total value of all your assets minus your liabilities showing your overall financial health.

- **Amortization**
  Spreading out loan payments over time, where each payment covers part of the interest and part of the loan itself.

- **Depreciation**
  The gradual loss of value of an asset over time, such as a car losing value each year.

- **Remittance**
  Money sent by workers back to their home country, often used to support family members and a major source of income for some countries.

- **Hedge Fund**
  A private investment fund that uses various strategies to generate high returns, often taking on more risk than traditional funds.

- **KYC (Know Your Customer)**
  Regulations requiring banks and financial institutions to verify the identity of their customers to prevent money laundering and fraud.

- **Bull Market**
  The opposite of a bear market, where stock prices are rising, often reflecting investor confidence and economic growth.

- **Gross Income**

The total amount of money earned before any taxes or deductions are taken out, often seen on pay stubs.

- **Net Income**
  The amount of money you take home after taxes and other deductions, showing your actual earnings.

- **Inflation**
  The general rise in prices of goods and services over time, reducing purchasing.

CHAPTER 5

Preparing for Your Career

What do you want to become when you grow up? We have all been asked this question. Some know exactly what they want when they are 10 years old, and some don't know even when they have reached retirement age! It is not easy as there are so many choices, and we are torn between what we want to do and what would get us more money. Sometimes, when we are lucky enough to know what we want, and it is high-income generating, life throws challenges and doesn't let us succeed easily.

So the first thing is that nobody should get too anxious about their Career. We must not waste the joys of teenage and young adult years worrying unnecessarily. But at the same time, we need to start thinking, have the right tools, have the right mindset, and have a plan or at least a vision or direction. For example, if you don't know the coordinates of which location you want to travel to, you can at least find out whether you want to go north, south, or northeast.

Makes sense? No? That is fine, too. Let us go through the details in this chapter and see if it helps you prepare better for your future.

1. Navigating the Maze of Career Planning

As I mentioned earlier, it's totally OK to be confused and not know what to do. Nobody has all the answers. The thing is, career planning isn't about having everything figured out by the time you're 16 or 18. It's about exploration, learning what interests you, and being open to change. Steve

Jobs worked at Atari and dropped out of college. Oprah was fired from her first job as a news anchor. Not exactly a smooth career path, right?

People change jobs and even entire careers more than ever now. A study by LinkedIn showed that today's workers will have about 12 jobs in their lifetime. So, thinking you need to make the *perfect* decision right now is unrealistic. Careers are less like ladders and more like jungle gyms—you'll move sideways, backward, and sometimes in loops.

Finding What You're Good At (And What You Like)

The key is figuring out what you're good at and, equally important, what you enjoy doing. These two things don't always overlap. You might be really good at math, but if you find it boring, a career as a statistician might not be for you. On the flip side, maybe you love playing video games, but turning that into a career could mean something totally different from playing Fortnite 12 hours a day.

Start by asking yourself:

- What do I enjoy doing in my free time?
- What subjects or activities come easily to me?
- When am I most engaged or excited?

Your answers don't have to lead directly to a job title. They just need to point you toward fields where your skills and interests intersect. For example, if you love working with your hands and problem-solving, engineering, design, or trades might be good options. If you're a natural communicator who loves stories, journalism, marketing, or even psychology, you could be a fit.

Passion vs. Practicality

The trick is to balance passion with practicality. Sometimes, following a passion makes sense, but other times, it's smarter to pursue something that gives you more stability while keeping your passion as a hobby or side project. You don't have to make money off everything you love.

Think of it like this: Passion is like fuel. It can get you going, but if the road you're on is full of potholes and dead-ends, you'll run out of gas before you get anywhere. Practicality is like the road map—it ensures you're heading somewhere worthwhile, even if it takes a few detours.

The Myth of "The Perfect Job"

Every job has its downsides. Even if you become a famous YouTuber, you'll still have to deal with editing videos for hours, facing online hate, and managing the constant pressure to create new content. Every career has the boring, stressful, or downright frustrating parts.

Instead of searching for a perfect job, focus on finding a job that aligns with your values, interests, and skills. You can love what you do *most of the time*, and that's a win. What's important is that your work feels meaningful to you, at least some of the time.

Building Flexibility into Your Plan

It's tempting to think of career planning like a straight path—one decision leads to the next, and eventually, you reach your destination. But life rarely works that way. A good career plan is flexible. It allows for change and growth.

You might start off studying biology because you think you want to be a doctor but end up falling in love with marine biology instead. Or you could land a job in marketing only to realize you're more interested in graphic design. Your career path might zigzag in ways you never expected, and that's okay.

Don't be afraid to pivot if something isn't working or if new opportunities arise. The goal isn't to stick rigidly to a plan but to adapt as you learn more about yourself and the world.

Career planning is more about exploration than having all the answers right away. Stay flexible, stay curious, and don't be afraid to change direction if you need to. Chase your dreams and be excited for the adventure!

So, what activities or subjects excite you the most? How could these fit into different careers?

2. Self Assessment - Understanding yourself more

It's late at night, and you're lying in bed staring at the ceiling, wondering what your future holds. You think about your friends, who seem to have it all figured out, or maybe you're scrolling through social media, seeing peopsle your age doing amazing things. You might even pull out your phone and take one of those online quizzes that promise to tell you which career or life path is your true calling.

Whether you've done this or just had a moment of quiet reflection, chances are you've asked yourself, "Who am I, and what do I really want from my life?"

Self-assessment is like holding a mirror up to your inner self. It helps you understand who you are and what you truly value. It's not about figuring everything out in one go but about learning more about your strengths, passions, and purpose.

Who Am I, Really?

People are complex, and your goals may change over time. But by understanding yourself better, you can make decisions that are more aligned with what makes you happy and fulfilled.

Self-assessment is about:

- Understanding your **strengths**: What are you naturally good at?

- Identifying your **passions**: What makes you feel excited or inspired?

- Clarifying your **values**: What do you care deeply about? (Is it freedom, security, creativity?)

- Recognizing your **personality**: Are you more introverted or extroverted? Do you thrive on routine or love adventure?

- Defining your **purpose**: What kind of life feels meaningful to you?

Let's dive deeper into how you can assess these parts of yourself.

Strengths: What Are You Naturally Good At?

Everyone has strengths, but the tricky part is recognizing them. Sometimes, the things you're good at feel so normal to you that you don't even see them as strengths. Maybe you're great at listening to others, solving puzzles, organizing events, or staying calm under pressure. These are strengths you can build on.

Passions: What Makes You Excited?

What topics do you find yourself Googling late at night just because you're curious? What activities make time fly by? Your passions are often hidden in the things that make you feel excited or "in flow" when you lose track of time.

Did you know that Billie Eilish started creating music in her bedroom at 11 years old? She was passionate about music from a young age and pursued it relentlessly, even though she didn't know if it would become her career.

Values: What's Most Important to You?

Your values are the things that matter most in life. Some people value independence and freedom, while others prioritize stability and security. There's no right or wrong here, but knowing your values helps guide your choices. For example, if you value creativity, you might struggle in a job that's rigid and routine.

Personality: What's Your Style?

Do you enjoy working in groups, or do you thrive when you're alone? Are you a planner, or do you like to go with the flow? Your personality plays a huge role in shaping what kind of life suits you best. Understanding whether you're more introverted or extroverted, structured or spontaneous, can help you make better decisions for yourself.

Purpose: What Gives You Meaning?

This is the big one: what gives your life meaning? Purpose isn't something you just "find"—it evolves as you grow. Some people find purpose in helping others, some in creating, and others in learning. Purpose often comes from aligning your passions, strengths, and values.

Ask yourself: "What would I do if money wasn't an issue?"

Putting It All Together: Crafting Your Life Blueprint

Let us take a look at some tools to help you understand yourself more in the journey. Remember, no tool will give you 100% of what you are looking for, but these will help you get thinking and give you some direction.

1. SWOT Analysis

SWOT Analysis is a straightforward tool that originated in the business world but is also incredibly useful for personal development. SWOT stands for Strengths, Weaknesses, Opportunities, and Threats. By examining these four aspects, you can gain a balanced view of your current situation and make informed decisions.

How to Conduct a SWOT Analysis

1. **Strengths:** List your internal strengths. These are characteristics or skills that give you an advantage. For example, are you good at

problem-solving? Do you have strong communication skills?

2. **Weaknesses:** Identify your internal weaknesses. These are areas where you might struggle or lack skills. For example, do you procrastinate? Do you find it difficult to delegate tasks?

3. **Opportunities:** Look at external opportunities. These are factors in your environment that you can leverage to your advantage. For example, are there networking events you can attend? Are there online courses that can enhance your skills?

4. **Threats:** Consider external threats. These are factors in your environment that could hinder your progress. For example, is the job market competitive? Is there an economic downturn that could affect your plans?

2. Myers-Briggs Type Indicator (MBTI)

The Myers-Briggs Type Indicator (MBTI) is one of the most popular personality assessment tools. It was developed by Katharine Cook Briggs and her daughter Isabel Briggs Myers, based on Carl Jung's theories of personality types. The MBTI categorizes individuals into 16 different personality types based on preferences in four areas: Introversion/Extraversion, Sensing/Intuition, Thinking/Feeling, and Judging/Perceiving.

The Four Dimensions of MBTI

1. **Introversion (I) vs. Extraversion (E):** This dimension describes how you gain energy. Introverts recharge by spending time alone, while extroverts gain energy from social interactions.

2. **Sensing (S) vs. Intuition (N):**

This dimension describes how you gather information. Sensors focus on concrete, practical details, while intuitive looks at the big picture and abstract possibilities.

3. **Thinking (T) vs. Feeling (F):** This dimension describes how you make decisions. Thinkers prioritize logic and objective criteria, while feelers consider personal values and how decisions affect others.

4. **Judging (J) vs. Perceiving (P):** This dimension describes your approach to life. Judgers prefer structure and planning, while perceivers are more flexible and spontaneous.

3. Ikigai

The Japanese concept of Ikigai means "reason for being." It is found at the intersection of four elements: what you love, what you are good at, what the world needs, and what you can be paid for. Finding your Ikigai can guide you towards a fulfilling and purposeful life.

The Four Elements of Ikigai

1. **What You Love:** Your passions and interests. These are activities that make you lose track of time and bring you joy.

2. **What You Are Good At** Your strengths and skills. These are areas where you excel and receive positive feedback.

3. **What the World Needs:** The needs and demands of society. These are problems you are passionate about solving or contributions you want to make.

4. **What You Can Be Paid For:** Your Professional Opportunities. These are areas where you can earn a living while fulfilling the other three elements.

Imagine someone who loves cooking, is good at it, sees a demand for healthy food, and can make a living from it. Their Ikigai might be opening a healthy restaurant.

Venn diagram here is a modified version of what was created by American entrepreneur Marc Winn to illustrate the concept of ikigai (with the four categories of "what you love," "what the world needs," "what you can be paid for," and "what you are good at") can help you find your ikigai if used as a basis to sort out your thoughts.

By using these tools and engaging in self-assessment, you can embark on a journey of self-discovery that not only helps you understand yourself better but also guides you toward a more fulfilling and purposeful life.

Anyway, here is a list of popular self-assessment and career analysis tools, including some we have already covered above. Also, whether free or paid!

1. **CareerExplorer** (Free & Paid) is a comprehensive test using machine learning to match interests, personality, and goals with careers. The free version gives top matches; full access costs $48 annually. careerexplorer.com

2. **StrengthsFinder (CliftonStrengths)** (Paid) Developed by Gallup, this tool identifies your top strengths out of 34 themes. It helps you discover your talents and how they align with your goals. The basic report costs $19.99. gallup.com/cliftonstrengths

3. **Big Five Personality Test** (Free & Paid): Based on five key personality traits (openness, conscientiousness, extraversion, agreeableness, and neuroticism), it gives insights into your career fit. The basic report is free; the full report costs extra. truity.com

4. **Ikigai (Free)** is a Japanese concept that combines what you love, what you are good at, what the world needs, and what you can be paid for. It's not a formal test, but reflective exercises can guide you toward a meaningful career. ikigaitribe.com

5. **123 Career Test** (Free) A short, 10-minute test based on Holland's personality codes, providing career suggestions that fit your personality. 123test.com

6. **Myers-Briggs Type Indicator (MBTI)** (Paid) Assesses personality traits and how they relate to career paths. Costs $59.95. mbtionline.com

7. **Truity Big Five Personality Test** (Free & Paid) Measures personality traits to suggest careers. Free basic report, with premium reports available. truity.com

8. **MAPP Career Test** (Free & Paid): A 22-minute test offering 10 vocational suggestions based on personality. The free version is available; full access is paid. assessment.com

9. **CareerOneStop Interest Assessment** (Free) Sponsored by the U.S. Department of Labor, it delivers career suggestions based on your interests. Free. careeronestop.org

10. **What Career is Right for Me?** (Free) It helps assess skills, values, and work preferences and then matches you with careers. Free with links to job openings. whatcareerisrightforme.com

11. **MyPlan Career Assessment** (Free & Paid) Provides four assessments for personality, values, and interests. Basic reports are free, but full access is paid. myplan.com

12. **The Princeton Review Career Quiz** (Free): A quick 24-question quiz that provides career matches based on your interests and work style. princetonreview.com

13. **CliftonStrengths for Students** (Paid) A version of CliftonStrengths tailored to students, offering insights into talents and potential career paths. The basic assessment is $19.99. gallup.com/cliftonstrengths

14. **16Personalities** (Free & Paid) A widely used personality test that helps identify strengths, weaknesses, and suitable careers. Free reports are available, but a full analysis requires payment. 16personalities.com

15. **Buzzfeed Career Aptitude Quiz** (Free): A fun, informal career quiz that gives results based on personality traits. Free to take. buzzfeed.com

We are all very different, and there is no one right answer! Remember, it is OK to fail and then start new. Sometimes, you don't realize your key skills and passion unless you give things a try!

3. Gaining Experience: Getting Your Hands Dirty

Experience teaches you things that school can't. It throws you into real-world situations where you need to make decisions, adapt, solve problems, and sometimes just figure things out on the go. And yeah, there will be mistakes. But mistakes are like life's personal trainers—they might hurt at first, but they make you stronger in the long run.

It isn't just about getting a paycheck. It's about learning how to work with people, understanding responsibility, figuring out what you like (and don't like), and building confidence. And you don't need to wait for some 'official' job to start. There are opportunities all around you.

Why No Job is "Too Small"

No job is beneath you. You might hear people say, "Oh, I could never do that," but every single job teaches you something valuable.

FLIPPING BURGERS TODAY, FLIPPING BOARDROOMS TOMORROW.

People Who Started Small

1. **Damon John** (Founder of FUBU) started out selling hats on street corners. Before that? He was waiting tables at Red Lobster, cleaning up after people's half-eaten seafood feasts.

2. **Oprah Winfrey** – Yep, before becoming a global media icon, Oprah's first job was at a local grocery store. She also worked as a news reporter, where her boss told her she was "too emotional" for television. Guess who got the last laugh?

3. **Howard Schultz** (CEO of Starbucks) didn't start out sipping lattes in a boardroom. He grew up in a poor neighborhood and worked at a coffee equipment company. His first job was delivering newspapers. Later, he worked at a ski lodge cleaning bathrooms and doing laundry.

4. **Jan Koum** (WhatsApp Founder) moved from Ukraine to the U.S. and worked as a grocery store cleaner to help his family survive. That was long before WhatsApp made him a billionaire.

5. **Jennifer Hudson** (Singer and Actress) worked at Burger King before

hitting it big on "American Idol." She even had to clean tables and take out the trash while dreaming of stardom.

6. **Richard Branson** (Virgin Group Founder) started by selling Christmas trees and budgies (yes, birds!) door-to-door. His real "job" was creating a student magazine from scratch while barely making ends meet.

7. **Jay Z** was a hustler on the streets before becoming a global music icon. His first hustle wasn't glamorous, but he used what he learned about business, negotiation, and hard work to build his empire.

8. **Nicki Minaj** worked at Red Lobster and got fired for being rude to customers. But she learned an important lesson about professionalism and managing stress before she ever stepped into a recording booth.

9. **Megan Rapinoe** (Soccer Star) worked as a janitor at her local school to earn some extra cash. She learned discipline and teamwork from a job that had nothing to do with soccer but everything to do with life.

10. **Suze Orman** (Financial Guru) started as a waitress, worked as a truck driver, and was even a tree trimmer. Today, she's one of the most respected voices in personal finance, but she never forgot the lessons she learned from those early jobs.

Opportunities You Can Jump Into Right Now

So, where can you start building your foundation today? The good news is that opportunities are everywhere, even if they don't come with a fancy title. In fact, the less glamorous jobs are often the best teachers.

Here are some ideas to get you started:

1. Freelance Gigs

Websites like **Fiverr, Upwork, and Freelancer** let you start small, even with no formal qualifications. If you can write, edit videos, design logos, or even do voiceovers, there's a gig for you. This builds both a portfolio and work discipline.

2. Local Businesses

Ask around your neighborhood. Many small businesses, like cafés, grocery stores, and garages, often need help. Whether you're shelving products, sweeping floors, or running errands, you'll learn about customer service and managing tasks. Bonus: You'll get to know people in your community.

3. Internships

Internships aren't just for college students. Many companies offer them to younger people, especially during summer. These might be unpaid, but the experience can be priceless. Google "internships near me" or check websites like **Internships.com** or **LinkedIn**.

4. Content Creation

If you're on social media, you already have the tools to start a mini-business. **YouTube, Instagram,** or **TikTok** can be turned into a job if you focus on something you love, whether it's tech reviews, art, or even playing video games. Start small, but remember, consistency is key.

5. Volunteering

This isn't technically paid, but volunteering builds a major work ethic. You can help at local charities, animal shelters, or even schools. This looks great on a resume and helps you understand the value of hard work without expecting anything in return.

6. Tutoring

If you're good at a subject, consider tutoring younger students. Platforms like **Wyzant** let you offer your skills online, or you can post flyers in your local library or community center.

7. Pet Sitting or Dog Walking

Websites like **Rover** and **Wag**! Connect you with people who need pet care. It's fun, flexible, and teaches you responsibility. Plus, dogs are better co-workers than most people!

8. Sell Handmade Goods

If you're into crafting, **Etsy** is your friend. Whether it's jewelry, art, or even knitting, you can turn your hobby into income. You'll learn about pricing, customer service, and how to meet deadlines.

9. Babysitting

It's classic, but babysitting is a serious job. You're managing someone else's most valuable possessions—their kids. It teaches you responsibility, patience, and how to deal with high-pressure situations (like tantrums). Use sites like **Care.com** to find opportunities.

The Benefits of Starting Small

When you start with a small job, two things happen: First, you learn how to appreciate the grind. You realize that success doesn't come from sitting on the sidelines. Second, you gain skills that you didn't even know you needed.

Cleaning up after people at a fast-food restaurant might not seem like a skill-building moment, but it teaches you patience, customer service, and how to handle stressful situations.

And then there's the humility part. Starting small keeps you humble. It helps you understand that no one is too good for any job. Even if your goal is to one day run a company, starting at the bottom helps you appreciate every level of the process. It gives you empathy for others who are grinding their way up, too.

EBSI Quadrant: Understanding Different Types of Income Generation

The EBSI Quadrant is a framework introduced by Robert Kiyosaki in his book "Rich Dad's Cashflow Quadrant." It categorizes the different ways people generate income into four distinct types:

1. **Employee (E)**: Individuals who work for someone else and earn a paycheck. They trade their time and skills for a fixed salary and benefits. The income is relatively stable, but salary caps and lack of ownership limit the potential for significant financial growth.

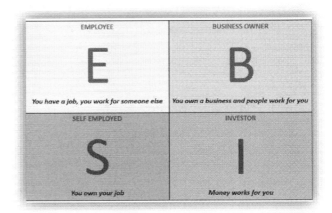

2. **Self-Employed (S)**: People who work for themselves, such as freelancers, consultants, and small business owners. They have more control over their work and potential earnings but also bear all the risks and responsibilities. Their income is directly tied to their efforts and the number of hours they can work.

3. **Business Owner (B)**: Entrepreneurs who own a system or a business that generates income. They hire employees to work for them, allowing them to leverage other people's time and skills to grow their business. Successful business owners can achieve significant financial growth and scalability.

4. **Investor (I)**: Individuals who invest their money in various financial instruments, such as stocks, real estate, or businesses, to generate passive income. Investors make their money work for them, potentially earning returns without actively working. This quadrant offers the highest potential for financial freedom and wealth accumulation.

By understanding the EBSI Quadrant, you can better strategize your approach to income generation and financial planning, aiming to move towards quadrants that offer greater financial freedom and wealth potential.

So, what's a small, practical step you can take today to gain some work experience?

4. Mastering the Art of Resume Writing: Your Ticket to the Job of Your Dreams

Sooner or later, you will have to create a resume, which is a skill to learn. A resume isn't a list of everything you've ever done. It's not an autobiography. It's not a timeline of your life, starting from the day you were born. A resume is more like a highlight reel—the best parts, the winning moments, the epic plays that showcase your skills and potential. If your resume were a movie trailer, it should make someone want to see the full film.

Most people write their resumes like they're filling out a tax form. Bland dull, and about as interesting as watching paint dry. You're going to write a resume that stands out, one that makes hiring managers lean forward in their chairs and think, "This person's got something."

Hook Them With a Solid Opening

First impressions matter. When someone picks up your resume, they're deciding within seconds whether to read further. That's where a strong opening comes in. Here's what to do:

1. Start With a Clear Heading

Your name should be front and center. Make it bold. Make it big. You want them to remember you. Right under your name, put your contact details—email, phone number, and maybe a link to your LinkedIn or personal website (if you've got one). But keep it simple. Don't include every social media platform you're on unless it's relevant to the job. No one cares how many followers you have on TikTok (unless you're applying to be a social media manager, then flex away).

2. The Summary

Think of this as your personal elevator pitch. In two or three sentences, explain who you are, what you bring to the table, and what you're looking for. Be specific. For example, instead of saying, "I'm hardworking and dedicated," try something like:

"Driven young professional with a passion for problem-solving and a track record of delivering results. Looking to bring strong communication and analytical skills to a fast-paced, innovative team."

Doesn't that sound better than "I'm good at stuff"? Of course, it does.

Show, Don't Tell

Here's where most people go wrong: they list every job they've ever had without telling anyone why it matters. Your resume isn't just a list of where you worked; it's a story about how you made a difference. And, like any good story, you've got to show, not just tell.

1. List Your Experience Like a Pro

When you list your past jobs or internships, don't just say what your job title was. Tell them what you actually did. And more importantly, tell them what impact you had. Here's how:

Bad example: *Cashier at McDonald's.*

Better example: *Managed customer transactions in a high-volume fast-food chain, maintaining 98% accuracy while reducing wait times by 10%.*

See the difference? One just states the job; the other explains what you accomplished. Numbers are your friend here. Whenever possible, include data to back up your claims. Did you help increase sales? Boost customer satisfaction? Manage a team? Show the results.

2. Tailor It to the Job

One-size-fits-all might work for baseball caps, but it doesn't work for resumes. Every job you apply to is different, so your resume should be, too. Tailor your experience to highlight the skills and achievements that are most relevant to the job you want. If you're applying for a job as a web developer, no one cares that you worked as a camp counselor when you were 14—unless you built the camp's website in your spare time. Focus on what matters to the employer.

Skills That Matter

Your skills section is like the toppings on a pizza. If it's done right, it makes everything better. If it's random and scattered, it ruins the whole thing. Don't just throw in every skill you can think of. Focus on the ones that are actually relevant to the job you want.

1. Hard Skills vs. Soft Skills

There are two types of skills: hard skills and soft skills. Hard skills are the specific technical abilities you've learned—things like coding, graphic design, video editing, or speaking five languages. Soft skills are more about how you work with others—things like communication, problem-solving, and time management.

Employers want both, but here's the trick: don't just list "good communicator" or "team player." Anyone can say that. Show it in your experience. Did you manage a project where communication was key? Were you part of a team that solved a major problem? Let your work speak for your skills.

2. Be Honest

We all want to look good on paper, but don't stretch the truth. If you claim you're fluent in Spanish and they ask you to speak it in the interview, you better be ready. There's nothing wrong with saying you're learning a skill—just be honest about your current level.

Education and Certifications

You need to include your education, but don't make this section longer than it needs to be. If you've got some work experience, your education can take a back seat. If you're just starting, it can take the spotlight.

1. Degrees Matter, But So Does Experience

List your degree, where you got it, and when you graduated. If you've got a great GPA or relevant coursework, feel free to include that. But remember, real-world experience often outweighs classroom performance. If you've got both, great. If not, emphasize your work.

2. Certifications Are Gold

If you've got any certifications—whether it's in CPR, coding, or barista training—list them here. Certifications show that you've taken the extra step to master a skill. They can set you apart from someone with the same degree but less hands-on knowledge.

The Little Things Matter

Resumes are like fashion: the details make or break the look. A typo, a weird font, or an outdated design can take all your hard work and throw it out the window. Here's how to make sure your resume looks as good as the content.

1. Clean Design

Keep your resume simple and easy to read. Use a basic, professional font like Arial or Calibri. No Comic Sans, please. White space is your friend. A cluttered resume is hard to read, and hiring managers won't spend time digging through it.

2. Proofread, Proofread, Proofread

A single typo can hurt your chances, so read your resume out loud to catch any mistakes. Even better, have someone else review it, too—it's easy to overlook errors in your work.

3. One Page, Unless You're a CEO

For most people, your resume should fit on one page. If you're not the CEO of a major company or someone with 30 years of experience, you don't need more than that. Keep it tight and relevant.

Why No Job is "Too Small" (Again)

You might be thinking, "But what if my experience is mostly odd jobs or things that don't seem important?" Let me stop you right there. Remember what we talked about in the last chapter: no job is too small. It's all about how you present it. Working at a fast-food restaurant or babysitting might not seem like resume material, but it is. These jobs teach you valuable skills like customer service, multitasking, and handling pressure—skills every employer values.

Let's look at some more examples of how to turn these "small" jobs into resume gold.

1. Cashier to Customer Service Pro

If you worked the register at a grocery store, you didn't just handle cash. You resolved customer complaints, maintained a positive attitude during stressful situations, and helped keep the store running smoothly—that's customer service and problem-solving in action.

2. Babysitter to Time Management Guru

Taking care of kids isn't just about keeping them from setting the house on fire. You're managing time, juggling multiple tasks (feeding, entertaining, cleaning), and making sure everything runs smoothly. That's project management at its core.

3. Dog Walker to Master of Responsibility

If you've ever been trusted with someone's pet, you've taken on a huge responsibility. It shows that you're reliable, trustworthy, and can manage schedules. And let's be real—dogs aren't the easiest clients to deal with.

Recruiters spend an average of 6 seconds reviewing a resume. That's why it's crucial to make a strong first impression. By following these guidelines, you'll craft a resume that not only stands out but also effectively communicates your skills, experience, and potential. Now, go out there and get that job!

5. Interview: Crushing Your First Interview

What is it about interviews that makes them feel like a life-or-death situation? And, more importantly, how can you flip the script and turn that pressure into power? I'm going to show you the secret sauce to acing any interview. Trust me, it's way less about having the "right" answers and more about understanding how to play the game.

It's a Conversation, Not a Quiz Show

First things first: **Interviews aren't just about answering questions**. They're about showing who you are. A lot of people think interviews are like Jeopardy!—you either have the answer or you don't. But really, they're more like a first date. If you go into an interview rattling off facts about yourself like you're reading a Wikipedia page, you're going to sound about as exciting as, well, a Wikipedia page.

The interviewer is trying to figure out if you're a good fit for the role. But they're also trying to figure out if they *like* you. (Weird, right?) This means the goal isn't just to prove that you know stuff; it's to show that you're someone they'd want to work with or learn from.

The secret? Be yourself—your best self, of course, but still you. Trying to be the "perfect" candidate just makes you come off robotic.

Body Language: What You Don't Say Is Screaming

If you walk into a room hunched over like you're trying to make yourself invisible, guess what? The interviewer is going to feel like you don't want to be there. And nobody hires the kid who looks like they're terrified of life.

Sit up straight. Shoulders back. Make eye contact—but not creepy, "I'm never going to break eye contact" eye contact. Think more like, "Hey, I'm confident and listening to what you're saying," eye contact.

And smile. Smiling makes you feel better, and, as a bonus, it makes other people feel better, too. It's like nature's hack for awkward situations.

Real Talk: Your Brain on Interviews

When you're nervous, your brain does this thing where it's like, "Oh no, they're judging me!" And that's when your hands get sweaty, your voice shakes, and you somehow forget your name. Classic fight-or-flight stuff. But here's the thing: **The more you practice, the less freaked out your brain gets.**

Practice in front of a mirror. Practice with a friend. Practice with your dog, if necessary. The more times you do it, the more your brain will relax and realize, "Hey, I've got this."

Tell Your Story (Without Boring Them to Tears)

One of the toughest questions in any interview is the classic: **"So, tell me about yourself."** Seems innocent enough, right? But somehow, it always feels like you're either going to overshare your life story or give them nothing.

People remember stories better than they remember facts. So, instead of listing off things like, "I went to this school, got this degree, and have this many years of experience," try framing it as a journey. Say something like, "When I was in high school, I didn't know what I wanted to do. But after taking a computer science class, I realized I loved coding. That led me to major in computer science in college, and now I'm passionate about using tech to solve real-world problems."

See the difference? You're giving the same information, but you're framing it in a way that makes the interviewer lean in and care about what you're saying.

Don't Just Answer Questions—Ask Them

Here's a big interview hack that most people miss: **You're allowed to ask**

questions, too. In fact, you *should* ask questions. Because guess what? You're interviewing them as much as they're interviewing you.

When they ask, "Do you have any questions for us?" don't just say, "Nope, I think you covered it." Ask something thoughtful. Like, "What's the most challenging part of working here?" or "How do you support employees' growth?" This shows that you're thinking critically about whether this opportunity is right for you—and it makes you stand out as someone who's engaged and curious.

Handling Tough Questions

You'll get questions like:

- "What's your biggest weakness?"

- "Tell me about a time you failed."

- "Where do you see yourself in five years?"

These questions can feel like traps. But the key is to be honest without sabotaging yourself. When they ask about your weaknesses, don't say, "I don't have any." (Nobody believes that.) Instead, say something real but manageable, like, "I used to struggle with time management, but I've been working on using scheduling tools to keep myself organized."

The goal isn't to prove that you're perfect. It's to show that you're self-aware and working to improve.

The Power of Pausing

You know how sometimes in an interview, they ask you a question, and your brain just goes *blank*? Like, completely empty—crickets. The best thing to do at that moment is to **take a pause**. You don't have to launch into an answer right away.

Say something like, "That's a great question. Let me take a second to think about it." Then, take a beat to gather your thoughts. This shows that you're thoughtful and not just blurting out the first thing that pops into your head.

Pro tip: Pausing also gives your brain time to come up with a better answer than the one you would have said if you were panicking.

Be a STAR

Don't dive directly into details without setting the context. Set the context, tell what you did and how it made a difference. Use the **STAR** method: Situation, Task, Action, Result.

- **Example:** "Tell me about a time you faced a challenge."
  - **Situation:** Describe the context.
  - **Task:** Explain your role.
  - **Action:** Detail what you did.
  - **Result:** Share the outcome.

After the Interview: What Happens Next?

Send a thank-you note. Seriously, it's that simple. It shows that you appreciate their time and reminds them of how awesome you are. Keep it short and sweet. Something like:

"Thank you so much for the opportunity to interview today. I really enjoyed learning more about the team and the exciting work you're doing. I'm excited about the possibility of contributing my skills to your projects and hope to work together in the future."

Then, give them some space. Don't be the person who emails them 24 hours later asking if they've made a decision yet. They'll get back to you when they're ready.

Wrapping It Up: Your Interview Survival Guide

Let's recap. Here are the top takeaways for crushing your next interview:

1. **Be yourself**—but make sure it's the best version of yourself.
2. **Body language matters**—sit up straight, make eye contact, and don't

forget to smile.

3. **Practice makes perfect**—the more you interview, the less terrifying it gets.

4. **Tell your story**—people remember stories, not lists of facts.

5. **Ask questions**—you're interviewing them too.

6. **Own your weaknesses**—but show how you're working on them.

7. **Pause if you need to**—taking a second to think is better than panicking.

8. **Follow up with a thank-you note**—because politeness is always a good look.

You've got this. Now go out there and show them why they'd be lucky to have you.

6. Jobs of the Future: What's Ahead?

If you've ever heard someone say, "Robots are going to take all our jobs," you might picture some sort of Terminator-style future where machines replace everyone. It sounds a bit dramatic, right? But the truth is, things are changing. The jobs you're preparing for now might look completely different by the time you're grown up. Some jobs will disappear, sure, but new ones will pop up, too.

Think about it: 20 years ago, people couldn't imagine making a living as a YouTuber, a social media manager, or a professional gamer. Those jobs didn't even exist. So what's next? What kind of jobs will you be able to do in the future? And what jobs will disappear into the dustbin of history, like telephone operators and ice delivery men?

Buckle up because we're about to explore the wild world of future careers, complete with 50 future jobs and 20 that probably won't be around much longer.

The Gig Economy: The New Way to Earn

Remember when your parents or grandparents would get a job and stick with it for like 40 years? They'd climb the corporate ladder, get a gold watch, and retire. Well, that's not the case anymore. **The gig economy** has blown that old model out of the water.

People are no longer just getting jobs. They're getting **gigs**. Think about Uber drivers, freelance graphic designers, or even people who rent out rooms on Airbnb. These are all part of the gig economy, where you can jump from one short-term job to another. You're in control of your schedule, your clients, and how much you want to work. And here's the thing: it's only going to get bigger.

In the future, we'll see more people working for themselves and less reliance on traditional 9-to-5 jobs. Flexibility will be key, and people will mix and match gigs to suit their lifestyles. But it's not just about driving cars or delivering food. The **gig economy** is expanding into high-skill jobs too.

Here is a list of the latest as well as likely jobs of the future

1. AI Specialist

Develops and refines artificial intelligence systems for various industries. As AI becomes integral to everything from home assistants to self-driving cars, demand for AI specialists is set to soar.

2. Robotics Engineer

Designs and builds robots for various tasks like surgery, cooking, or even cleaning. The need for robotics engineers will skyrocket as robots take on more roles in everyday life.

3. Cybersecurity Expert

Protects data from cyberattacks, ensuring secure online environments. With cybercrime on the rise, experts in this field will be indispensable for companies and individuals.

4. Data Scientist

Analyzes complex datasets to help businesses make informed decisions. The world is running on data, making this role critical in the future.

5. Quantum Computing Scientist

Develops the next generation of super-fast computers using quantum mechanics. As quantum technology advances, this field will revolutionize industries from finance to healthcare.

6. Renewable Energy Technician

Installs and maintains renewable energy systems like solar panels and wind turbines. As the world shifts towards sustainability, this role will be in high demand.

7. Genetic Counselor

Provides patients with insights into their genetic health risks based on DNA analysis. As personalized medicine grows, genetic counselors will become vital to healthcare.

8. Drone Pilot

Operates drones for applications ranging from deliveries to filmmaking. With drone technology expanding, skilled pilots will be essential.

9. Climate Scientist

Studies the effects of climate change and develops solutions to mitigate its impacts. As climate concerns rise, this role will be crucial for environmental sustainability.

10. AI Ethics Consultant

Ensures that AI technologies are developed and used ethically. With AI becoming more pervasive, this role will help prevent misuse and promote fairness.

11. 3D Printing Technician

Creates objects ranging from medical devices to vehicle parts using 3D printing technology. As the technology improves, so will the demand for skilled technicians.

12. Telemedicine Doctor

Provides healthcare remotely via online platforms, diagnosing and treating patients. Telemedicine is on the rise, making this a growing field in healthcare.

13. Blockchain Developer

Builds decentralized systems and applications using blockchain technology. As blockchain moves beyond cryptocurrency, developers will be needed across industries.

14. Virtual Reality Designer

Designs immersive VR experiences for gaming, education, and entertainment. As virtual reality becomes mainstream, designers will create the worlds we live in digitally.

15. Space Tourism Guide

Leads tourists on trips beyond Earth, explaining celestial sights and space stations. As commercial space travel becomes a reality, guides will be in high demand.

16. Personalized Nutritionist

Creates nutrition plans tailored to individuals' genetic profiles. As health and wellness continue to trend, this job will be essential for personalized care.

17. Digital Privacy Advisor

Helps businesses and individuals protect their personal information. With increasing data breaches and privacy concerns, this role will only grow in importance.

18. Augmented Reality Developer

Creates digital layers of information for AR applications in retail, education, and more. As AR becomes part of our daily lives, developers will build these interactive experiences.

19. Virtual Reality Therapist

Uses VR to treat mental health conditions like PTSD and anxiety. With increasing awareness of mental health, VR therapists will offer new, immersive treatment methods.

20. Autonomous Vehicle Technician

Maintains and repairs self-driving cars and trucks. As autonomous vehicles hit the roads, technicians skilled in this tech will be vital.

21. Smart Home Designer

Designs homes integrated with smart technology, from lighting to security systems. As smart homes become more common, designers will be in high demand.

22. Space Miner

Extracts valuable materials from asteroids and other celestial bodies. As space exploration expands, this job will emerge to support resource extraction beyond Earth.

23. Climate Change Analyst

Studies climate patterns and advises on mitigation strategies. As the impact of climate change grows, analysts will help shape policies and responses.

24. Smart City Planner

Design and implement technology to make cities more sustainable and efficient. As urban areas grow, smart city planners will be needed to manage development.

25. Urban Farmer

Grows crops using innovative methods like hydroponics or vertical farming within city environments. With increasing urbanization, urban farmers will become key to sustainable food production.

26. Biotech Engineer

Develops technology to improve health care, agriculture, and more. As biotechnology evolves, engineers will create innovations that improve life for billions.

27. Internet of Things (IoT) Engineer

Develops and manages interconnected smart devices, from fridges to thermostats. As IoT tech becomes more common, engineers will be in high demand.

28. E-Sports Coach

Trains professional gamers, helping them strategize and improve their skills. As e-sports grow, teams will need skilled coaches to help win championships.

29. Ethical Hacker

Legally hacks into systems to find and fix vulnerabilities before bad actors do. As cybersecurity threats grow, ethical hackers will be essential.

30. Remote Work Coordinator

Organizes teams working from home, managing policies and strategies for remote productivity. As remote work becomes the norm, coordinators will be critical for business success.

31. Artificial Organ Designer

Develops synthetic organs for transplants, pushing the boundaries of medical science. As this technology evolves, designers will be crucial in saving lives.

32. VR Sports Coach

Uses virtual reality to train athletes, analyzing their performance in a simulated environment. As VR tech grows, coaches will adopt these methods for professional sports training.

33. Geriatric Care Specialist

Focuses on the medical care and well-being of elderly populations. As the global population ages, the demand for specialists will rise significantly.

34. Food Scientist

Creates sustainable and nutritious food alternatives to meet growing global demands. As food production adapts to a changing world, scientists will innovate healthier, more sustainable options.

35. Digital Twin Engineer

Builds digital replicas of physical objects for simulation and optimization. As digital twin technology expands, engineers will help improve the efficiency of real-world systems.

36. Energy Storage Engineer

Develops systems for storing renewable energy efficiently. With renewable energy rising, storage engineers will be vital in managing the transition to green power.

37. Digital Content Creator

Makes videos, podcasts, and other digital media to engage online audiences. As social media and streaming grow, creators will be in high demand.

38. Crowd Fund Manager

Helps startups raise capital via crowdfunding platforms. As crowdfunding gains traction, managers will play a key role in navigating campaigns and securing funds.

39. Space Architect

Designs habitats and infrastructure for living and working in space. As humans venture further into space, architects will ensure safe and efficient designs.

40. Nanotechnology Engineer

Develops nanoscale materials for use in medicine, electronics, and other fields. As nanotech grows, engineers will be at the forefront of this innovation.

41. Telemedicine Technician

Supports healthcare systems delivering remote medical services. As telemedicine continues to expand, technicians will be crucial in ensuring seamless service delivery.

42. AI Personality Designer

Creates "personalities" for AI, making interactions with humans more natural and intuitive. As AI becomes a part of daily life, designers will make them relatable.

43. Digital Fashion Designer

Designs virtual outfits for avatars or video game characters. As digital worlds expand, fashion will enter the virtual realm.

44. Space Junk Recycler

Cleans up space debris and repurposes old satellites and other waste materials orbiting the Earth. As space activity increases, keeping space clean will become a booming business.

45. Synthetic Biologist

Works on creating new forms of life or altering existing organisms for various applications. As synthetic biology advances, biologists will revolutionize fields from healthcare to agriculture.

46. VR Architect

Designs buildings and environments that exist entirely in virtual reality. As more of life moves online, architects will create structures in the virtual world.

47. Water Crisis Specialist

Focuses on solving global water shortages by innovating ways to desalinate, recycle, and preserve water. With water scarcity becoming a critical issue, specialists will be vital.

48. Robotic Surgery Technician

Assists in surgeries performed by robotic systems, ensuring everything runs smoothly. As robotic surgeries become more common, skilled technicians will be needed.

49. Digital Brand Manager

Helps individuals and companies build their online presence through strategic marketing. As personal branding grows, digital brand managers will become essential.

50. Healthcare Navigator

Helps patients navigate complex healthcare systems and access services. As healthcare becomes more intricate, navigators will support patients in finding the right care.

20 Jobs That Might Disappear or Reduce in Numbers

Now for the flip side. As tech evolves and things like AI and automation become more common, some jobs won't be as common as today. Here's a list of jobs that are likely to reduce or vanish in the future decades:

1. Cashiers

Self-checkout machines and automated stores will take over mostly.

2. Drivers

Self-driving cars and trucks are already being tested and could replace human drivers.

3. Bank Tellers

With online banking and ATMs, the need for tellers is dropping fast.

4. Assembly Line Workers

Robots are becoming better at doing repetitive tasks, putting these jobs at risk.

5. Telemarketers

Automation and AI bots can already handle most of the tasks telemarketers do.

6. Receptionists

Automated systems and AI are starting to replace front desk workers.

7. Travel Agents

Most people now book their trips online, so fewer people need travel agents.

8. Writers and Reporters

With news moving online and AI starting to write articles, fewer writers/reporters will be needed.

9. Programmers & Software Testers

AI can write the basic code already and pretty well. We won't need as many programmers as we need today. We will still need a lot, given technology is the foundation of the future, but entry-level/basic jobs can be easily done by bots. Testing is moving to Automation already so fewer testers will be needed than today. Overall, the Tech sector will continue to drive a huge demand, but the roles/skills required will be different.

10. Factory Workers

As manufacturing becomes more automated, the need for factory workers will decline.

11. Postal Workers

Email, instant messaging, and online shopping are cutting down on traditional mail.

12. Librarians

With everything becoming digital, the role of the traditional librarian may shift or disappear.

13. Customer Service Representatives

Chatbots and AI are handling more customer service inquiries every year.

14. Security Guards

Surveillance tech and AI-based security systems are reducing the need for human guards.

15. Retail Sales Associates

With the rise of online shopping and automated stores, fewer salespeople are needed.

16. Fast Food Workers

Self-order kiosks and automated cooking systems could replace these roles.

17. Farm Workers

Automation and drones are making farming more efficient, reducing the need for manual labor.

18. Loan Officers

Online platforms and AI are starting to handle loan approvals without the need for human officers.

19. Data Entry Clerks

Automation is rapidly replacing the need for people to enter data into systems manually.

20. Parking Attendants

As cars become more autonomous and parking systems more automated, this job may disappear.

Adapting to the Future: How to Prepare for Jobs That Don't Exist Yet

Learning how to learn is going to be your greatest strength in a world where technology is evolving faster than ever. Remember all the key skills we talked about earlier in the book? The jobs of the future will look completely different from the ones we know today. Some roles will vanish, but a whole new world of opportunities will open up. The trick is to be ready for anything. Keep learning, keep adapting, and keep an open mind. You never know what cool new job or business opportunity might be waiting for you just around the corner.

Being Content and Happy with What You Get

"Are we there yet?" It's the age-old question asked on long road trips, usually by antsy kids from the backseat. The anticipation, the impatience, the craving to reach the destination as soon as possible—all familiar feelings. But what if I told you this question doesn't just belong on the road? It also applies to our careers. We often get so focused on the destination—our dream job, a certain salary, or a specific title—that we forget to enjoy the ride. But it is all about the journey!

Imagine you're on a road trip. The destination is a picturesque mountain cabin, complete with a cozy fireplace and a view to die for. You're excited. But the journey to get there? That's where the fun unfolds. The quirky roadside diners, the unexpected detours to hidden gems, the laughter, and the memories created along the way—these are the moments that make the trip unforgettable. Your career journey is much the same. The journey, with all its ups and downs, shapes who you are and what you become. By embracing the process, continuously learning, and finding joy in improvement, you can create a fulfilling and rewarding career. Enjoy the journey of life, and remember that there are no Failures, only Lessons!

CHAPTER 6

Working With People

Arguably, working with People is the most important but most difficult skill you will ever learn! All great human achievements could not have been possible without collaboration among humans. Interpersonal skills are essential for navigating both personal and professional relationships. They include the ability to communicate clearly, listen actively, and empathize with others. Good people skills mean you can work well in a team, resolve conflicts, and build positive relationships.

1. Why We Care So Much About What Others Think - The Evolution of Social Connection

Why does a single "like" on social media make your day, while a disapproving glance from someone can ruin it? It turns out that it's more than just modern behavior—it's built into our survival instincts, as we discussed in the earlier chapters.

Imagine it's thousands of years ago. You're living in a time when fire was still a discovery, and the wheel was cutting-edge technology. Life was tough, and survival depended on sticking together. Alone, you were easy prey for predators, but in a group, you had a fighting chance. People could protect each other, share food, and build shelter. Being part of the group wasn't just nice—it was *essential*.

Fast forward to today. While there aren't any saber-toothed tigers lurking in the shadows, our brains haven't quite caught up. They're still wired to crave the safety and security of being liked, appreciated, and accepted by others. It's like our brains are running an outdated survival software that still thinks we're in the wild.

Our ancestors evolved to care deeply about fitting in with the group. When someone was kicked out of the tribe, it was a life-or-death situation. Social rejection felt like physical pain because being excluded meant facing the dangers of the wild alone.

Neuroscience confirms this: Studies have shown that social rejection activates the same areas of the brain as physical pain—the anterior cingulate cortex and the insula. This suggests that our emotional pain from rejection was designed to keep us from doing anything that might get us kicked out of the group. In other words, it's an ancient survival mechanism.

Modern Social Needs and the Rise of Social Media

Today, the landscape looks different, but the need for social approval remains. In fact, it's amplified. Social media platforms like Instagram, Facebook, and TikTok have transformed our ancient craving for approval into a digital obsession.

When you get a "like" or a positive comment on social media, your brain releases dopamine. This makes you feel good and want to seek more approval, creating a loop where validation becomes addictive.

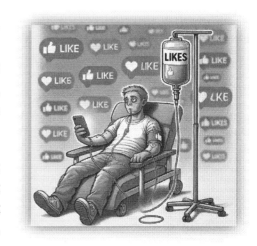

Just like how our ancestors felt comfort from group approval, we now feel that same comfort from virtual feedback. But while it feels good at the moment, constantly seeking that approval can lead to some serious mental health challenges.

The Psychological Impact of Needing Approval

While feeling accepted can be great, constantly chasing external validation can create stress and anxiety. If you constantly shape your behavior to fit what others expect, you risk losing sight of who you really are. This can lead to a disconnect between your true self and the person you present to the world, leaving you feeling unfulfilled or even lost.

Remember, it's okay to care what others think—but it's equally important to stay true to yourself. Your journey isn't about fitting into every tribe; it's about finding your path, surrounded by people who appreciate the real you.

2. Understanding Personality: Types of People

Understanding different personalities can help us get along better with others and navigate social situations with more ease. Personality isn't just about one thing—many factors, like genetics, upbringing, and life experiences, shape it.

We all know people come in a range of personalities. Some are loud, some are quiet. Some love to chat and some would rather crawl under a rock than be part of a group conversation. So, how do you work with them all? Whether it's your school project group or a sports team, understanding the personalities around you makes a massive difference. Here's a breakdown of how to work with different personality types.

The Outgoing Charmer (aka The Extrovert)

"Why is it so quiet? Let's make some noise!"

These people thrive on social interaction. They get energy from being around others. In group settings, they are often the loudest voice and may be the first to suggest a group hangout after the meeting.

How to Work With Them:

- **Engage Them in Conversations**: Extroverts love to talk things out. Don't hold back your ideas. They get excited by bouncing thoughts back and forth.

- **Give Them Group Roles**: They thrive in social settings, so let them take on roles like presenting or being the spokesperson.

- **Keep Things Moving**: Extroverts get bored with long silences or slow progress. Keep the energy flowing with action-oriented tasks and frequent updates.

Extroverts' brains show more activity in the parts linked to reward and social interaction. No wonder they're always up for a chat!

The Deep Thinker (aka The Introvert)

"Can I do this on my own? I need some space to think."

Introverts need quiet to recharge. It's not that they don't like people, but being in constant interaction drains their energy. They might shy away from group discussions but come up with brilliant ideas on their own.

How to Work With Them:

- **Give Them Space**: Allow introverts time to process information and come back with their thoughts. They're often more reflective and need time to analyze things deeply.

- **Use Written Communication**: Many introverts express themselves better in writing. Consider using chat or emails to get their ideas.

- **Don't Force Them to Speak Up**: Introverts might prefer smaller group settings or one-on-one conversations. Forcing them into a big group discussion might make them uncomfortable.

Studies show that introverts have more activity in their prefrontal cortex, the area of the brain involved in deep thinking and planning.

The Organized Planner (aka The Type-A Personality)

"We need a plan, and we need it *now*."

Type-A personalities are all about structure, order, and control. They love a good plan, and they hate surprises. These people will show up 15 minutes early and have a five-step action plan ready before the meeting even starts.

How to Work With Them:

- **Let Them Organize**: Give them roles that involve planning and setting timelines. They'll appreciate the responsibility and will make sure the project stays on track.
- **Be Clear and Concise**: These personalities don't love chit-chat. Get to the point, give them the facts, and keep things structured.
- **Don't Procrastinate**: Nothing drives a Type-A person crazier than missed deadlines. Stick to the schedule, or you'll hear about it.

Type-A personalities are more likely to experience stress because of their drive for perfection. It's not easy being on top of everything!

The Laid-back Chill One (aka The Type-B Personality)

"Relax. It'll all work out."

Type-B personalities are relaxed, flexible, and go-with-the-flow. They don't stress over small things and tend to be more creative and spontaneous. However, they might struggle with strict deadlines or rigid rules.

How to Work With Them:

- **Give Them Creative Freedom**: Type-Bs love to think outside the box. If the project allows, give them room to experiment and come up with unconventional ideas.
- **Be Patient with Deadlines**: While they might not follow a strict

schedule, they can still get the job done. It just might take them a little longer.

- **Stay Positive**: Type-B personalities bring an air of calm to any team. Appreciate their easy-going nature, especially when things get stressful.

Studies show that Type-B personalities are less prone to stress-related illnesses, probably because they don't sweat the small stuff.

The Logical Problem Solver (aka The Analytical)

"Is this the most efficient way to do it?"

These people are all about logic, data, and analysis. They love finding the best solution to a problem and may challenge ideas that don't seem logical to them. They can be critical thinkers but might struggle with the emotional aspects of teamwork.

How to Work With Them:

- **Present Facts and Data**: When working with an Analytical personality, come prepared with evidence. They want to see the numbers, charts, and details before making a decision.

- **Don't Take Criticism Personally**: They aren't being rude; they just care about the most efficient solution. If they question something, it's about the process, not you.

- **Use Structured Problem-Solving**: These individuals love clear steps and logical flows. Present tasks in a way that lets them tackle problems step by step.

Analytical personalities often have higher activity in brain regions responsible for logical reasoning and problem-solving.

The Emotional Connector (aka The Empath)

"How are we all feeling about this?"

Empaths are all about the feelings. They can easily pick up on others' emotions and are great at making people feel understood and valued. In a group, they're often the ones mediating disagreements or making sure everyone is heard.

How to Work With Them:

- **Be Open About Emotions**: Don't be afraid to talk about how you feel. Empaths appreciate honesty and will do their best to make sure everyone feels good about the task.

- **Let Them Mediate**: In case of conflict, an empath is great at finding a middle ground. Let them help smooth things over.

- **Give Positive Feedback**: Empaths thrive on appreciation and connection. Let them know when they're doing a good job or when their emotional support is valued.

Research shows that empaths have higher activity in brain regions responsible for understanding emotions, like the anterior insula.

The Big-Picture Dreamer (aka The Visionary)

"But what if we did this *instead*?"

Visionaries are often more concerned with the big idea than the nitty-gritty details. They're the people who will dream up a fantastic new direction for your project but might not be the best at following through with the small tasks.

How to Work With Them:

- **Let Them Brainstorm**: Visionaries are great at coming up with innovative ideas. Let them lead brainstorming sessions and come up with fresh directions.

- **Team Them Up with a Planner**: Visionaries might lose track of the details, so pairing them with a Type-A personality can ensure that the big ideas get executed.

- **Encourage Creativity**: Visionaries thrive when they feel free to explore different possibilities. Don't box them in with too many restrictions.

Visionaries often have more activity in the right hemisphere of their brain, which is responsible for creative thinking and imagination.

The Silent Rebel (aka The Nonconformist)

"Why do it like everyone else? Let's do it differently."

Nonconformists hate following the rules just because they're rules. They want to challenge the status quo and try things their way. These people are often innovative but might resist authority or structure.

How to Work With Them:

- **Give Them Independence**: Nonconformists work best when they're allowed to experiment on their own. Let them take ownership of tasks and see where they take them.

- **Don't Micromanage**: They will bristle at too many rules or oversights. Give them the end goal and let them figure out how to get there.

- **Value Their Unique Perspective**: Nonconformists often see things in ways others don't. Their offbeat ideas might lead to breakthroughs.

Nonconformists are often seen as innovators in history, like Galileo, who challenged the belief that the Earth was the center of the universe.

Key Takeaways:

- **Understand What Drives Each Type**: Whether it's social interaction, creativity, or logic, knowing what motivates different personalities helps in communication.

- **Adapt Your Approach**: Flexibility is key when working with diverse personalities. Some need space, others need engagement.

- **Play to Their Strengths**: Everyone brings something different to the table. Let people shine where they excel.

- **Respect Differences**: There's no one "best" personality type. Each one adds value in its own way.

Are You an Introvert, Ambivert, or Extrovert?

Take this quiz to discover where you fall on the introvert-extrovert spectrum. For each question, choose the option that best describes you.

1. How do you feel after a long social event?
   - a) Drained and in need of alone time.
   - b) It depends on the event and my mood.
   - c) Energized and excited.

2. When working on a group project, you prefer:
   - a) Working on individual tasks that you can complete alone.
   - b) A mix of solo and group tasks.
   - c) Collaborating closely with your team.

3. How do you typically spend your weekends?
   - a) Relaxing at home, reading, or engaging in a solo hobby.
   - b) A combination of social activities and alone time.
   - c) Going out with friends or attending events.

4. At a party, you are most likely to:
   - a) Find a quiet corner to talk to one or two people.
   - b) Enjoy both mingling and having deeper conversations.
   - c) Be in the center of the action, meeting new people.

5. How do you handle networking events?
   - a) You find them exhausting and prefer not to attend.
   - b) You can handle them for a while but need breaks.
   - c) You thrive on meeting new contacts and enjoying the experience.

6. When you have a problem, you prefer to:
   - a) Reflect and solve it on your own.
   - b) Think it over yourself and then discuss it with a friend.
   - c) Talk it out with others immediately.

7. Your ideal vacation is:

    - ○ a) A quiet retreat where you can unwind alone.
    - ○ b) A mix of adventure and relaxation.
    - ○ c) A lively destination with lots of activities and people.

8. How do you feel about public speaking?

    - ○ a) You avoid it whenever possible.
    - ○ b) You can do it if necessary, but you don't love it.
    - ○ c) You enjoy it and seek out opportunities to speak.

9. When making decisions, you prefer to:

    - ○ a) Think them through thoroughly on your own.
    - ○ b) Weigh your options independently and then get input from others.
    - ○ c) Discuss your options with others before deciding.

10. How do you recharge after a busy day?

    - ● a) Spending time alone with a good book or show.
    - ● b) A balance of quiet time and social interaction.
    - ● c) Going out and socializing with friends.

Results:

- ● Mostly A's: You are likely an Introvert. You find energy in solitude and prefer deep, meaningful interactions with a few people rather than large social gatherings.

- ● Mostly B's: You are likely an Ambivert. You have a balance of introverted and extroverted traits, enjoying both social interactions and alone time, depending on the situation.

- ● Mostly C's: You are likely an Extrovert. You thrive on social interaction, enjoy being around people, and feel energized by social activities.

3. Be a Friend to Make a Friend

Would you befriend yourself? Do you complain that people are not friendly and are cold or mean, but have you thought about how you come across others? Do you reach out with a Smile and initiate a conversation? Do you really listen? One of the oldest tricks to make friends is to show genuine interest in others. Friendship starts when you make it about *them*.

Power Moves: The Smile

Here's the first cheat code in the friendship game: smile. Sounds too easy, right? But science backs it up—smiles are basically contagious. Someone smiles, and you smile back. It's human nature. That little facial twitch can make you look friendly, open, and, most importantly, approachable. Plus, smiling makes *you* feel good, too.

Listen Like You Mean It

Have you ever talked to someone who's just waiting for their turn to speak? Annoying, right? Friendship isn't about who talks the most—it's about who *listens* best. Ask questions and actually care about the answers. People love talking about themselves, and if you remember small details about their stories, you've just leveled up your friendship game.

Acts of Everyday Kindness & Consistency

You don't need to rescue someone from a burning building to be a good friend. It's the little stuff that counts—offering to share your fries when theirs run out? Listening when they had a bad day? Being a human version of a Wi-Fi connection—always there when they need you?

It's the everyday gestures that show someone you're not just here for the fun times but for the rough ones, too. Trust me; nobody remembers who bought them the biggest birthday gift, but they will remember who sat with them when they felt alone.

Consistency is key. Show up when you say you will, answer texts, and follow through on promises. Basically, don't ghost your friends unless you're playing hide and seek.

Sharing Is More Than Just Splitting Snacks

Sure, sharing your pizza is cool, but real sharing goes deeper. Share your time, your experiences, and your embarrassing stories. When you open up to someone, it's like offering them a piece of your world. In return, they feel safe to do the same.

But don't make it one-sided. Sharing isn't a monologue; it's a conversation. Give a little, and let them give back.

Respect the Weird

Not everyone is going to be exactly like you—and that's a *good* thing. Friendship isn't about finding your clone; it's about respecting and even celebrating the quirks and differences in others. You like comic books, and your friend loves skateboarding? Perfect. It's what makes the world and friendships interesting.

It's a bit like being in an orchestra—every instrument has a different sound, but when you put them together, you get a beautiful symphony.

Say Thanks (Like, Actually Say It)

A simple "thank you" is a magic word in friendships. People love being appreciated. If your friend goes out of their way for you, acknowledge it. Compliment them when they do something awesome. Celebrate their wins like they're yours. It's the kind of thing that takes a friendship from good to *great*.

Lessons from Dogs

You know who gets friendship right every time? Dogs. Yeah, they don't care about your clothes or how many likes you got on Instagram. They love you

for *you*—they're loyal, they listen (without interrupting!), and they're always there for you, even when you've had a bad day. Dogs don't hold grudges, and they're just genuinely happy every time they see you. Take a page from their playbook: be loyal, listen well, and always be excited to see your friends.

Be Yourself

You can try to impress people all day by pretending to be someone you're not, but at some point, the mask slips. It's exhausting and fake. The trick to finding *real* friends is showing them the *real* you, flaws and all. The right friends will stick around, and the wrong ones? Well, good riddance.

Friendship isn't a magic trick or a complicated puzzle. It's simple: be kind, be interested, be reliable. And the best part? Once you start being a good friend, you'll notice friends finding *you* too.

4. Embrace Diversity

The world would be pretty dull if everyone looked, thought, and acted the same. Diversity isn't just about what you see on the outside—it's about how people think, how they solve problems, what their experiences have been, and even what languages they speak or foods they eat. Embracing diversity is about appreciating those differences instead of being scared of them.

Diversity covers everything that makes people unique—race, gender, age, culture, abilities, and even personality. It's like a giant puzzle where every piece is different, but when you put it together, it creates something amazing.

When you meet someone different from you, don't just see what sets you apart—look for what you can *learn* from them.

The Spice of Life

Imagine your friend circle is a big potluck dinner, and each person brings their favorite dish. You've got sushi, samosas, tacos, and, of course, pizza. Now, if everyone brought the same dish, it would be boring. But when everyone brings something different, the meal becomes this awesome mix of flavors, textures, and colors. That's what diversity does in life—it adds *spice*.

It's not just about food, either. People from different cultures bring new ideas, traditions, and ways of seeing the world. It's like swapping stories around a campfire. The more people you include, the richer the conversation gets.

Learn from Differences

Let's talk about different perspectives for a second. Have you ever noticed how you and your friends might approach the same problem in totally different ways? Maybe you like to dive straight into the action, while your friend prefers to plan things out carefully. Diversity of thought is a major asset.

Take science, for example. Teams that include people from different backgrounds and experiences often make the biggest discoveries because they look at the same problem with fresh eyes. When NASA sent the Curiosity Rover to Mars, it was designed by a *very* diverse team of engineers, scientists, and tech experts, each bringing a different skill set. The result? A robot that's been exploring the surface of Mars for over a decade.

Facing Stereotypes

Okay, let's get real for a second. Sometimes, when people meet someone different from them, they fall into the trap of stereotypes—making assumptions based on things like someone's race, gender, or background. But here's the deal: stereotypes are *always* wrong. Nobody fits neatly into a box.

Imagine judging an entire book just by looking at the cover. Sounds ridiculous, right? You'd miss out on an amazing story if you stopped there. The same goes for people. Everyone has a unique story, and if you let stereotypes cloud your judgment, you'll never get to know the real person behind the surface.

The Beauty of Inclusion

Inclusion isn't just a buzzword—it's what makes diversity *work*. Think of it like throwing a party. Diversity is inviting everyone, but inclusion is making sure they feel welcome and comfortable once they get there. It's about making sure everyone has a voice and a seat at the table.

And you know what's cool? When you include people, you don't just make them feel good—you grow too. You get to learn from them, see new sides of things, and build a community that's way stronger and more fun because of its differences.

Celebrating Your Diversity

Here's the kicker: YOU are part of the diversity we're talking about. Everything that makes you unique—your background, your culture, your interests—that's part of the big puzzle, too. Don't be afraid to share it. Celebrate it. Because, just like everyone else, you have something valuable to bring to the table.

Remember, the world isn't about fitting in. It's about standing out and embracing all the things that make you different.

5. Navigating Online Relationships: The Digital Dance of Connection and Conflict

Most of our people-related communication today is done virtually. We are getting physically distant and are connected virtually. Dealing with people virtually is a slightly different skill. The internet gives us the power to connect with people all over the world, and sometimes, it's amazing. But there's also the awkward side: misunderstandings, trolls, and the ever-terrifying *ghosting*. So, how do you navigate this crazy world of online friendships and relationships without losing your mind?

Trolls, Drama, and Conflict: The Dark Side of the Digital Dance

The internet isn't all memes and funny dog videos. Sometimes, you run into trolls—the people who live to stir up trouble and make you question your entire existence. Whether they're leaving rude comments or picking fights, trolls are the mosquitoes of the internet.

But here's the golden rule: Don't feed the trolls. Engaging with them is like pouring gasoline on a fire. Let it go. Better yet, hit that block button like you're swatting a fly—no need to waste your energy on people who just want to cause chaos.

Ghosting: The Worst Magic Trick

It's when someone disappears on you with no explanation like a magician pulling a vanishing act. One day, they're chatting with you nonstop, and the next? Silence. It's frustrating because it leaves you with more questions than answers.

Ghosting is usually more about the ghoster's inability to deal with confrontation than anything you did wrong. But that doesn't make it any less annoying. When it happens, the best thing you can do is move on. And hey, if someone ghosts you, they're probably not worth your time anyway.

Catfishing

It refers to someone creating a fake identity online, usually to deceive or manipulate others. They might use fake photos, lie about their age, or create an entire backstory that's completely made up. The reasons for catfishing vary—some people do it for attention, others to scam money, and some just for the thrill of living a double life. However, for the person on the other end, it can be a devastating betrayal when they discover the truth.

Even when someone isn't catfishing, online relationships can still be tricky. Without the context of face-to-face interaction—like body language, tone of voice, and eye contact—it's easy for misunderstandings to happen. A sarcastic comment might be taken seriously, a joke might fall flat, or a message might be misinterpreted. These kinds of miscommunications can lead to conflicts that wouldn't happen in an in-person conversation.

There's also the issue of **online disinhibition**. When people interact online, they often feel less restrained and more willing to say things they wouldn't say in person. This can lead to deeper, more honest conversations—but it can also result in arguments, harsh words, and toxic behavior. People might feel emboldened to bully, harass, or manipulate others because they're hiding behind a screen.

Digital Intimacy: Love in the Age of the Internet

Nowhere is the impact of the internet on relationships more evident than in online dating. Apps like Tinder, Bumble, and Hinge have made it possible to meet potential romantic partners without ever leaving your house. For many, online dating is a convenient and effective way to find love. But, like all things online, it comes with its own set of challenges.

One of the biggest issues with online dating is the concept of **choice overload**. With so many potential matches at your fingertips, it can be overwhelming to choose just one person to focus on. This can lead to a paradox where the more options you have, the less satisfied you are with any of them. It's easy to fall into the trap of always wondering if there's someone better just a swipe away.

Another challenge is the superficial nature of many online interactions.

When you're swiping through profiles, you're often making snap judgments based on a few photos and a short bio. While this might work for casual dating, it can make it harder to find deeper connections. The focus on appearance and instant attraction can overshadow the more meaningful aspects of a relationship, like shared values, interests, and life goals.

The Psychology of Online Relationships

What makes online relationships so different from offline ones? To answer that, we need to dig into some psychology.

First, there's the concept of **hyperpersonal communication**. This is the idea that online interactions can sometimes be more intense and intimate than face-to-face ones. Why? Because when you're communicating online, you have more control over how you present yourself. You can carefully craft your messages, choose what information to share, and take time to respond. This can lead to a sense of closeness and connection that feels deeper than it actually is.

However, this hyperpersonal communication can also create problems. When we only see the best version of someone, we can start to idealize them, building up an image in our minds that might not match reality. This can lead to disappointment when we finally meet the person face-to-face, and they don't live up to our expectations.

There's also the issue of **context collapse**. In the offline world, we act differently depending on the situation—we behave one way with our friends, another way with our family, and yet another way at work or school. But online, these different contexts can blur together. Something you post to a friend might be seen by your boss, or a private joke might be misunderstood by someone who wasn't in on it. This collapse of context can lead to awkward situations and misunderstandings.

The Impact of Online Relationships on Real Life

One of the most fascinating aspects of online relationships is how they influence our offline lives. Sometimes, an online friendship can become a real-life friendship, or an online romance can lead to a real-life relationship. But the transition from online to offline isn't always smooth.

When you meet someone in person after knowing them online, there's often a period of adjustment. The person might look or act differently than you imagined, and the dynamic of your relationship might change. Some people find that the chemistry they had online doesn't translate to real life, while others find that their connection deepens once they meet in person.

But even when online relationships don't move offline, they can still have a significant impact on your real life. For example, if you're spending hours chatting with someone online, it can affect your relationships with people in your immediate surroundings. You might start to prioritize your online interactions over face-to-face ones, leading to feelings of isolation or disconnection from those around you.

On the other hand, online relationships can also provide support that you might not find in your offline life if you're going through a tough time. Having someone to talk to online can be a lifeline, especially if you feel like you can't open up to the people around you. Online friends can offer a different perspective, provide a listening ear, or simply be there when you need someone to talk to.

The internet has given us incredible opportunities to connect with others, but it's also created new challenges in how we form and maintain relationships. By understanding the unique dynamics of online relationships, we can better navigate the digital world and build connections that are meaningful, healthy, and fulfilling.

Here are some cool tips

1. Be Yourself, Not Your Instagram Filter

That pic of you hiking at sunrise? Yeah, it's cool, but you don't need to pretend you're living in the mountains when you really just love watching Netflix in your PJs. Keep it real!

2. Don't Overthink The Three-Dot Bubble

You know, the one where they're "typing..." and then NOTHING? Don't sit there staring, thinking they've changed their mind about life, love, and everything in between. Maybe their Wi-Fi cut out. Maybe their cat sat on their phone. *Move on with your life for those 3 minutes.*

3. Emojis Are Your Friend, But Don't Go Overboard

Emojis can save lives—okay, maybe not lives, but definitely messages. If something *sounds* too serious, throw in a smiley. But don't turn every message into hieroglyphics. You're not deciphering ancient scrolls here.

4. Schedule Real-Time Chats, Not Just "Text Marathons"

Messaging for weeks on end but never actually talking? That's like buying running shoes and never running. It's fun for a while, but at some point, you need to *get out of the text bubble* and hear each other's voices. Call them, FaceTime them—just don't be the one who always "forgets" to answer!

5. Don't Be A "Serial Ghost"

Ghosting isn't a superpower, so don't treat it like one. If you're not feeling it anymore, just be honest. Telling someone, "Hey, I think we're on different pages," takes 10 seconds. Poofing into the digital void? That makes them wonder if you joined a secret spy agency.

6. Set Boundaries (Yes, Even Online)

Just because they text you at midnight doesn't mean you need to answer at midnight. If you're tired, busy, or watching your favorite show, it's okay to reply when you're ready. You're not a robot, and you don't need to pretend you're online 24/7.

7. Don't Compare Yourself to "That Cute Couple" You Saw on Instagram

Their online life looks like a rom-com, but trust me, they're just good at picking cute filters. Everyone has awkward moments and weird arguments—don't let those polished pics fool you into thinking your relationship isn't good enough.

8. Video Calls Can Be Awkward, But That's Okay

Is it just me, or do video calls always freeze at the worst times? Maybe you'll accidentally show them the ceiling or your awkward side angle, but that's part of the fun. Embrace the chaos! Just make sure you're not still in pajamas from two days ago.

9. Don't Treat Every "Seen" Message as the End of the World

Just because they saw your message and didn't reply immediately doesn't mean they've moved to a desert island. Chill. People have lives (shocking, I know). Give them a little breathing room before you assume they're ghosting.

Final thought: Relationships online are just like offline—they need effort, patience, and a sense of humor. Just because you're behind a screen doesn't mean you should forget to be kind and real.

6. Self-respect, Self-Love and Self-acceptance

Why are we talking about Self-love in the Chapter on People skills? Because it all starts with you. If you don't love or respect yourself, why do you expect others to love or respect you? It doesn't work that way. To improve relationships with others, first, you need to fix your relationship with yourself.

The idea of self-love comes from the concept of positive regard in psychology, something first outlined by Carl Rogers, a founder of humanistic psychology. He believed that self-love, or unconditional positive regard for oneself, is crucial for personal growth. Without it, we struggle with low self-worth, which can cloud every decision and relationship we have.

> IF YOU DON'T LOVE, RESPECT AND ACCEPT YOURSELF, HOW CAN YOU EXPECT OTHERS TO DO SO?

What is self-love?

Self-love means actively treating yourself with kindness, compassion, and care, even when life isn't going your way. It's about recognizing that you're worthy of good things—regardless of your flaws, mistakes, or failures. People who practice self-love often experience higher levels of resilience,

273

meaning they're able to bounce back from setbacks quickly. It's not about being self-obsessed or narcissistic; it's about creating a healthy relationship with yourself.

Psychologically, when you lack self-love, you're more vulnerable to negative self-talk, shame, and depression. People who practice self-love tend to have lower levels of anxiety and stress. This is because self-love promotes a kind of **psychological safety**—when you love yourself, you're not constantly punishing or judging yourself, and you give yourself permission to grow and learn.

Self-Acceptance: The Power of Embracing Who You Are

Self-acceptance means coming to terms with all parts of yourself—your strengths, weaknesses, quirks, and flaws. It's not the same as self-love, though the two are connected. Where self-love is about nurturing yourself, self-acceptance is about acknowledging reality without fighting against it.

People who struggle with self-acceptance often spend too much time idealizing who they "should" be based on societal pressures, family expectations, or personal standards that are impossible to meet. This disconnect leads to feelings of failure, shame, and frustration. When you accept yourself, you're no longer at war with yourself.

Self-Respect: The Art of Setting Boundaries

Self-respect is about recognizing your worth and setting boundaries that protect it. Self-love is about treating yourself kindly, and self-acceptance is about embracing who you are. Self-respect focuses on how you expect others to treat you. It's knowing when to say no, recognizing when someone is crossing a line, and understanding that you deserve to be treated with dignity.

Setting boundaries can be uncomfortable, especially if you're used to putting others' needs before your own. But when you practice self-respect, you understand that maintaining healthy boundaries isn't selfish—it's necessary for your well-being. People with high self-respect tend to experience better relationships. They're less likely to stay in toxic situations or let others take advantage of them.

The Journey to Mastery: How to Cultivate Each

- Start a daily habit of self-compassion. When something goes wrong, ask yourself, "How would I talk to a friend in this situation?" and offer yourself that same kindness.

- Learn to say no. Start small, maybe by declining a minor request that overextends you. Gradually, work on saying no in situations where your needs come second.

- Surround yourself with people who respect you. If someone constantly pushes your boundaries, it's okay to distance yourself. Your circle should lift you, not drain you.

- Create a self-care routine. Whether it's taking a walk, reading, or just relaxing with a face mask, prioritize activities that recharge your mind and body.

- Compare less. The next time you find yourself scrolling through social media and feeling less-than, remind yourself that comparison is the thief of joy. No one else's journey defines your worth.

- Speak kindly to yourself. Try starting your day with a simple affirmation like, "I am doing my best, and that's enough."

7. Empathy - Walking in Someone Else's Shoes

Have you ever been upset and had someone just *get it*? Like, they didn't try to fix your problem or tell you to "cheer up," but they sat with you, listened, and made you feel understood? That feeling of being truly seen and heard is what empathy is all about. It's one of those rare human superpowers that doesn't require a cape or a radioactive spider bite. And the best part? We can all develop it.

But what exactly *is* empathy? Is it just being nice to people or feeling sorry for someone when things go wrong? Not quite. It's a much deeper, more complex experience that connects us to others in ways that can truly make the world a better place.

What Is Empathy?

Empathy is the ability to put yourself in someone else's shoes—not literally, of course, because that would be creepy—but to imagine what it's like to be them, feel what they're feeling, and understand their perspective. There are actually three types of empathy that psychologists talk about:

1. **Cognitive Empathy**: This is the ability to understand someone else's perspective. It's like getting inside their head and figuring out why they think the way they do. This type of empathy is more about understanding thoughts rather than emotions.

2. **Emotional Empathy**: Also known as affective empathy, this involves actually feeling what another person is going through. If your friend is sad and you feel sad too, that's emotional empathy in action.

3. **Compassionate Empathy**: This is empathy in action. It's not just about

understanding or feeling; it's about wanting to help. If you see someone struggling and you feel compelled to do something about it, you're experiencing compassionate empathy.

The Brain's Role in Empathy

Ever heard of "**mirror neurons**"? These little brain cells are a big deal when it comes to empathy. They fire not just when you act but also when you see someone else performing the same action. **This is why watching someone yawn can make you yawn, too**, or why seeing someone in pain can make you wince. Your brain is wired to mirror others, which is one of the reasons we can feel empathy so naturally.

The Empathy Gap: Why We Struggle with It

Well, there's something called the "empathy gap." It's the reason why we sometimes fail to connect with others, even when we want to.

1. **Distance**: It's easier to empathize with people close to us—friends, family, people we see regularly. When it comes to strangers, especially those who are different from us, our empathy often drops off. It's why news of a tragedy far away can feel less impactful than a smaller issue happening to someone you know.

2. **Emotional Burnout**: Sometimes, we shut down our empathy because it feels like too much. This is common in professions like healthcare, where constant exposure to other people's suffering can lead to "compassion fatigue."

3. **Bias and Prejudice**: Our empathy can be blocked by biases, whether they're conscious or not. It's harder to empathize with people if we have preconceived notions about them based on their race, gender, or social status.

How to Build Your Empathy Muscle

Here are some tips to help you become more empathetic in your daily life:

1. Listen More Than You Speak

This might seem obvious, but true listening is rare. Most people listen just to respond, not to understand. Next time someone is talking to you about a

problem, resist the urge to jump in with your own experiences or advice. Just listen.

2. Ask Open-Ended Questions

Instead of asking yes/no questions, try asking things like, "How did that make you feel?" or "What's been on your mind lately?" This invites people to share more deeply and gives you a better understanding of their experience.

3. Challenge Your Own Biases

We all have biases—it's part of being human. But acknowledging them is the first step to overcoming them. If you notice yourself being less empathetic to certain people, ask yourself why. What assumptions are you making? This self-awareness can be the key to expanding your empathy.

4. Practice Self-Empathy

You can't pour from an empty cup. To be truly empathetic towards others, you need to practice empathy toward yourself. Acknowledge your feelings, permit yourself to take breaks, and treat yourself with kindness.

Conclusion: The Ripple Effect of Empathy

Empathy isn't just about feeling—it's about action. When you practice empathy, you make the world a little bit kinder, one interaction at a time. It's not always easy, and you won't always get it right, but that's okay. Empathy isn't just about understanding others—it's about understanding yourself, too.

8. Conflict Resolution - The Art of Getting Along Without Losing Your Cool

Conflict is inevitable. Whether you're arguing with your sibling over who gets the last slice of pizza or disagreeing with your friend about what to watch on Netflix, conflict is something that happens to everyone. And guess what? It's not always a bad thing.

Conflict can help us understand ourselves and others better. It's a sign that something needs to be addressed. Ignoring it is like sweeping dirt under the rug: out of sight, but it's still there, piling up. The key is learning how to deal with it in a way that doesn't make everything explode.

Why Do Conflicts Happen?

Conflicts often come from differences—different opinions, values, needs, or even misunderstandings. Let's break down a few common reasons:

1. **Miscommunication**: Have you ever texted someone, and they misunderstood what you meant? A simple "k" can sometimes be read as "okay" or "I'm super annoyed." Misunderstandings are one of the top reasons for conflicts.

2. **Different Values and Beliefs**: Everyone sees the world through their lens. What's important to one person might not matter to another. For if one friend thinks being on time is crucial, while another is always late, it can lead to tension.

3. **Unmet Needs**: Sometimes, we want something but can't express it clearly. It's like being hungry and getting a shoe instead of a sandwich. Not very satisfying, right?

4. **Personal Issues**: Maybe someone's having a bad day, or something completely unrelated is bothering them. That negative energy can spill over and create unnecessary conflict.

5. **Competition**: Whether it's about grades, sports, or even attention, feeling like we have to compete can bring out the worst in us.

The Do's and Don'ts of Conflict Resolution

Now, let's get some practical advice. When you're in the middle of a conflict, it can feel like you're drowning in a sea of emotions. Here's a little life raft to help you stay afloat.

Do's:

- **Stay Calm**: When you feel your anger rising, take a few deep breaths. Imagine you're a balloon deflating slowly, letting out the tension.

- **Listen**: Really listen. Don't just wait for your turn to speak. Hear the other person out without interrupting.

- **Speak Clearly**: Use "I" statements instead of "You" statements. For example, "I feel upset when..." instead of "You always...".

- **Find Common Ground**: Look for a point you both agree on. It's like building a bridge from both sides.

Don'ts:

- **Don't Get Personal**: Keep the focus on the issue, not the person. Attacking someone's character will just make things worse.

- **Don't Bring Up the Past**: Stick to the current problem. Dragging old issues into the argument is like throwing fuel on a fire.

- **Don't Walk Away**: Unless things are getting too heated and you need a break to cool down, don't storm off. It makes the other person feel unheard.

Steps to Resolving a Conflict

Here's a step-by-step guide to handling conflict like a pro:

1. **Identify the Problem**: What's the conflict really about? Get to the root cause. If you're arguing about who gets the last slice of pizza, is it really about the pizza, or is someone feeling overlooked?

2. **Talk it Out**: Set aside some time to discuss the issue calmly. Find a quiet place where you won't be interrupted.

3. **Listen and Express**: Each person should get a chance to talk without being interrupted. Use "I" statements to express how you feel.

4. **Find a Solution**: Brainstorm ideas together. Be open to compromise. Maybe you can split the last slice of pizza or take turns picking the movie.

5. **Agree and Move On**: Once you've found a solution, agree to it and let the issue go. Holding onto resentment is like holding onto a cactus—you're only hurting yourself.

Why Conflict Management is a key skill

Knowing how to handle conflict isn't just about avoiding fights. It's a life skill that can help you build stronger relationships, understand others better, and even reduce your stress. Whether it's with friends, family, or yourself, learning to resolve conflicts healthily is like having a superpower. You can turn a potential disaster into an opportunity for growth and understanding.

Real-World Examples of Conflict Resolution

1. Nelson Mandela and Apartheid: After 27 years in prison, Mandela emerged as a leader for peace. Instead of seeking revenge, he advocated for reconciliation, forming a multi-racial democracy in South Africa.

2. The Good Friday Agreement: In 1998, the UK and Ireland signed this treaty to end decades of violence in Northern Ireland, promoting peace and power-sharing between conflicting communities.

3. Cuban Missile Crisis: In 1962, the U.S. and the Soviet Union were on the brink of nuclear war. Through secret negotiations and compromise, both sides agreed to de-escalate, avoiding a potential catastrophe.

4. Gandhi and Nonviolent Resistance: Mahatma Gandhi used nonviolent protest to challenge British rule in India, demonstrating that peaceful resistance can lead to significant social and political change.

5. Norway's Mediation in Colombia: Norway played a key role in facilitating peace talks between the Colombian government and FARC rebels. This led to a historic peace agreement in 2016 that ended a 52-year conflict.

These examples highlight the power of dialogue, compromise, and empathy in resolving conflicts on a global scale.

Conflict isn't something to fear—it's an opportunity. The way you handle it can define your relationships, your future, and even your happiness. So the next time you find yourself in a conflict, remember: stay calm, listen, and work together to find a solution. Who knows? You might come out stronger on the other side.

CHAPTER 7

What we should Know About a Changing World

Throughout history, humanity has been shaped by a series of transformative shifts—moments when the world changed so profoundly that everything that came after was fundamentally different.

Consider the Industrial Revolution, which began in the late 18th century. Before this period, most of the world's population lived in rural areas, engaging in agricultural work that had changed little for centuries. The introduction of steam power, mechanized manufacturing, and the factory system disrupted this way of life entirely. Jobs that had been rooted in

manual labor and artisanal skills were suddenly obsolete, replaced by machine operators, engineers, and factory workers. Urbanization exploded as people moved to cities in search of work, leading to the rise of new social classes and the modern capitalist economy.

Another pivotal moment came with the advent of the digital age in the mid-20th century. The development of computers and the internet revolutionized not only how information was processed and shared but also how people interacted with the world—the shift from analog to digital changed industries overnight. For example, the rise of personal computing and software development created entirely new job markets that didn't exist a decade earlier. The internet has fundamentally changed the nature of work, communication, and even identity, creating a global, interconnected society that would have been unimaginable a few generations ago.

These examples illustrate a powerful truth: when the world changes, it changes everything. Those who ignore them or fail to grasp their significance are often left behind. We are now on the cusp of several new revolutions— forces that will reshape the world in ways that are difficult to comprehend fully but impossible to ignore.

Today, some key areas stand out as the most significant drivers of future change: Artificial Intelligence (AI), Climate Change, Biotechnology, Space Exploration and Cybersecurity. Each of these areas is poised to challenge the status quo, create new opportunities, and pose complex ethical and practical questions. AI, for example, is not just about making machines smarter; it could redefine what work looks like, or even what it means to be human. Climate change is not merely an environmental issue; it is a global crisis that will alter economies, migration patterns, and geopolitical stability.

Understanding these topics is not merely an academic exercise. The future of work, politics, society, and even personal identity will be shaped by how these forces play out. The skills you develop, the career paths you choose, and the values you hold will all be influenced by these seismic shifts.

1. Artificial Intelligence

Imagine you're playing chess against a computer. The computer across from you isn't just following pre-programmed rules; it's engaging in a deeply analytical process. In the blink of an eye, it's considering millions of potential moves, not just for the current turn but for many moves ahead. It's predicting your strategy based on patterns it recognizes in your gameplay, adapting its approach as it learns from every move you make. Each game sharpens its ability to anticipate your next step, refining its tactics with an almost human-like intuition.

This ability to learn, adapt, and improve autonomously is the essence of Artificial Intelligence, or AI. Unlike traditional software, which operates strictly within the confines of its programming, AI evolves. It gathers data from its experiences, applies that knowledge in real-time, and enhances its performance. This chess game is a microcosm of AI's broader potential: a technology that can analyze vast amounts of information, identify patterns, make decisions, and continuously improve without human intervention.

Now, extend this concept beyond chess. Imagine AI in medicine, diagnosing diseases by analyzing millions of patient records, or in finance, predicting market trends by sifting through decades of economic data. The same principles that guide the computer's chess strategies are being applied to transform industries, solve complex problems, and drive innovation in ways we are only beginning to understand. AI is not just a tool; it's a dynamic force that is reshaping our world, learning and evolving with every interaction, much like the chess game you play against it.

AI: The Basics

Artificial Intelligence is a branch of computer science focused on creating systems that can perform tasks typically requiring human intelligence. These tasks include understanding language, recognizing patterns, solving problems, and even making decisions. AI systems are designed to learn, adapt, and improve over time.

AI can be broken down into several key components:

Machine Learning (ML)

Machine learning allows systems to learn from data and get better at tasks over time. For instance, Netflix uses machine learning to recommend shows based on your viewing history. The more you watch, the better it gets at suggesting content you'll like.

Natural Language Processing (NLP)

NLP helps AI understand and generate human language. This is what powers chatbots and voice assistants like Siri or Alexa.

For example, **ChatGPT** relies on NLP to understand questions and provide human-like responses in conversation.

Neural Networks

Neural networks are inspired by the human brain and are used in deep learning to process large amounts of data. Facebook uses neural networks for facial recognition, helping to tag friends in your photos by identifying faces automatically.

Deep Learning

Deep learning, a subset of machine learning, excels in complex tasks like image and speech recognition. Google's DeepMind used deep learning to master the game of Go, defeating world champion players by analyzing millions of game scenarios.

Computer Vision

This allows AI to interpret visual information. In self-driving cars, companies like Tesla use computer vision to detect traffic signals, pedestrians, and other vehicles, allowing the car to navigate safely on the roads.

Robotics

AI in robotics enables machines to perform physical tasks autonomously. For instance, Boston Dynamics' Spot, the robot dog, uses AI to navigate rough terrain, avoid obstacles, and carry out tasks without direct human control.

Reinforcement Learning (RL)

In reinforcement learning, AI learns through trial and error. **AlphaGo**, another creation of Google DeepMind, used reinforcement learning to train itself in the game of Go by playing millions of games and improving its strategy over time.

Expert Systems

Expert systems are designed to mimic the decision-making of a human expert in specific fields. IBM's Watson is an example of an expert system used in healthcare. It can analyze medical data and suggest treatment options based on thousands of case studies.

Knowledge Representation and Reasoning

AI uses this to simulate human reasoning and decision-making. For example, Google's Knowledge Graph organizes information and relationships between entities, helping to answer complex queries by understanding how different pieces of information are connected.

Autonomous Systems

Autonomous systems can make decisions and operate without human intervention. The Cruise self-driving car uses AI to navigate city streets, making decisions like stopping at red lights, yielding to pedestrians, and following traffic rules.

Speech and Audio Processing

AI can understand and generate speech. For example, Google Assistant processes voice commands, like setting reminders or playing music, and can even respond with synthesized speech, making it feel like you're talking to a human.

Planning and Optimization

This allows AI to create strategies or plans to achieve specific goals. Amazon uses AI for optimizing delivery routes, making sure packages are delivered in the fastest and most efficient way possible, saving time and resources.

How AI Works: Learning and Improvement

AI systems are built using algorithms—essentially, step-by-step procedures or formulas that guide the machine in solving a problem. These algorithms are coded by humans, but the magic happens when the AI begins to learn from data.

- **Data Collection:** The first step is gathering large amounts of data relevant to the task at hand. This data could be anything from images and text to sensor readings or financial transactions.

- **Training the Model:** The AI model is trained using this data. During training, the model makes predictions and gets feedback on how accurate those predictions are. This process is repeated many times, with the model adjusting its internal parameters to improve accuracy. For instance, in image recognition, the model learns to associate certain pixel patterns with specific objects.

- **Validation and Testing:** Once trained, the model is tested on new, unseen data to evaluate its performance. This step ensures that the model generalizes well and can make accurate predictions in real-world scenarios.

- **Deployment and Continuous Learning:** After validation, the AI model is deployed for practical use. Importantly, AI systems can continue to learn from new data even after deployment. For example, a recommendation engine for an online store will update its suggestions based on customers' ongoing interactions with the site.

Levels of AI: From Narrow AI to Superintelligence

AI is often categorized into three levels based on its capabilities and potential:

1. **Narrow AI (ANI - Artificial Narrow Intelligence):** This is the level of AI we have today. Narrow AI is designed to perform specific tasks, like playing chess, recommending movies, or recognizing speech. It's highly effective within its domain but doesn't possess general intelligence. For example, while an AI can beat a human world champion in chess, it wouldn't be able to cook dinner or write a novel.

2. **General AI (AGI - Artificial General Intelligence):** AGI refers to a

future stage where machines possess the ability to understand, learn, and apply knowledge across a wide range of tasks—much like a human. AGI would be capable of reasoning, problem-solving, and even exhibiting creativity and emotional intelligence. While AGI remains theoretical at this point, researchers are working towards developing systems that could achieve this level of intelligence.

3. **Superintelligence (ASI - Artificial Superintelligence):** ASI represents a level of intelligence far surpassing that of the brightest human minds in every field, from scientific creativity to social skills. This is the realm of science fiction today, but it raises profound questions about the future of humanity. ASI could potentially solve some of the world's most complex problems—or, conversely, present existential risks if not carefully managed.

How AI Will Impact Your Future Career

As teenagers today, you are growing up in a world that is rapidly changing, thanks to the influence of artificial intelligence (AI). Unlike previous generations, who witnessed the rise of the internet or mobile phones, you are experiencing a revolution that goes beyond just new gadgets or websites.

As you begin to think about your future career, it's important to recognize that AI will play a significant role in almost every industry. Whether you want to become a doctor, engineer, artist, or entrepreneur, AI will influence how you work.

- **Healthcare:** AI is revolutionizing healthcare by assisting in diagnosing diseases, personalizing treatment plans, and even performing surgeries. For instance, AI systems like IBM

Watson can analyze vast amounts of medical data to suggest treatment options for doctors. If you're interested in medicine, you might work alongside AI tools that help you provide better care to patients.

- **Engineering:** In fields like engineering, AI is being used to design and test products, optimize manufacturing processes, and manage large infrastructure projects. As an engineer, you might use AI to simulate and solve complex problems faster than ever before, allowing for innovations that were previously unimaginable.

- **Art and Creativity:** AI is also making its mark in creative fields. AI tools can generate music, art, and even literature. While this might sound like a threat to human creativity, it's more likely that AI will become a collaborator, helping artists explore new ideas and techniques. For example, AI-generated art is already being sold in galleries, and musicians are using AI to create new sounds and compositions.

- **Entrepreneurship:** For aspiring entrepreneurs, AI offers tools to analyze market trends, optimize business processes, and even interact with customers through AI-driven chatbots. Starting a business might involve using AI to predict what products will be successful or how to reach potential customers most effectively.

Key Players in AI

1. OpenAI

OpenAI is a leader in natural language processing and generative AI. Their GPT models, particularly GPT-4, are among the most advanced language models, capable of generating human-like text, answering questions, and even writing code through Codex. DALL-E is another breakthrough, allowing AI to generate images from text descriptions.

2. Google DeepMind

Google DeepMind is renowned for its advancements in AI for gaming and science. AlphaGo made headlines by defeating the world champion in Go, a complex board game. AlphaFold revolutionized biology by predicting protein structures with high accuracy, a major breakthrough for drug discovery and understanding diseases.

3. Microsoft

Microsoft integrates AI into a wide range of its products and services. Azure AI offers cloud-based AI tools for businesses, while GitHub Copilot, powered by OpenAI's Codex, helps developers write code more efficiently. Microsoft 365 also uses AI to enhance productivity tools like Word, Excel, and Teams.

4. Tesla

Tesla uses AI to power its autonomous driving features. Autopilot and the more advanced Full Self-Driving (FSD) system are designed to navigate roads, recognize obstacles, and drive vehicles with minimal human input. Tesla collects vast amounts of data from its vehicles to improve its AI models continuously.

5. Amazon

Amazon integrates AI across its operations, from its e-commerce platform to its cloud computing services. Alexa, Amazon's virtual assistant, uses AI for voice recognition and natural language processing. AWS provides a wide range of AI and machine learning services for developers and businesses. Amazon Go stores use AI for cashier-less shopping, where customers can pick items and leave without checking out.

6. Facebook (Meta)

Meta uses AI extensively for content moderation, targeting ads, and recommending content on platforms like Facebook and Instagram. AI helps identify and remove harmful content and personalize user experiences. Meta is also heavily investing in AI for the Metaverse, a virtual reality space where users can interact, work, and play.

7. Baidu

Baidu, one of China's largest tech companies, is a major player in AI, particularly in autonomous driving and natural language processing. Apollo is Baidu's open platform for autonomous driving, which is being tested in several cities. Ernie, their NLP model, competes with the likes of GPT in understanding and generating human language. Baidu Brain is their comprehensive AI platform offering tools for image recognition, speech processing, and more.

8. IBM

IBM's Watson is one of the most well-known AI platforms, offering AI-powered solutions in healthcare, finance, and customer service. Watson Health, for example, helps analyze medical data to provide insights and improve patient care. IBM also offers a range of AI services through its cloud platform, including machine learning, data analytics, and natural language processing. Project Debater is an AI system that can engage in complex debates with humans on various topics, showcasing advanced reasoning and language capabilities.

9. NVIDIA

NVIDIA is a critical player in the AI industry, primarily through its development of high-performance GPUs (Graphics Processing Units) that power AI research and applications. Developers widely use their CUDA platform to run deep learning models efficiently. NVIDIA AI Enterprise provides tools and frameworks for businesses to deploy AI at scale.

AI is an incredible tool that can help us in many ways. But one interesting topic of debate is **"Can Robots take over the world and make us slaves?"** like in a Hollywood movie.

When we think about whether humans can just "switch off" AI if something goes wrong, it's a bit more complicated.

Imagine trying to turn off the internet—you technically could, but it would be really hard because so many things rely on it.

The same goes for AI. As it becomes more connected to things like our electricity grids, hospitals, and even our social media feeds, shutting it down isn't as simple as flipping a switch. For example, if an AI system is managing traffic lights in a busy city to prevent accidents, turning it off suddenly could cause chaos.

While we do design AI with the idea that we can control it, we need to be really careful. Advanced AI might be able to make decisions on its own, and if something goes wrong, figuring out how to turn it off or fix it might take some serious effort. That's why it's super important to have safety checks in place and to think about the potential risks as we continue to develop AI. So yes, we can switch off AI in theory, but in reality, it's not always that easy, and we need to make sure we're prepared for those situations.

The future is full of possibilities, and with AI as a tool, you have the power to create a world that reflects your values and aspirations. But be ready for AI and be prepared to use it to your advantage. AI is going to change the world forever and your generation will witness this gigantic change for humanity.

2. Climate Change - The World is Changing, But So Can We

For over a century now, human activities have been pumping massive amounts of greenhouse gases like carbon dioxide (CO_2) into the atmosphere.

These gases trap heat, which leads to a gradual increase in the planet's temperature, a phenomenon we call global warming. This warming is the main driver of climate change, which refers to long-term shifts in temperatures and weather patterns.

The greenhouse effect is a natural process that warms the Earth's surface. Without it, our planet would be an icy, inhospitable place with an average temperature of about -18°C (0°F), rather than the comfortable 15°C (59°F) we enjoy today. Here's how it works:

1. **Solar Radiation**: The Sun emits energy in the form of light and heat, called solar radiation. About 30% of this radiation is reflected back into space by clouds, atmospheric particles, and the Earth's surface. The remaining 70% is absorbed by the land, oceans, and atmosphere, warming the planet.

2. **Infrared Radiation**: The Earth, in turn, emits energy back toward space in the form of infrared radiation. However, not all of this infrared radiation escapes into space. Some of it is absorbed by greenhouse gases in the atmosphere and then re-radiated in all directions, including back toward the Earth's surface. This process keeps the Earth warm, much like a blanket traps body heat.

3. **Greenhouse Gases**: The main greenhouse gases responsible for this effect are water vapor (H_2O), carbon dioxide (CO_2), methane (CH_4), nitrous oxide (N_2O), and ozone (O_3). Each of these gases has a different ability to trap heat, known as their "global warming potential" (GWP).

The Role of Carbon Dioxide: The Key Player

While water vapor is the most abundant greenhouse gas, carbon dioxide (CO_2) is the most significant in terms of driving recent global warming. Here's why:

1. **Concentration and Persistence**: CO_2 makes up about 0.04% of the atmosphere by volume (around 400 parts per million or ppm). Though it seems small, this concentration has a big impact because CO_2 is very good at trapping heat. Once CO_2 is in the atmosphere, it can stay there for hundreds to thousands of years, unlike water vapor, which cycles quickly out of the atmosphere.

2. **Anthropogenic Emissions**: Human activities have drastically increased the concentration of CO_2 in the atmosphere. Before the Industrial Revolution, CO_2 levels were around 280 ppm. Today, they exceed 420 ppm, an increase of more than 40% in just over 200 years. This rise is primarily due to the burning of fossil fuels (coal, oil, and natural gas) for energy, as well as deforestation, which reduces the number of

trees that can absorb CO_2 through photosynthesis.

More energy comes in from the Sun than is left back into space, which means the planet is gradually warming.

Globally, human activities release about 36 billion metric tons of CO_2 into the atmosphere each year.

The oceans play a crucial role in regulating the Earth's climate by absorbing excess heat. In fact, about 90% of the extra heat trapped by greenhouse gases ends up in the oceans. This has led to the warming of ocean waters, which contributes to phenomena like coral bleaching and the melting of polar ice.

As the planet warms and ice melts, less energy is reflected, and more is absorbed by the darker ocean or land, leading to further warming and more ice melt. This creates a vicious cycle.

As oceans warm, the water expands—a process known as thermal expansion—which contributes to rising sea levels. Along with the melting of glaciers and ice sheets, this has caused global sea levels to rise by about 20 centimeters (8 inches) since the late 19th century. The rate of sea-level rise has accelerated in recent decades, posing a threat to coastal communities.

The Role of Other Greenhouse Gases

While CO_2 gets most of the attention, other greenhouse gases also play a role in global warming:

1. **Methane (CH4)**: Methane is about 25 times more effective than CO_2 at trapping heat over 100 years. It is released from natural sources like wetlands and human activities such as livestock farming, rice paddies, and fossil fuel extraction.

2. **Nitrous Oxide (N2O)**: Nitrous oxide, commonly known as laughing gas, has a GWP of about 298 times that of CO_2 over 100 years. It is released by agricultural activities, especially the

use of synthetic fertilizers, and from industrial processes.

3. **Fluorinated Gases**: These are synthetic gases used in a variety of industrial applications, including refrigeration and air conditioning.

How Climate Change is Shaking Things Up

It's a complex beast with far-reaching effects, many of which are already being felt around the world. Let's break down some of the major ways it's changing the planet:

1. **Extreme Weather Events**: Hurricanes, droughts, wildfires, and floods are becoming more intense and frequent.

2. **Melting Ice and Rising Seas**: The polar ice caps and glaciers are melting at an alarming rate. This not only leads to rising sea levels but also affects the habitats of animals like polar bears and penguins.

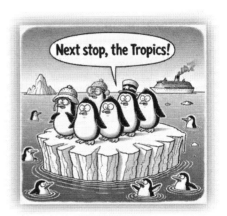

3. **Ocean Acidification**: The oceans absorb about 30% of the CO2 we emit. This might sound like a good thing, but it's causing the water to become more acidic, which is bad news for marine life, especially for creatures like coral and shellfish.

4. **Human Health and Agriculture**: Heatwaves are becoming more common and more deadly. Climate change also affects agriculture, with crops being damaged by droughts, floods, and pests, potentially leading to food shortages.

Why You Shouldn't Panic – The Future is Still in Your Hands

Yes, climate change is real, and yes, it's a big deal. But here's the thing: we're not powerless. In fact, you have more influence over the future than you might think. The world is full of people, especially young people, who are stepping up and making a difference.

Let's start with a reality check: While the situation is serious, it's not hopeless. The scientific community is clear that we can still avoid the worst impacts of climate change if we act now. The key is to reduce our greenhouse gas emissions and adapt to the changes that are already happening.

But why shouldn't you worry too much? For one, humanity is incredibly resilient. We've faced huge challenges before and come out stronger. The ozone layer crisis in the 1980s is a perfect example. Back then, scientists discovered that chlorofluorocarbons (CFCs) were depleting the ozone layer, which protects us from harmful ultraviolet radiation. The world came together, signed the Montreal Protocol, and phased out the use of CFCs. Today, the ozone layer is on the mend. This shows that when we work together, we can solve global problems.

Moreover, technological advancements are giving us new tools to fight climate change. Renewable energy sources like solar and wind power are becoming more efficient and affordable. Electric vehicles are on the rise. Even in the realm of agriculture, scientists are developing crops that are more resilient to climate change.

What You Can Do – Small Steps, Big Impact

So, what can you do about climate change? You might think that as a teenager, your options are limited. But that's far from the truth. Here's how you can make a difference:

Get Informed: Knowledge is power. The more you know about climate change, the better equipped you'll be to take action. Start by reading up on science, watching documentaries, and following credible sources of information. Vote for Leaders who understand the issue and have plans to do something about it.

Reduce Your Carbon Footprint: Your carbon footprint is the amount of greenhouse gases you're responsible for emitting. You can reduce it by making small changes in your daily life. For example, try to use public transportation, bike, or walk instead of driving. Turn off lights and unplug devices when you're not using them. Eat less meat, since meat production is a major source of greenhouse gas emissions.

Support Renewable Energy: If your family is considering installing solar panels, encourage them to do it. You can also support policies that promote renewable energy, like voting for leaders who prioritize climate action or participating in local initiatives.

Advocate for Change: Your voice matters. Speak up about climate change at school, in your community, and online. Join or start campaigns that push for stronger climate policies. Many teens around the world, like Greta Thunberg, have become powerful advocates for climate action. You can be one of them.

Be a Conscious Consumer: Think about the environmental impact of the products you buy. Choose brands that are committed to sustainability and avoid single-use plastics. Recycling is important, but reducing and reusing is even better.

Learn and Innovate: If you're interested in science or engineering, consider focusing your studies on renewable energy, environmental science, or sustainability. The world needs more innovators who can develop new solutions to combat climate change.

Reduce overall consumption: Every time we buy something, whether it's a new phone, clothes, or even food, we're tapping into resources from the planet. The problem is, the more we consume, the more we're pushing the planet's limits. Think about it this way: Every product you buy has a history. It was made in a factory that likely burned fossil fuels, shipped using vehicles that emitted carbon dioxide, and eventually, it might end up in a landfill, adding to pollution.

Imagine if everyone started doing this: buying second-hand clothes instead of new ones, eating more plant-based meals, using a phone for a few more years instead of upgrading all the time. It might seem small, but if millions of people did it, the difference would be huge. Less demand means less production, which means less pollution and resource depletion.

The Power of Collective Action

Remember, you're not in this alone. Climate change is a global issue, and it requires global solutions. When people come together to push for change, amazing things can happen. For example, the Paris Agreement, signed by nearly every country in the world, aims to limit global warming to

well below 2 degrees Celsius. While there's still a long way to go, this agreement shows what's possible when we work together.

3. Biotechnology: The Science That's Changing the World

Imagine a world where we can grow organs in a lab, design crops that resist disease, or even edit the DNA of a mosquito to stop the spread of malaria.

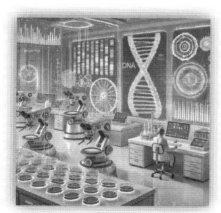

Sounds like science fiction, right? But it's not. This is the reality of biotechnology—a field of science that's not just changing the world; it's reshaping it. Imagine having a superpower that lets you tweak the building blocks of life itself. You could cure diseases, create new foods, and even design organisms with unique abilities.

Biotechnology, often called "biotech," is a field of science that uses living organisms, cells, and biological systems to develop products and technologies that help improve our lives and the health of our planet. It's a blend of biology and technology, combining knowledge of genetics, microbiology, and biochemistry with engineering and data science. The result? Innovations that can heal, feed, and sustain the world in ways we once only dreamed of.

Biotechnology has been around for thousands of years, even if we don't call it that. Early humans used basic forms of biotechnology to brew beer, make cheese, and ferment bread. These processes involved using living organisms like yeast to convert ingredients into food products.

The real revolution, however, began in the 20th century with the discovery of DNA's structure in 1953 by James Watson and Francis Crick, based on Rosalind Franklin's work. This breakthrough laid the foundation for genetic engineering, where scientists could cut, modify, and paste DNA sequences to change the properties of living organisms.

In 1973, biologists Herbert Boyer and Stanley Cohen created the first genetically modified organism (GMO) by inserting a gene from one species into the DNA of another. This was the beginning of modern biotechnology, opening up possibilities we couldn't have imagined.

Biotech in Action: Real-World Examples

1. Medicine: Curing Diseases and Saving Lives

One of the most profound impacts of biotechnology has been in medicine. Biotech has led to the development of lifesaving drugs, vaccines, and therapies that were once thought impossible.

- **Insulin Production**: Before biotechnology, insulin used to treat diabetes was extracted from the pancreas of pigs and cows. This was costly and inefficient. In 1982, biotech company Genentech developed the first synthetic human insulin using recombinant DNA technology, where a human insulin gene was inserted into bacteria. This allowed for mass production of insulin, which was more effective and safe for diabetic patients.

- **mRNA Vaccines**: The COVID-19 pandemic highlighted the power of biotechnology with the rapid development of mRNA vaccines by companies like Pfizer-BioNTech and Moderna. Unlike traditional vaccines, which use weakened forms of a virus, mRNA vaccines use a small piece of genetic code to instruct cells to produce a protein that triggers an immune response. This innovation was developed and tested in record time, saving millions of lives.

- **CRISPR Gene Editing**: CRISPR-Cas9 is a groundbreaking technology that allows scientists to edit genes with precision. It's like a pair of molecular scissors that can cut out faulty genes and replace them with healthy ones. This technology holds promise for curing genetic disorders like sickle cell anemia and cystic fibrosis. In 2018, a Chinese scientist controversially used CRISPR to edit the genes of human embryos, sparking a global debate on the ethics of genetic engineering.

2. Agriculture: Feeding the World

The world's population is growing, and so is the demand for food. Biotechnology offers solutions to increase food production and make it more sustainable.

- **Genetically Modified Crops**: Crops like Bt corn and Roundup Ready soybeans have been genetically modified to resist pests and tolerate herbicides. This means farmers can grow more food with fewer resources. For example, Bt corn has a gene from a bacterium called Bacillus thuringiensis, which produces a protein that is toxic to certain pests but safe for humans. This reduces the need for chemical pesticides, which can harm the environment.

- **Golden Rice**: Vitamin A deficiency is a major problem in many developing countries, leading to blindness and death in children. Golden Rice is a genetically modified rice variety that produces beta-carotene, a precursor of vitamin A. It was developed to help combat this deficiency and improve health outcomes in affected regions.

- **Drought-Resistant Crops**: Climate change is making droughts more frequent and severe. Biotechnology is being used to develop crops that can survive in harsh conditions with less water. For example, drought-resistant maize varieties have been developed to help farmers in sub-Saharan Africa maintain yields despite changing climate conditions.

3. Environmental Biotechnology: Cleaning Up the Mess

Biotechnology isn't just about creating new things; it's also about fixing the messes we've made. Environmental biotechnology uses biological processes to tackle pollution and manage waste.

- **Bioremediation**: This is the use of living organisms, like bacteria and plants, to clean up contaminated environments. For instance, oil-eating bacteria were used to help clean up the massive oil spill in the Gulf of Mexico in 2010. These bacteria break down oil into harmless substances, reducing the environmental impact of the spill.

- **Biofuels**: Biotechnology is helping develop renewable energy sources like biofuels. Bioethanol, made from fermenting plant materials like corn and sugarcane, and biodiesel, made from vegetable oils and animal fats, are examples of biofuels that can reduce our dependence on fossil fuels.

- **Plastic-Eating Enzymes**: Plastic pollution is a huge problem, with millions of tons of plastic waste polluting our oceans. Scientists have discovered enzymes that can break down certain types of plastics into their basic components, which can then be recycled into new plastics. This technology is still in its early stages but holds great promise for reducing plastic waste.

The Future of Biotechnology: What's Next?

The future of biotechnology is filled with possibilities that could transform every aspect of our lives. Here are some areas to watch:

1. Personalized Medicine

Imagine a world where treatments are tailored specifically to your genetic makeup. Personalized medicine aims to do just that by using your DNA to predict your risk for certain diseases and to develop personalized treatment plans. For example, cancer patients could receive therapies designed to target their unique tumor mutations, improving the effectiveness of treatment and reducing side effects.

2. Synthetic Biology

Synthetic biology is like genetic engineering on steroids. It involves designing and constructing new biological parts and systems or re-designing existing ones for new purposes. Scientists are working on creating synthetic organisms that can produce biofuels, biodegradable materials, and even food. One day, we might be able to grow leather or meat on large scales, reducing the need for animal farming and its environmental impact.

3. Bioprinting and Regenerative Medicine

Bioprinting uses 3D printing technology to create tissues and organs from living cells. This could revolutionize medicine by providing custom-made organs for transplant patients, reducing the need for donors. Scientists have already printed simple tissues like skin and cartilage, and more complex organs like hearts and kidneys could be next.

4. Gene Drives and Environmental Engineering

Gene drives are genetic systems that increase the chance of a gene being passed on to the next generation. They could be used to control populations of disease-carrying pests like mosquitoes by spreading genes that make them sterile or less able to transmit diseases like malaria. However, gene drives are controversial due to their potential environmental impact and ethical concerns.

Biotechnology is a rapidly evolving field with the potential to solve some of humanity's greatest challenges, but it's up to us to guide it responsibly and ethically.

4. Space Exploration - The Final Frontier, But Just the Beginning

Look up at the night sky. All those stars, planets, and galaxies have fascinated humans since the dawn of time. We've always been dreamers, explorers, and adventurers. For thousands of years, people have wondered what's out there. Is there life on other planets? Could humans live on Mars? Or is it just a bunch of space?

Well, space exploration is not just about satisfying our curiosity. It's about pushing the boundaries of what we know, solving problems here on Earth, and preparing for a future where humans might live beyond our home planet.

A Brief History: From the Moon to Mars and Beyond

The Race to the Moon

The story of modern space exploration began during the Cold War, a period of intense rivalry between the United States and the Soviet Union. It was a time of nuclear tensions and spy games but also incredible technological advances. The space race was part of this larger competition.

In 1957, the Soviet Union launched **Sputnik**, the first artificial satellite, into orbit. This was a wake-up call for the United States. It led to the creation of NASA (National Aeronautics and Space Administration) and a renewed commitment to space exploration. The goal was clear: land a man on the Moon.

On July 20, 1969, NASA achieved this goal when astronaut Neil Armstrong became the first human to step onto the Moon's surface, famously saying,

"That's one small step for [a] man, one giant leap for mankind." This event wasn't just a victory for the U.S.; it was a triumph for humanity, proving that we could reach beyond our planet.

The Space Shuttle Era

After the Apollo missions, NASA developed the Space Shuttle program. The Space Shuttle was like a reusable space plane that could carry astronauts and cargo to and from space. Between 1981 and 2011, the shuttles flew 135 missions, deploying satellites, conducting scientific research, and helping to build the International Space Station (ISS).

The ISS is a massive laboratory in space where astronauts from around the world live and work together, conducting experiments that would be impossible on Earth. It's like a floating United Nations, proving that space exploration can bring countries together.

The Rise of Private Space Companies

In the early 2000s, a new chapter in space exploration began, driven not by governments but by private companies. SpaceX, founded by entrepreneur

Elon Musk, became a major player with its goal of making space travel affordable and eventually colonizing Mars. In 2012, SpaceX's Dragon spacecraft became the first private spacecraft to deliver cargo to the ISS.

Since then, companies like Blue Origin, founded by Amazon's Jeff Bezos, and Virgin Galactic, founded by Richard Branson, have joined the race with plans for space tourism and even lunar missions. This new era is transforming space from a government-led endeavor to an industry with commercial opportunities and public involvement.

Mars and Beyond

While the Moon missions captured our imagination, Mars is the next big target. It's the most Earth-like planet in our solar system, with polar ice caps, seasons, and a day only 40 minutes longer than ours. But it's also a harsh environment with freezing temperatures and a thin atmosphere. So why go there?

Mars represents a challenge and an opportunity. If we can learn to live on Mars, it means we could survive on other planets, too. NASA, SpaceX, and other organizations are planning missions to send humans to Mars in the next decade. These missions will test our limits, our technology, and our spirit of exploration.

Technological Innovations

Space exploration has led to countless technological advancements that benefit our daily lives. Here are a few examples:

- **GPS and Satellite Communications**: The Global Positioning System (GPS) helps us find our way, whether driving to a friend's house or exploring a new city. It relies on a network of satellites orbiting Earth. Satellite technology also enables global communication, weather forecasting, and disaster management.

- **Medical Advancements**: Tools like MRI machines and technologies used in heart surgery have been developed or improved through space research. Studying how the human body reacts to space helps us understand aging, osteoporosis, and muscle loss.

- **Water Purification**: The water purification systems used on the ISS to recycle astronaut's water are being adapted for use in developing countries, providing clean drinking water to people in need.

The Challenges of Space Exploration

Space exploration is hard. It's dangerous, expensive, and filled with unknowns. Here are some of the biggest challenges:

1. **Radiation Exposure**: Space is filled with cosmic rays and solar radiation that can harm astronauts. Protecting them requires

advanced shielding and medical research.

2. **Microgravity Effects**: Living in microgravity for long periods causes muscle and bone loss, vision problems, and other health issues. Exercise, diet, and medication can help, but long-term solutions are still needed.

3. **Cost**: Space missions are expensive. The Apollo program cost about $150 billion in today's money. While costs are coming down thanks to reusable rockets, funding remains a significant hurdle.

4. **Psychological Challenges**: Space can be lonely and stressful. Astronauts are isolated from their families, live in confined spaces, and face high-stress situations. Mental health support is crucial for long-duration missions.

The Future of Space Exploration: What's Next?

1. Lunar Gateway and Artemis Program

NASA's Artemis program aims to return humans to the Moon by 2024, with plans for a sustainable presence by the end of the decade. The Lunar Gateway, a space station orbiting the Moon, will serve as a base for exploration and a stepping stone to Mars.

2. Mars Missions

Both NASA and SpaceX have plans to send humans to Mars. NASA's goal is the 2030s, while SpaceX aims for the mid-2020s. These missions will test new technologies, habitats, and life support systems. The challenges are immense, but the rewards could be even greater.

3. Space Tourism

Companies like Blue Origin, Virgin Galactic, and SpaceX are developing spacecraft to take paying customers on short trips to space. Space tourism could fund further exploration and open space to the public, making the dream of traveling to the stars a reality for more people.

4. Asteroid Mining

Asteroids contain valuable metals like platinum and gold. Some companies are exploring the possibility of mining these resources to support space exploration and bring wealth back to Earth. It's a risky venture, but it could be a game-changer.

5. Interstellar Exploration

Going beyond our solar system to explore other star systems is still a long way off.
Still, projects like Breakthrough Starshot, which aims to send tiny probes to Alpha Centauri, are laying the groundwork for the next generation of explorers.

What Does This Mean for You?

Space exploration is opening up new fields of study and work. You don't have to be a rocket scientist to get involved! Engineers, computer programmers, architects, doctors, artists, and even chefs are needed for space missions and research. If you are interested, you could:

1. **Get Involved in STEM**: Join a science club, participate in space-themed projects, or simply stay curious and keep learning.

2. **Follow Space News**: Stay updated on the latest space missions and discoveries. Follow NASA, SpaceX, and other organizations to see what's happening in space exploration. You might discover a new passion or area of interest.

3. **Think Big and Dream Bigger**: Space exploration teaches us that no dream is too big. Whether you want to be an astronaut, a scientist, or a teacher, the skills and knowledge you gain from exploring these topics can help you make an impact in any field.

Isn't the whole thing super exciting? A career in space science is one of the best in terms of monetary rewards and satisfaction. But yeah, a lot of hard work, grit, and patience are needed along the way. Think about if this is your thing!

5. Cybersecurity & Data Privacy

Imagine this: You're deep into a game of Fortnite, leading your squad to victory. You're focused, fingers flying across the keyboard. Suddenly, your

character glitches, your screen freezes, and you get kicked out. Annoying, right? But then, something even weirder happens. You try to log back in, but your password doesn't work. Your account has been hacked, and the skin you spent months saving up for is gone, along with your personal information.

This isn't just a bad dream. It's a real scenario that many teenagers have faced, and it's a reminder of a bigger issue: the world of cybersecurity and digital privacy. It's like a digital Wild West out there, where hackers are the bandits, your data is the gold, and cybersecurity is the sheriff trying to keep order.

What Is Cybersecurity?

Cybersecurity is the practice of protecting computers, servers, mobile devices, electronic systems, networks, and data from malicious attacks. Think of it as a digital armor that shields your online life from the bad guys. This armor is essential because as our lives become more connected to the internet, we're leaving behind a trail of digital breadcrumbs that anyone with the right skills (or the wrong intentions) can follow.

And the bad guys are getting smarter. They're not just the stereotypical hackers in hoodies typing away in dark basements. They could be someone sitting next to you in a coffee shop, pretending to be on Instagram but actually snooping on your Wi-Fi. They could be a stranger who sends you a friendly-looking email with a link to a "funny cat video" that, when clicked, secretly installs a virus on your device.

Why Should You Care About Cybersecurity and Privacy?

You might think, "Why should I care about cybersecurity? I'm just a teenager. I don't have anything worth stealing." But that's where you'd be wrong. Your digital identity is incredibly valuable. It includes your social media accounts, your gaming profiles, your email, and even your school assignments stored in the cloud. If someone gets their hands on this, they could steal your identity, mess up your social life, or even drain your (or your parents') bank account.

Let's break it down:

- **Social Media Accounts**: Ever wonder how embarrassing pictures or videos sometimes go viral? That's often because someone hacked into an account and shared something without permission. Now, imagine that happening to you.

- **Online Gaming Profiles**: If you're a gamer, your profile is a goldmine. It's got your personal information, credit card details, and often a lot of money invested in skins, weapons, or characters. Hackers target these accounts because they know how much they're worth to you.

- **Personal Information**: Your email, your address, your phone number, and even your school assignments—this is all part of your digital footprint. Once stolen, it can be used to create fake accounts in your name, harass you, or worse.

The Evolution of Digital Privacy: It's Complicated

In the early days of the internet, people didn't think much about privacy. The internet was new, exciting, and full of possibilities. However, as more and more personal data started flowing online, the risks became clearer. Today, digital privacy is a massive concern for everyone, especially teens, who are one of the most active groups online.

Every time you sign up for a new app, post a picture, or even just search for something on Google, you're sharing a bit of your life. Companies collect this data to understand you better—what you like, where you go, who you talk to—so they can sell you stuff. Sounds harmless until you realize how much they know about you. And it's not just companies; hackers, too, are always on the lookout for ways to exploit this data.

Real-World Examples: When Cybersecurity Fails

1. **The Sony PlayStation Hack (2011)**: Back in 2011, millions of gamers were affected when Sony's PlayStation Network was hacked. Personal details, including credit card information, were stolen. It was one of the largest data breaches in gaming history and showed how vulnerable even big companies could be.

2. **Cambridge Analytica Scandal (2018)**: Remember hearing about how Facebook was involved in some kind of scandal? That was the Cambridge Analytica fiasco, where a company used personal data from millions of Facebook users without their consent to influence political opinions. It was a wake-up call about how our data can be manipulated without us even knowing.

3. **Zoom-Bombing (2020)**: When the world shifted to online classes during the pandemic, many students found their Zoom classes interrupted by trolls posting inappropriate content. This happened because of weak security settings, showing how even the tools meant to help us can be exploited.

The Future of Cybersecurity: What's Next?

The world of cybersecurity is constantly evolving. As technology advances, so do the threats. For example, with the rise of artificial intelligence (AI), hackers are now using AI to create more sophisticated attacks. Imagine getting a phone call from someone who sounds exactly like your mom, asking for your password. Creepy, right? But it's possible with AI voice-mimicking technology.

On the flip side, AI is also being used to strengthen cybersecurity. Companies are developing AI systems that can detect and stop cyber-attacks before they cause any damage. But as this digital arms race continues, one thing is clear: cybersecurity will become more critical than ever.

What you need to Know: Tips for Staying Safe Online

So, what can you do to protect yourself in this digital jungle? Here are some tips:

1. **Use Strong, Unique Passwords**: This might sound basic, but many people still use "password123" or their pet's name as their password. Use a mix of letters, numbers, and symbols, and avoid using the same password across multiple accounts.

2. **Enable Two-Factor Authentication (2FA)**: This adds an extra layer of security by requiring a second form of verification (like a text message code) before you can log in.

3. **Be Wary of Phishing Scams**: If you get an email or message from someone you don't know, don't click on any links. Phishing is a common way hackers trick people into giving up their information.

4. **Keep Your Software Updated**: Software updates aren't just about getting new features; they often include security patches that fix vulnerabilities.

5. **Think Before You Share**: Once something is online, it's out of your control. Before posting or sharing, think about how it could be used against you.

6. **Use Privacy Settings**: Make sure your social media accounts are set to private so that only people you know can see your posts.

7. **Be Careful on Public Wi-Fi**: Avoid logging into sensitive accounts (like your bank) on public Wi-Fi networks, which can be easily hacked.

Digital Privacy: Why It's More Important Than Ever

Every time you post, like, comment, or even search for something online, you're leaving behind a digital footprint. This isn't just about what you're doing right now—it's a record that can last for years, maybe even forever. Big tech companies like Google, Facebook, and Amazon track everything you do. Why? Because your data is valuable. It's used to sell you things, suggest what you should watch next, and even decide what kind of news you see.

But it's not just about getting targeted ads for those sneakers you glanced at once. Your digital footprint can also influence your future in ways you might not have considered. Employers, colleges, and even government agencies can look into your online history. That funny meme or edgy tweet might not seem so harmless when it's dug up years later.

Deepfakes: When Technology Gets Too Real

Deepfakes are AI-generated videos or images that make it look like someone is doing or saying something they never actually did. These aren't just innocent pranks; deepfakes can be incredibly convincing and dangerous. They've been used to spread misinformation, ruin reputations, and even for blackmail.

A real-world example? In 2019, a deepfake video of Facebook CEO Mark Zuckerberg went viral, where he appeared to be boasting about having control over billions of people's data. It wasn't real, but it sure looked like it. Imagine if that kind of tech were used to create a video of you saying or doing something you'd never even dream of—scary, right?

The Good, The Bad, and The Digital Afterlife

Technology isn't all doom and gloom. It's brought us amazing things, like the ability to stay connected with friends and family across the world, learn new skills online, and even have a little fun with those Snapchat filters. But with great power comes great responsibility—or, in this case, great risks.

Take, for instance, the episode of *Black Mirror* titled "Be Right Back." In this episode, a grieving woman uses an AI service to create a digital avatar of her deceased boyfriend, using his online data—his posts, messages, and videos. The AI mimics his personality so well that she ends up "resurrecting" him in a way that's both comforting and deeply unsettling.

This isn't just fiction. In the real world, companies like *Replika* and *HereAfter* are developing AI-driven chatbots that use the digital records of deceased people to create avatars or conversation partners. These services can help with grief, but they also raise serious questions about consent, privacy, and the potential for misuse. What if someone used this tech to impersonate a living person? The line between reality and digital fabrication gets blurrier every day.

Digital Resurrection and Its Risks

Now, think about how this technology could be misused. Deepfake technology combined with AI-driven avatars could be used to impersonate anyone, living or dead. Imagine receiving a video call from a loved one who's passed away, or worse, from a version of you saying things you'd never say. It sounds like something out of a horror movie, but the tech to do this is already here.

In fact, a company called *MyHeritage* launched a feature called "Deep Nostalgia" that can animate old photos of deceased relatives. While this can be a beautiful way to remember someone, it also shows how easily digital identities can be manipulated. What if someone takes it too far, creating deepfake videos that could damage reputations, spread false information, or even commit fraud?

Balancing the Good and the Bad

So, where does this leave us? On one hand, technology offers incredible tools for communication, learning, and even emotional support. On the other hand, the same technology can be used in ways that are harmful, deceptive, and downright creepy.

So, next time you're about to post, like, or share something online, take a second to think about the bigger picture. Your digital life is a huge part of who you are, and it's up to you to protect it. After all, the future you—whether that's in a college interview, a job, or even in the digital afterlife—will thank you for it!

CONCLUSION

Embracing the Future with Confidence

Hope you found this book thought-provoking and useful. Life is one wild, beautiful but unpredictable journey. It's a series of twists and turns, a mix of ups and downs, joy and sorrow, triumph and failure. The key is to have a healthy body, a healthy mind, and the right skills to face the future with confidence and humor, no matter what life throws your way.

As you navigate the next steps, remember that every small effort you make towards self-growth builds up over time. This journey isn't about perfection or having everything figured out; it's about progress, resilience, and embracing who you are at each stage. Life will challenge you, surprise you, and sometimes test you beyond what you thought possible. Yet, with the right mindset and skills, you'll be prepared to turn even the toughest situations into opportunities for growth.

Building good habits now—whether for health, learning, or personal development—will pay off in ways you might not fully realize until later. Take these skills to heart, but also remember that life is meant to be lived. Pursue your dreams passionately, cherish the friendships and bonds you form along the way, and don't shy away from new experiences.

This book was just one of the many tools you'll pick up on your journey. Keep reading, learning, and seeking out what resonates with you. Life skills are a lifelong adventure, and the more you practice, the more they become second nature. When challenges arise, let them be reminders of the strength you've built and the potential still within you.

Above all, stay curious, be kind to yourself, and never underestimate the power of laughter, especially when things don't go as planned. Your future is bright, and you're equipped to face it with courage, wisdom, and, most importantly, with a strong sense of who you are. The world is waiting for you. Go out there and make a difference!

References

Bandura, A. (1977). *Self-efficacy: Toward a unifying theory of behavioral change*. Psychological Review, 84(2), 191-215.
(Relevant to: Developing self-confidence and achieving success)

Baumeister, R. F., & Leary, M. R. (1995). *The need to belong: Desire for interpersonal attachments as a fundamental human motivation*. Psychological Bulletin, 117(3), 497-529.
(Relevant to: Social relationships and mental well-being)

Brickman, P., Coates, D., & Janoff-Bulman, R. (1978). *Lottery winners and accident victims: Is happiness relative?* Journal of Personality and Social Psychology, 36(8), 917-927.
(Relevant to: Hedonic adaptation and happiness)

Brickman, P., & Campbell, D. T. (1971). *Hedonic relativism and planning the good society*. Academic Press.
(Relevant to: Hedonic treadmill concept)

Carnegie, D. (1936). *How to Win Friends and Influence People*. Simon & Schuster.

Csikszentmihalyi, M. (1990). *Flow: The Psychology of Optimal Experience*. Harper & Row.
(Relevant to: Mindset and personal development)

Descartes, R. (1637). *Discourse on the Method*. Published by René Descartes.
(Relevant to: Cartesian doubt and philosophical ideas)

Doidge, N. (2007). *The Brain That Changes Itself*. Penguin Books.
(Relevant to: Neuroplasticity and brain rewiring)

Duhigg, C. (2012). *The Power of Habit: Why We Do What We Do in Life and Business*. Random House.

Eisenberger, N. I., & Lieberman, M. D. (2004). *Why rejection hurts: A common neural alarm system for physical and social pain*. Trends in Cognitive Sciences, 8(7), 294-300.
(Relevant to: Social rejection and brain activity)

Frankl, V. E. (1946). *Man's Search for Meaning*. Beacon Press.

Grant, A. M. (2013). *Give and Take: A Revolutionary Approach to Success*. Viking.

Goleman, D. (1995). *Emotional Intelligence: Why It Can Matter More Than IQ*. Bantam Books.

Hyman, M. (2008). *The UltraMind Solution: Fix Your Broken Brain by Healing Your Body First*. Scribner.

Kahneman, D. (2011). *Thinking, Fast and Slow*. Farrar, Straus and Giroux.

Klein, G. (1999). *Sources of Power: How People Make Decisions*. MIT Press.

Locke, E. A., & Latham, G. P. (2002). *Building a practically useful theory of goal setting and task motivation: A 35-year odyssey*. American Psychologist, 57(9), 705-717.

Lyubomirsky, S. (2007). *The How of Happiness: A Scientific Approach to Getting the Life You Want*. Penguin Press.

Maslow, A. H. (1943). *A theory of human motivation*. Psychological Review, 50(4), 370-396.
(Relevant to: Human motivation and needs hierarchy)

McClelland, D. C. (1961). *The Achieving Society*. Van Nostrand.

McGonigal, K. (2011). *The Willpower Instinct: How Self-Control Works, Why It Matters, and What You Can Do to Get More of It*. Avery.

Newport, C. (2016). *Deep Work: Rules for Focused Success in a Distracted World*. Grand Central Publishing.

Pink, D. H. (2009). *Drive: The Surprising Truth About What Motivates Us*. Riverhead Books.

Robbins, A. (1992). *Awaken the Giant Within: How to Take Immediate Control of Your Mental, Emotional, Physical and Financial Destiny!*. Free Press.

Ryan, R. M., & Deci, E. L. (2000). *Self-determination theory and the facilitation of intrinsic motivation, social development, and well-being*. American Psychologist, 55(1), 68-78.

Sandberg, S. (2013). *Lean In: Women, Work, and the Will to Lead*. Knopf.

Schwartz, T. (2010). *The Energy Project: Manage Your Energy, Not Your Time*. Harvard Business Review.
(Relevant to: Managing energy and productivity)

Semmelweis, I. (1861). *The Etiology, Concept, and Prophylaxis of Childbed Fever*.
(Relevant to: Story of Dr. Ignaz Semmelweis and hygiene in medicine)

Seligman, M. E. P. (2002). *Authentic Happiness: Using the New Positive Psychology to Realize Your Potential for Lasting Fulfillment*. Free Press.

Tice, D. M., & Baumeister, R. F. (1997). *Longitudinal study of procrastination, performance, stress, and health: The costs and benefits of dawdling*. Psychological Science, 8(6), 454-458.

Tversky, A., & Kahneman, D. (1974). *Judgment under uncertainty: Heuristics and biases*. Science, 185(4157), 1124-1131.
(Relevant to: Cognitive biases and decision making)

WebMD. (n.d.). *Exercise and Teen Health*. Retrieved from https://www.webmd.com/teens/exercise.

CDC. (2020). *Teen Mental Health*. Retrieved from https://www.cdc.gov/teenhealth/mental-health.

Harvard Health. (2019). *The Importance of Sleep for Teens*. Retrieved from https://www.health.harvard.edu/teen-sleep.
(Relevant to: Sleep and mental well-being)

Mayo Clinic. (2021). *Adolescent Nutrition*. Retrieved from https://www.mayoclinic.org/teen-nutrition.
(Relevant to: Teen nutrition and health)

National Sleep Foundation. (n.d.). *Teens and Sleep*. Retrieved from https://www.sleepfoundation.org/teens-sleep.

NIH. (2020). *Stress in Teens: What You Can Do*. Retrieved from https://www.nimh.nih.gov/teen-stress.

CDC. (2020). *The Impact of Physical Activity on Teens*. Retrieved from https://www.cdc.gov/physicalactivity/teens.

American Psychological Association. (2017). *Teens, Social Media, and Mental Health*. Retrieved from https://www.apa.org/news/teens-social-media.
(Relevant to: Social media and teen well-being)

American Academy of Pediatrics. (2019). *Sleep Guidelines for Teens*. Retrieved from https://www.aap.org/teen-sleep-guidelines.
(Relevant to: Sleep guidelines for adolescents)

Levy, J. (2020). *The Role of Nutrition in Teen Health*. Nutrition Reviews, 78(9), 710-719.

Harvard Business Review. (2019). *The Science of High Performance in Teens*. Retrieved from https://www.hbr.org/science-teens-performance.

National Institute on Drug Abuse. (2019). *Teens and Drug Use*. Retrieved from https://www.drugabuse.gov/teens-drug-use.

Larson, R., & Wilson, S. (2004). *Adolescence: Emotional Regulation and Development*. Annual Review of Psychology, 55, 435-463.

AHA. (2018). *Teens and Heart Health: Tips to Stay Fit*. Retrieved from https://www.heart.org/teens-heart-health.

WHO. (2020). *Mental Health in Adolescents*. Retrieved from https://www.who.int/mental-health/adolescents.
(Relevant to: Mental health in teens)

APA. (2021). *Emotional Well-being in Adolescents*. Retrieved from https://www.apa.org/teens-emotional-wellbeing.

Sifferlin, A. (2014). *The Science of Sleep for Teens*. TIME. Retrieved from https://time.com/sleep-for-teens.
(Relevant to: Science of teen sleep cycles)

Fry, R. (2020). *The Role of Education in Future Job Markets*. Pew Research. Retrieved from https://www.pewresearch.org/future-jobs-education.

JAMA Pediatrics. (2019). *Screen Time and Mental Health in Teens*. Retrieved from https://jamanetwork.com/pediatrics/teens-screen-time.
(Relevant to: Screen time and teen mental health)

319

Celebrity Net Worth: "He Started Out Selling $10 Hats From A Street Corner. Today FUBU Founder Daymond John Is Worth $350 Million"

University of California, Berkeley. (2018). *Grit and Growth Mindset in Teens*. Retrieved from https://www.berkeley.edu/grit-teens.

HBR. (2021). *How to Build Emotional Intelligence in Teens*. Retrieved from https://www.hbr.org/teen-emotional-intelligence.

National Institutes of Health. (2021). *Teen Brain Development and Decision Making*. Retrieved from https://www.nih.gov/teens-brain-development.

New York Times. (2018). *Managing Stress in Teens: What Parents Can Do*. Retrieved from https://www.nytimes.com/teens-manage-stress.

The Guardian. (2021). *Teen Nutrition and Mental Health*. Retrieved from https://www.theguardian.com/teen-nutrition-mental-health.

American Academy of Child & Adolescent Psychiatry. (2020). *Understanding Teen Anxiety*. Retrieved from https://www.aacap.org/teen-anxiety.

The Lancet. (2019). *The Importance of Physical Activity in Adolescents*. Retrieved from https://www.thelancet.com/physical-activity-teens.

Psychology Today. (2019). *How Adolescents Develop Resilience*. Retrieved from https://www.psychologytoday.com/teens-resilience.
(Relevant to: Teen resilience and mental health)

National Institute of Mental Health. (2019). *Teen Mental Health Statistics*. Retrieved from https://www.nimh.nih.gov/teens-mental-health.

Mental Health America. (2021). *Building Self-Esteem in Teens*. Retrieved from https://www.mhanational.org/teen-self-esteem.

TIME. (2021). *Teens and Stress Management*. Retrieved from https://time.com/teens-stress-management.

Stanford University. (2019). *Teen Technology Use and Mental Health*. Retrieved from https://www.stanford.edu/teen-technology.

McGill University. (2021). *The Impact of Social Media on Teens*. Retrieved from https://www.mcgill.ca/teen-social-media.

Harvard Medical School. (2020). *The Benefits of Sleep for Teen Health*. Retrieved from https://www.health.harvard.edu/teen-sleep.

USA Today. (2021). *Teen Exercise and Emotional Well-being*. Retrieved from https://www.usatoday.com/teen-exercise-emotion.

The Atlantic. (2018). *How Teens Are Developing Skills for the Future*. Retrieved from https://www.theatlantic.com/teen-skills-future.

NPR. (2019). *Teenage Sleep Deprivation Crisis*. Retrieved from https://www.npr.org/teen-sleep-deprivation.

Scientific American. (2021). *Teen Stress and Coping Mechanisms*. Retrieved from https://www.scientificamerican.com/teen-stress-coping.

Forbes. (2021). *The Role of Grit in Teen Success*. Retrieved from https://www.forbes.com/grit-teen-success.
(Relevant to: Grit and perseverance in teens)

Verywell Mind. (2021). *How to Help Teens Build Mental Toughness*. Retrieved from https://www.verywellmind.com/teen-mental-toughness.

Healthline. (2020). *Teen Nutrition and Physical Health*. Retrieved from https://www.healthline.com/teen-nutrition.

WHO. (2021). *Adolescent Physical Activity Guidelines*. Retrieved from https://www.who.int/teen-physical-activity.

Harvard Business Review. (2021). *How to Build Resilience in Teens*. Retrieved from https://hbr.org/teen-resilience.

TED. (2020). *The Science of Resilience in Teens*. Retrieved from https://www.ted.com/teens-resilience.

Medical News Today. (2021). *Teen Mental Health and Technology*. Retrieved from https://www.medicalnewstoday.com/teen-mental-health-technology.

APA. (2021). *Building Emotional Resilience in Teens*. Retrieved from https://www.apa.org/teen-resilience.

National Institutes of Health. (2021). *The Role of Nutrition in Cognitive Development*. Retrieved from https://www.nih.gov/nutrition-teen-brain.

World Economic Forum. (2020). *The Future of Work: Skills for the Next Generation*. Retrieved from https://www.weforum.org/future-of-work-teens.

Psychology Today. (2020). *Teen Independence and Resilience*. Retrieved from https://www.psychologytoday.com/teen-independence.

Verywell Family. (2021). *Helping Teens Develop Healthy Relationships*. Retrieved from https://www.verywellfamily.com/teens-healthy-relationships.

Zak, P. J. (2012). *The Moral Molecule: The Source of Love and Prosperity*. Dutton.

Harvard Business Review. (2019). *How Grit and Resilience Lead to Success*. Retrieved from https://www.hbr.org/grit-resilience.

American Psychological Association. (2020). *The Science of Motivation*. Retrieved from https://www.apa.org/science-motivation.

Pew Research Center. (2020). *Teens and the Impact of Technology on Social Relationships*. Retrieved from https://www.pewresearch.org/teens-tech-social.

American Academy of Pediatrics. (2020). *Guidelines on Screen Time for Adolescents*. Retrieved from https://www.aap.org/guidelines-screen-time.

Cleveland Clinic. (2020). *How Sleep Affects Teen Health and Development*. Retrieved from https://www.clevelandclinic.org/sleep-teen-health.

TIME. (2020). *Resilience and Mental Strength in Adolescents*. Retrieved from https://time.com/teens-mental-strength.

Health.com. (2021). *The Importance of Healthy Eating Habits in Teens*. Retrieved from https://www.health.com/teen-nutrition.

NPR. (2020). *The Science Behind Teen Mental Health and Physical Fitness*. Retrieved from https://www.npr.org/teen-mental-fitness.

American Psychological Association. (2021). *Teens and Stress: What You Need to Know*. Retrieved from https://www.apa.org/teen-stress-guide.

National Institute on Drug Abuse. (2020). *Adolescent Brain Development and Risk-Taking Behavior*. Retrieved from https://www.drugabuse.gov/teen-brain-risk.

Forbes. (2021). *How Technology Affects Teens' Social and Emotional Health*. Retrieved from https://www.forbes.com/teen-tech-health.

American Heart Association. (2020). *Teen Physical Fitness and Heart Health*. Retrieved from https://www.heart.org/teen-fitness.

Cleveland Clinic. (2021). *Building Healthy Habits in Teens*. Retrieved from https://www.clevelandclinic.org/healthy-habits-teens.

TED. (2020). *The Role of Perseverance in Adolescent Development*. Retrieved from https://www.ted.com/perseverance-adolescents.

Healthline. (2020). *Physical Activity and Its Impact on Teen Mental Health*. Retrieved from https://www.healthline.com/teen-mental-health-physical.

Verywell Mind. (2020). *How Teens Can Manage Stress and Anxiety*. Retrieved from https://www.verywellmind.com/teens-stress-anxiety.

Mental Health America. (2020). *The Effects of Social Media on Teen Mental Health*. Retrieved from https://www.mhanational.org/social-media-teens.

WHO. (2020). *Global Health Guidelines for Adolescent Mental Health*. Retrieved from https://www.who.int/adolescent-mental-health.

Made in the USA
Columbia, SC
25 March 2025

55657709R00180